# FUNDAMENTALS OF
# ELECTRONIC
# COMPUTERS:
## Digital and Analog

PRENTICE-HALL INTERNATIONAL, INC., *London*
PRENTICE-HALL OF AUSTRALIA, PTY., LTD., *Sydney*
PRENTICE-HALL OF CANADA, LTD., *Toronto*
PRENTICE-HALL OF INDIA PRIVATE LTD., *New Delhi*
PRENTICE-HALL OF JAPAN, INC., *Tokyo*

# FUNDAMENTALS OF ELECTRONIC COMPUTERS:
## Digital and Analog

**Matthew Mandl**

SENIOR INSTRUCTOR
TECHNICAL INSTITUTE
TEMPLE UNIVERSITY

Prentice-Hall, Inc., Englewood Cliffs, New Jersey

Current printing (last digit):

10 9 8

Library of Congress Catalog Card Number 67-18921
Printed in the United States of America

Dedicated to my wife, Kay

# PREFACE

**Fundamentals of Electronic Computers** discusses all aspects of *digital* and *analog* computer circuitry, organization, codes, and programming factors. It is a medium-level book intended for those who have a basic knowledge of d-c and a-c electronic fundamentals, including introductory principles of solid-state circuitry. For an understanding of the analog computer technology discussed in Chapters 11 and 12, a prerequisite in the calculus fundamentals is helpful.

Since the publication of the author's *Fundamentals of Digital Computers* (1958) the state of the art has reached a high level in terms of miniaturization, programming simplicity, extended versatility in the fields of computational ability and data processing, as well as in the highly sophisticated auxiliary equipment which greatly facilitates computer data acquisition and output printing or display of computational results. Hence, the need for a new text was indicated to cover these various areas in the light of modern practices. In addition, the theory and operational characteristics of analog computers have been included so that all phases of electronic computers would be covered.

The basic differences between the digital and analog computers are discussed in the first chapter. Included are the type of signals encountered and the variety of nonlogic circuits found in computers. This chapter also serves as a review of electronic circuit fundamentals.

Computer arithmetic is covered in the second chapter for an immediate acquisition of the binary principles necessary in the study of logic circuitry. In the third chapter the principles of Boolean algebra are combined with logic-gate discussions to unify the two allied subjects and to show their inter-relationships. All phases are thoroughly explored and illustrated with truth tables, Karnaugh maps, and Venn diagrams.

The text has been organized to provide an orderly and sequential presentation of the material. Each new topic builds upon the subject matter previously learned. Thus, the treatment of accumulators and counters precedes discussions of special codes and notations so the latter can be exemplified by practical applications. This is followed in logical order by the more complex calculation circuitry.

Because of the great variety of storage systems, this topic is covered extensively in Chapter 7 — this includes coverage of microminiaturization, modules and chips, and allied subjects. Similar treatment is accorded the input and output devices in Chapter 8.

The essential factors relating to programming are introduced in Chapter 9, and programming procedures with illustrative examples involving equation computations and data processing are given. Basic aspects of FORTRAN, COBOL, and ALGOL are also included. The final two chapters cover analog computer principles, auxiliary equipment, and programming methods. Several examples of computer trainer equipment are given in the Appendix.

At the end of each chapter appropriate questions and problems are given, each relating to some aspect of the material covered in the particular chapter. Since circuit drawing practices offer some instructional advantages, assignments of this nature have been included at various intervals.

MATTHEW MANDL

*Yardley, Pennsylvania*

# CONTENTS

## 5. Special Codes and Notation   115

## 6. Calculation Circuits   133

## 7. Storage Systems and Component Logic   164

# FUNDAMENTALS OF
# ELECTRONIC
# COMPUTERS:
## Digital and Analog

# BASIC TYPES,
# CIRCUITS,
# AND SIGNALS

**1**

**Introduction.** Modern electronic computers are the result of years of intensive engineering research and the constant improvements in components and circuitry which have been made as the state of the art advanced. In consequence, computers have reached a high level of performance and find extensive applications in the data-processing field, in guided-missile and satellite projects, in the solving of complex problems in scientific laboratory work or other engineering research, in industrial process control, and in various other areas. Their primary advantages are speed of operation, accuracy, vast storage capacity, and ability to handle complex problems or process data in extraordinarily brief intervals of time for the material handled.

In this chapter the basic differences between the digital and analog computers are explained, followed by a discussion of the sections, circuits, and signals encountered in the digital computers. Digital computer coverage is continued through Chapter 10, followed by analog computer principles.

## Digital versus Analog

The digital computer is a *counting* device, as opposed to the analog computer, which is fundamentally a *measuring* device. The digital

1

computer has basic functions of addition, multiplication, subtraction, and division and performs many mathematical functions and processes by iterative (repetitive) methods. Inherently, it operates in a progressive and *sequential* manner as it performs the instructions (program) which have been fed to it. In such a computer the presence, absence, and repetition rate of the signals are important factors, and not signal amplitude.

In an analog computer the data fed into it are acted upon *simultaneously*. As opposed to the digital computer, the amplitudes of the analog signals determine their numerical value. Both types, however, are capable of solving problems with speeds far in excess of those obtained with the mechanical office type of calculators. Each is capable of doing complex calculations in minutes as compared to days, weeks, or even months by other means.

The digital computer can be compared to the adding machine in its functional aspects, except that the electronic device will solve problems of a much more complex or involved nature than the desk type of adding machine. It handles numbers or coded alphabetic characters and performs with them required calculations, comparisons, and other arithmetic functions. The digital computer is more versatile than the analog with respect to the nature and variety of work it can do, and the data it can process.

The analog computer relates *physical* changes and variables (gear rotation, changes of shaft positions, etc.) in the form of mathematical equations. The analog computer, by analogy, thus interprets the physical changes and indicates the significance which such changes have with respect to the device or unit as a whole. The analog computer is useful in industrial automatic processes, guided missile and radar work, and other systems where the effects of physical variables must be mathematically coordinated for proper function and to achieve an end result. Analog computers are limited in application primarily to the problems related to a particular sytem. Such computers can be likened to the slide rule, and as with the latter, accuracy is limited by the design. For accuracy to a number of decimal places, an enormously large slide rule would have to be employed for fractional divisions to be ascertained. Actually, however, the accuracy and precision of computations in both types of computers are exceptionally good in the type of problems each handles. A clarification of the essential differences requires a brief summary of the definitions of accuracy and precision with respect to computers. Accuracy in an electronic computer relates to how closely a solution of a problem approaches the actual answer. *Precision* of a solution is indicative of the closeness or sharpness of the answer to the actual sum. For instance, 3.14159 is of greater precision than 3.14, even though the latter suffices for a statement of the numerical value of *pi*. How precise a digital computer is relates to the capacity of the digits in any circuit group and the degree of error in round-off. (Round-off errors are those which keep accumulating during the processing of a problem because of rounding off the various results, or answers, to the number of significant figures under consideration.)

In analog computers an increase in precision means design and circuitry increase, whereas in digital computers precision can be increased without any necessity of increasing the number of circuits, because an increase in precision can be obtained by increasing the time required for an answer. It is not unusual to encounter more than twenty significant figures in digial computers, while analog computers operate with four or five significant figures. The amount of precision required depends on application and can be built into the machine as required.

The comparison of digital and analog computers to the desk calculator and slide rule, respectively, is made only to indicate broad similarities. To carry the analogy further, the applications of the slide rule and the adding machine differ, even though there are a number of similar computations which can be handled by each device. So it is with the analog and digital computers; each has a specific application, even though in a broad sense there can be some overlapping of calculating operations. (Analog computer principles start with Chapter 11.)

## Digital Development

Ever since man first learned to count and to use numbers for performing arithmetic operations, he has endeavored to simplify and speed up such processes by employing some means other than the tedious method of writing down the numbers and going through the rather slow mental procedures of calculating routines. Even before writing instruments were invented, at the dawn of civilization, the fingers of the hands were used for counting purposes. Use of the digits (digital counting) is undoubtedly the basis for our present-day system of numbers using the base 10.

The earliest form of the digital type of computer, from which all modern computers — no matter how complex — stem, is the *abacus*. This simple, yet effective, digital machine finds mention in history as being used by the Egyptians as early as 450 B.C. In the form used then it consisted of a grooved clay board which used round pebbles in the grooves. Historical evidence indicates crude types of the abacus to have been employed even some centuries preceding its use by the Egyptians. Later, modified forms of the early abacus appeared in Japan, China, and other countries, that consisted of a wood frame with wires or rods on which wood beads were strung. Each group of beads represents a *place* in the decimal system, such as tens, hundreds, thousands, etc. The abacus is still in use in China and Japan, and a skilled operator can compete in noteworthy fashion even with a modern desk calculator for speed in the common forms of addition, multiplication, etc. It is of interest that a particular type of computer notation is based on the number representation of the abacus, as is discussed in Chapter 5.

In briefly summarizing how machine computers evolved, mention must be made of the Scottish mathematician John Napier (1550–1617), who made some valuable contributions to mathematics. Napier is credited with the invention of logarithms (1614), coining the word and publishing the famous tables. With John Briggs, he converted logarithms to the base 10 and also introduced the decimal point in numerical notations. Napier was also first to use tables of trigonometric functions. He originated a multiplication process which utilized numbering rods (1617). The numbering rods were often referred to as *Napier's bones*.

It was not until 1642, however, that the first type of adding machine, or desk calculator, appeared. This was invented by Blaise Pascal (1623–1662), the French scientist. The device employed simple wheels in the form of gears and its functions were confined solely to addition and subtraction. Subsequently, other mathematicians improved Pascal's earlier calculation device by the addition of the multiplication process employing repeated additions, but mechanical imperfections hampered progress.

One of the most brilliant pioneers in the development of the digital computer was Charles Babbage (1792–1871), who conceived a mechanical machine embracing virtually all the principles of the modern type. In 1822 he built an operational model, which he called a *difference engine* which was capable of preparing mathematical tables to the sixth decimal place. Encouraged with the reception of this device, he proposed one which would operate to 20 decimal places. He gained financial support from the British government and the project continued for many years.

In 1833 he formulated plans for a more complex machine known as the *analytical engine*. This unit was to be designed with programming features (method and process of calculation) as well as memory (storage of numbers) by employing two sets of cards — one set for the purpose of selecting the type of operation to be performed and the other set indicating the numerical values to be processed. The arithmetic processes were to be performed with toothed wheels, and the answer was to be printed out. Thus he envisioned a mechanical device which has the operational characteristics of the modern digital computer, but almost 100 years elapsed before a practical counterpart was actually assembled.

While Babbage's ideas were inspirational conceptions of an advanced nature, he encountered the drawbacks of imperfect materials, lack of precision in tools, and lack of understanding among his associates of the potentials of his analytical engine. Approximately ten years later the government withdrew financial support and the project was abandoned.

The first key-driven type of adding machine was patented as early as 1850, but it was not until 1886 that Dorr E. Felt brought out the first really practical key-driven adding machine. This was patented in 1887 as the *Comptometer*, and in 1889 Felt added the printing feature (*Comptograph*) making it the first practical machine to print out answers. Subsequently, other desk type of calculators appeared on the market, and by 1920 the development of small electric motors permitted the calculating machines to be electrified, which simplified the ease of operation.

As industries grew in size, their record storage and computing requirements became more complex and intricate. The demand then arose for greater speed in handling accounts, filing records, and maintaining bookkeeping processes. Coinciding with this demand for high speed was the rapid development of the electronics field, with the advent of diodes, vacuum tubes, and transistors, plus the design of appropriate circuits lending themselves to adaptation in computer circuitry. Hence, the design of all-electronic computers solved the problems of expanding business growth.

The first *special purpose* computer using the electrical principles (relays, etc.) was completed in 1940 by the Bell Telephone Laboratories. Special purpose computers in great variety have been manufactured since then. *Special purpose* refers to machines designed to handle a particular task related to a particular business or project, such as the handling of airline passenger lists, traffic tabulations, keeping track of train schedules, etc.

The first *general purpose* digital computer also employing electrical principles on a large scale was developed by Harvard University in 1944 and built with the assistance of the International Business Machines Corporation (IBM). *General purpose* refers to the ability of a computer to handle a variety of mathematical problems.

The Harvard computer used electric relays and electromagnetic clutches in the arithmetic section, and punched cards were employed for feeding information into the machine as well as for storing mathematical data. Compared with all-electronic calculators, however, this computer had limited storage facilities and, because of its mechanical aspects, was incapable of the high-speed operations performed by later types. Chronologically, however, it was the forerunner of modern digital computers.

Around 1942 the Moore School of Engineering of the University of Pennsylvania developed the first all-electronic type of digital computer. This computer was named the ENIAC (Electronic Numerical Integrator and Calculator) and contained approximately 18,000 vacuum tubes. It was designed primarily for solving problems of trajectory for the Ballistics Research Laboratories at the Aberdeen Proving Grounds.

Subsequently, other electronic computers of large-scale dimensions stemmed from the original ones developed and included such types as the TRANSAC, BISMAC, SEAC, BINAC, UNIVAC, etc. In the modern types, the tubes have been replaced by solid-state diodes and transistors. In addition, printed circuits, modules, and other miniaturization techniques have reduced sizes to a remarkable degree compared with the older types.

## Basic Computer Sections

The basic sections of a modern digital computer are shown in Fig. 1-1. They consist of input devices for entering the information and calculation processes into the computer, storage devices for retaining information, control sections which operate the computer according to the instructions placed into the device, the arithmetic

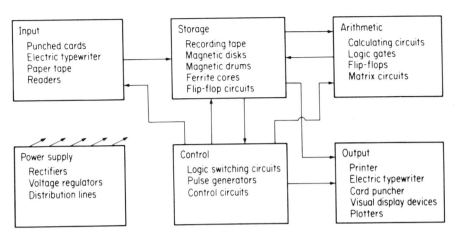

**Fig. 1-1. Basic sections of digital computers.**

section where calculations are performed, and output devices which produce the results of the calculations and processes. In addition, a power supply unit furnishes the necessary voltage and current for the various circuits.

The sequence of instructions is placed into storage initially, in addition to the figures, numbers, and other data to be used in the calculations. The control section will then act on the instructions in storage by channeling the stored numbers to the respective parts of the arithmetic section. Once the calculation has been completed, the control section will either store the result of the calculations or channel it to the output devices in accordance with the instructions which have been stored initially.

The input devices can consist of punched cards, paper tape, or an electric typewriter. These devices are used by the operator of the computer to place instructions and other information into the memory, as shown by the arrow from the input devices block to the storage devices block in the figure. The input consists of such information as instructions which are interpreted by the machine with respect to the processes involved in calculation, the various numbers or groups of numbers to be used in the arithmetic processes, as well as other alphabetic or numerical information. Automatic data reading (by optical means) may also be employed as described in Chapter 8.

The storage section of the computer may consist of magnetic drums, ferrite cores, or other devices which have the ability to store electric signals. The storage section of the computer must obtain all the information and numbers related to a particular calculation or process from the input device before the computer can act on such information. Also, the storage devices may retain information to be used at a later date or store the results of calculations for reuse in subsequent arithmetic processes.

The control section of the computer contains electronic gating and switching circuits, electronic control circuits, and interconnecting networks which link the various computer sections. The control section must interpret the information and instructions which are retained in the storage section, and it must transmit the results of such interpretations to the computer sections for initiating the calculation processes.

The arithmetic section contains adders, multipliers, dividers, and subtracters. These calculation devices are electronic and are made up of transistor and diode circuitry. It is in the arithmetic section that calculations are performed at incredible speeds as compared to those of the ordinary desk calculators.

The results of the calculations or other processes performed by the computer are obtained from the output devices. The output devices can consist of punched cards which retain the information resulting from the calculations, or of paper tape which is also punched according to a specific code that interprets the results. Also employed are electric typewriters which automatically type out the information procured from the computer. Printers may be utilized which print one or more copies of the information obtained from the computer.

The power supply section consists of transformers, rectifiers, and voltage regulator devices quite similar to the power supplies for other electronic devices.

The placement of information into the computer by means of the input devices is known as *read-in*, and the procurement of information from the output devices is known as *read-out*. The instructions which indicate to the computer what processes are to be performed are coded, that is, specific alphabetic or numerical designations are given to each particular process. Locations of specific storage areas are also coded and each location is known as an *address*. An entire sequence of coded instructions, plus addresses, is known as a *program*. The applications of all these terms, plus additional discussions of them, are covered in subsequent chapters.

## Digital Signals

A digital computer uses a pulse type of signal having a single polarity. The presence of a pulse signal denotes the unit value 1, while the absence of a pulse indicates zero. Depending on the type of circuits utilized and the speed of operation, pulse durations may be $\frac{1}{2}$ microsecond or less, with a microsecond or two separation between individual pulses. If zero representations are present between two pulses, the interval between them would be dependent on the number of zeros represented.

If the design engineers of a computer elect to use positive pulses to represent ones, the presence of a negative pulse would represent zero. Similarly, if a computer uses negative pulses to represent ones, the presence of positive pulses at any time would be equivalent to the absence of pulses, and hence would be equal to zero. Unwanted pulses are clipped in subsequent circuitry or applied to circuits which reject the unwanted polarity.

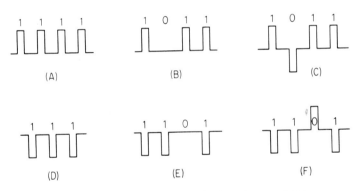

**Fig. 1-2. Number representation by pulse waveforms.**

Typical pulse trains are shown in Fig.1-2. In A, four positive pulses are shown, representing the number 1111. In B, the second pulse from the left is missing, hence the representation is 1011. The same numerical value is indicated in C since the positive pulses only are of significance, and the negative pulse thus equals zero. For a computer using negative pulses, the train would appear as in D, where the result is the numerical value 111. In E, the missing pulse produces a value of 1101. In F, the 1101 value is again present because the positive pulse does not count as a digit.

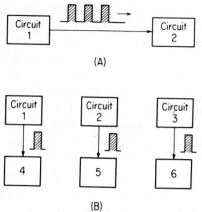

(A)

(B)

**Fig. 1-3. Serial and parallel modes.**

Pulse trains representing a specific numerical value are routed through various circuits of the computer in either a *serial form* or a *parallel form.* This is shown in Fig. 1-3, where the serial form is represented in A. Here, pulses from the first circuit are fed to the second circuit in *sequential order,* that is, one at a time. This represents a serial form of pulse train transfer. Thus, the numerical value of 111 is coupled from one circuit to another.

Another method of transferring the 111 is to do it *simultaneously,* that is, to have the three pulses applied in parallel form as shown in B. Here, each of the upper circuits contains a single digit pulse. Thus, the 111 representation is stored in three separate sections, permitting the pulses to be applied to the lower circuits during the same time interval. In a digital computer some of the various circuit and storage devices are capable of serial train read-in and read-out of information, while others are capable of parallel operation (or both serial and parallel), as more fully discussed in subsequent chapters.

Because the digital computer recognizes numerical values only by the presence or absence of pulses, it operates under the base-2 (binary) system as fully detailed in the next chapter. While this system may appear to impose limitations, digital operations are actually simplified and the error factor minimized. In addition, alphabetical or alphanumerical (combined numbers and letters) representations present no serious difficulty, as shown later.

### Signal-generating Circuitry

The pulse type of signals used in a computer must be obtained by electronic generators which produce waveforms having the required repetition rate (frequency). In order to produce pulses of proper amplitude and duration, other circuits are required to shape, modify, and amplify the signals to obtain the desired pulse type of wave forms. The basic signal-generating circuits are discussed in this section, and signal shaping, modification, and amplification are covered later. Not all the circuits discussed in this chapter may be included in a particular computer, since the circuit selection depends on the degree of signal modification and amplification necessary. The basic circuitry involved in signal generation and modification, however, is discussed for familiarization with the various types which may be encountered.

The circuits in this chapter are conventional types also found in other electronic equipment. The so-called *logic* circuits, which are used almost exclusively in computer and counting systems, are discussed in detail in subsequent chapters.

## Crystal Oscillator

A *crystal oscillator* is so named because it employs a piezo-quartz-crystal slab as the frequency-stabilizing device. The crystal oscillates at a frequency dependent upon the thickness of the crystal and the type; hence, when included in a signal-generating circuit, it maintains a constant frequency with negligible drift during oscillator operation. A typical crystal oscillator is shown in Fig. 1-4.

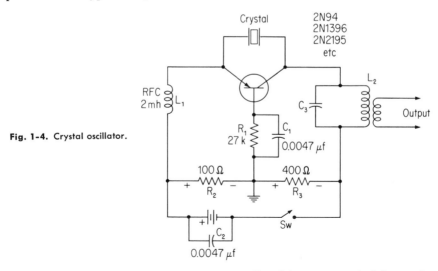

**Fig. 1-4. Crystal oscillator.**

In this circuit a PNP transistor is utilized in a grounded-base circuit. The base is at *signal ground* because of the low reactance of capacitor $C_1$, which shunts the base resistor $R_1$. A single power source is utilized as shown, shunted by resistors $R_2$ and $R_3$, which form a voltage divider and thus provide the necessary forward and reverse bias potentials without the necessity for utilizing two batteries or power devices. As shown, the voltage drop across $R_2$ makes the emitter positive with respect to the base and thus satisfies the necessary forward bias for the emitter base. Similarly, the voltage drop across $R_3$ applies a negative potential to the collector with respect to the base and thus furnishes the reverse bias. For an NPN transistor the battery would be reversed, so that the emitter would be negative with respect to the base and the collector positive.

As shown, the crystal is connected between the emitter and collector and hence acts as a feedback path between the output and input circuits to provide the necessary regeneration to sustain oscillation. In addition, the crystal slab determines the signal frequency of the oscillator. The resonant circuit is composed of the inductor $L_2$ and the capacitor $C_3$, with the output inductor coupled to $L_2$ as shown.

The base network ($R_1$ and $C_1$) serves to stabilize the circuit. The voltage drop across $R_1$ opposes the forward bias potential established across $R_2$ and hence reduces the forward bias by an amount equal to the voltage drop across $R_1$. If transistor conduction increases because of temperature change or for other reasons, there will be a larger voltage drop across $R_1$ and the forward bias will be reduced to compensate for the undesired conduction increase. Capacitor $C_1$ has a bypass effect across $R_1$ to prevent the degeneration which would occur if signal variations prevailed across $R_1$. A radio-frequency choke (RFC) isolates the emitter section from the power source. Capacitor $C_2$ has a bypass effect for signal currents around the power source, or battery.

The crystal oscillator produces a sinewave type of signal which must be clipped if square waves are desired, as shown later. The square waves, in turn, have to be clipped if pulses are desired, by removing either the positive or the negative alternations.

## Blocking Oscillator

The blocking oscillator (as well as the multivibrator discussed next) is a relaxation oscillator which has a signal frequency determined by resistance-capacitance (RC) values. The relaxation oscillators are capable of having the frequency of their signals locked in with respect to frequency by an external synchronizing signal. Block-ing oscillators function on the principle of periodically permitting transistor conduction and blocking current flow. A typical blocking

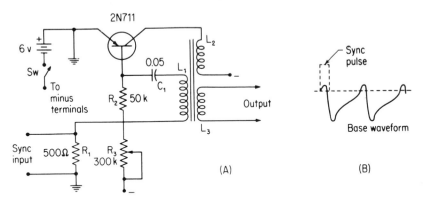

**Fig. 1-5. Blocking oscillator.**

oscillator is shown in A of Fig. 1-5. When the switch is closed, cur-rent flow through the transistor rises and thus represents a changing signal amplitude. Because such current flow occurs through induc-tance $L_2$, the fields which are produced will induce a voltage in the winding $L_1$. The two transformer windings are so polarized that the signal induced across $L_1$ increases the negative potential applied to the base and thus increases conduction. During conduction, however, capacitor $C_1$ charges with a polarity which is positive toward the transistor base. This positive polarity applies a reverse bias to the emitter-base section, and the transistor is driven into the cutoff region. Conduction stops until capacitor $C_1$ discharges through the resistive network to re-establish normal forward bias. The transistor will then again conduct and the cycle of operation will repeat itself. The out-put signal is obtained from a third winding $L_3$, as shown.

In B of Fig. 1-5 is shown the base waveform above and below the conduction level. If a synchronizing pulse is applied to the circuit during (or slightly prior to) the conduction period, the frequency of the signal produced by the blocking oscillator will be locked in by the frequency of the incoming synchronizing signal. This synchronizing pulse is applied across resistor $R_1$, as shown.

Resistor $R_3$ aids in synchronizing the frequency of the input signal with that of the free-running frequency of the blocking oscillator. Ad-justment of this resistor provides the most stable synchronization.

## Astable Multivibrator

A multivibrator is also a relaxation type of signal generator which depends on $RC$ constants for determining the frequency of the signals produced. Also like the blocking oscillator, the astable multivibrator is free-running and continuously produces an output signal. A typical circuit using NPN transistors is shown in Fig. 1-6.

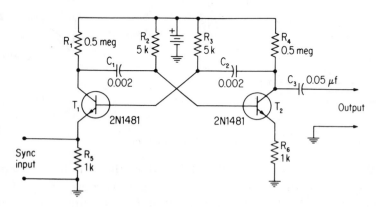

**Fig. 1-6.** Astable multivibrator.

Since NPN transistors are employed, the forward bias between emitter and base requires that the emitter be made negative with respect to the base. This condition is satisfied for the circuit shown in Fig. 1-6 by returning the emitter to ground, which is common with the negative power-source terminal. For the required positive potential for the collectors of the NPN transistors, series resistors connect to the positive battery terminal as shown.

When power is first applied to the multivibrator, one transistor will start to conduct more quickly than the other, despite a symmetrical circuit and identical transistors. If, for instance, transistor $T_1$ starts to conduct sooner than transistor $T_2$, the rising current through $R_1$ will develop a voltage drop across this resistor and the collector voltage for $T_1$ will start to decline. This *change* of voltage across the collector is toward the negative (ground) potential, and this is felt at the base of transistor $T_2$. The negative potential at the base of $T_2$ reduces the forward bias for this transistor and current flow declines. The decrease in current through collector resistor $R_4$ decreases the voltage drop across this resistor, and hence the collector voltage for $T_2$ rises. This increase in the positive potential at the collector of $T_2$ is felt at the base of $T_1$ because of the coupling capacitor $C_2$. In consequence, the forward bias applied to the base of $T_1$ is increased, and conduction through $T_1$ increases an additional amount. The process continues (in a very short time interval) until transistor $T_1$ conducts at full saturation. When this occurs, transistor $T_2$ is cut off and no longer is there a *change* in conduction. Now, the charge which had developed across $C_2$ will hold transistor $T_2$ in its nonconducting state until capacitor $C_1$ discharges sufficiently to release the cut-off bias applied to transistor $T_2$. When capacitor $C_1$ has discharged sufficiently, transistor $T_2$ is permitted to conduct and current flows through resistor $R_4$, decreasing the potential at the collector of $T_2$. This negative change of potential is felt at the base of $T_1$ and reduces the forward bias for this transistor until $T_1$ is cut off and $T_2$ conducts fully. This is now a state which is the reverse of the original and the process starts over again and the oscillator continues to produce an output signal. As with other relaxation oscillators, the frequency of the signals produced by the multivibrator is determined by the time constants of the resistors and capacitors involved in the complete circuit.

The waveforms at the collector and base circuits of the multivibrator are shown in Fig. 1-7. The rising collector voltage for $T_1$ is caused by this transistor's changing to a nonconduction state. This

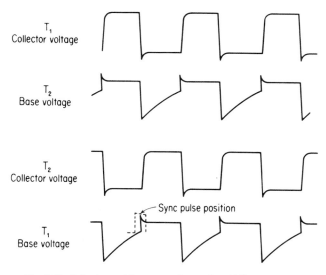

**Fig. 1-7.** Collector and base waveforms of multivibrator.

rise in positive potential is applied to the base of $T_2$ and increases forward bias which causes conduction. The result is a lowering of the collector voltage because of the drop across the collector resistor. This decreased voltage is felt at the base of $T_1$ which cuts off this transistor. After capacitor discharge, the states reverse themselves as shown in Fig. 1-7. The collector voltages change to form square-wave signals which have a frequency determined by the resistance-capacitance components of the circuit. For a longer time constant, capacitor charge and discharge rate is slowed down, resulting in a lower frequency. On the other hand, if the time constant is made shorter by decreasing the value of the capacitance or resistance (or both), the charge and discharge rates occur more rapidly and frequency rises.

The application of input sync pulses across $R_1$ will lock in the oscillator if the frequency of the synchronizing signal is not too far removed from the free-running frequency of the multivibrator. If the sync signal arrives at or near the time that the base reaches its conduction level, lock-in will occur. This is shown by the dotted outline in the lower waveform drawing for $T_1$ in Fig. 1-7.

### Monostable Multivibrator

The monostable multivibrator is a relaxation oscillator which, when triggered, produces an output pulse of a predetermined duration. The circuit is also known as a *one-shot* or *start-stop* multivibrator. It differs from the astable multivibrator in not being a free-running type. Instead, an output signal is produced only for the application of a pulse to the input. Because the monostable multivibrator will produce a pulse of a predetermined width, it is useful for converting a train of pulses having various widths to a pulse train in which each pulse has the same width as others. Because of its characteristics, it can also be utilized as a delay system — to delay pulses for a certain time interval, as shown later in this chapter, and for purposes detailed more fully in subsequent chapters. A typical monostable multivibrator using NPN transistors is shown in Fig. 1-8.

For this design, an additional power source $B_2$ is placed between the collector of $T_2$ and ground. Battery $B_1$ is the conventional power source for furnishing the necessary forward and reverse bias potentials.

Because an NPN transistor has a forward bias which is negative for the emitter and positive for the base, the inclusion of $B_2$ at $T_2$ pro-

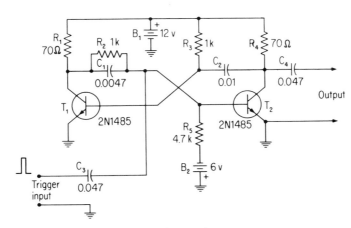

Fig. 1-8. Monostable (one-shot) multivibrator.

vides a reverse bias and hence cuts off this transistor and thus prevents conduction through it. During this time no voltage drop occurs across the collector resistor $R_4$, and hence the potential at the collector is equal to that of the voltage source $B_1$. Transistor $T_1$, however, has the necessary positive forward bias applied to the base by resistor $R_3$, and the negative potential for the emitter is obtained through the ground circuit which is common to the negative terminal of $B_1$. Thus, $T_1$ conducts at saturation and $T_2$ is cut off.

When a positive-polarity trigger pulse is applied to the input as shown in Fig. 1-8, a positive polarity appears at the base of $T_2$ and causes this transistor to go into its conducting state. Now the current flow through $R_4$ causes a voltage drop to occur, and the collector potential declines toward the ground level. This voltage change toward the negative potential is coupled by capacitor $C_2$ to the base of $T_1$ and hence reduces the forward bias and decreases conduction for the $T_1$ transistor. In consequence, the voltage drop across $R_1$ decreases and causes the collector voltage for $T_1$ to rise. The increase in positive potential applied to the base of transistor $T_2$ increases the forward bias on this transistor and increases conduction. The process is repeated and in a very short time interval $T_1$ is cut off and $T_2$ conducts fully.

When the trigger pulse drops to zero, the positive potential which had been applied to the base of $T_2$ is removed and a brief interval of time elapses before capacitor $C_2$ assumes its original charge level to permit $T_1$ to conduct again. When this occurs, the decreased voltage at the collector of $T_1$ no longer is capable of overcoming the reverse bias applied to the base by $B_2$ and hence $T_2$ cuts off. Thus the original state again prevails, and the conduction to nonconduction period of $T_2$ produces an output pulse having a duration controlled by circuit constants.

## Schmitt Trigger

The Schmitt trigger circuit shown in Fig. 1-9 is one which has a switching sensitivity related to the amplitude of the triggering pulse

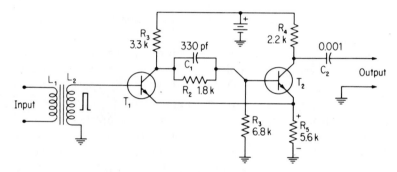

**Fig. 1-9. Schmitt trigger.**

applied to the circuit. It is useful in computer applications for re-forming and reshaping the computer signal pulses as well as for reforming and reshaping square waves and sinusoidal waveforms. It is also useful for d-c signal-level detection and for the suppression of noise signals which fall between pulses of the computer as well as for ridding pulses of transient overshoot signals.

As shown in Fig. 1-9, two NPN transistors are used though PNP types could also be used instead, with battery potential reversals.

With no input signal applied, the circuit remains in a stable state. Resistors $R_1$, $R_2$, and $R_3$ form a voltage divider network between the positive and negative supply terminals. Thus, the voltage drop which occurs across $R_3$ would have a positive potential at the base of $T_2$ and a negative potential at the emitter, providing the necessary forward bias for the NPN transistor. The necessary reverse bias for the collector of $T_2$ is supplied by the positive terminal of the power source, using $R_4$ as the series resistor. Thus, the bias requirements for $T_2$ are present, and this transistor conducts at saturation. During this time the current flow through $R_4$ develops a voltage drop across this resistor, decreasing the collector voltage level below that of the positive terminal of the battery. Similarly, a voltage drop develops across the emitter resistor $R_5$, producing a polarity across the resistor as shown. Because the emitter of $T_1$ is common with that of $T_2$, a voltage drop across $R_5$ also prevails for the emitter of $T_1$. The low resistance of $L_2$ provides the necessary return connection to the bottom of $R_5$ which makes the base of $T_1$ negative with respect to the emitter. Since this is a reverse bias condition, transistor $T_1$ is in a nonconducting state. Thus, the complete trigger circuit remains in this state until an input pulse is applied.

When an input pulse of sufficient amplitude is applied to the circuit, it nullifies the reverse bias applied to the input of transistor $T_1$ and permits this transistor to conduct. When this occurs, the voltage across $R_1$ rises and the collector voltage drops to a lower value.    This voltage reduction is also felt at the base of $T_2$ and decreases its conduction. When less current flows through $T_2$ and $R_5$, the voltage drop across $R_5$ declines and the effective forward bias applied to $T_1$ is now increased, which causes additional conduction through $T_1$. The voltage drop across $R_1$ increases to a greater amount, causing an additional potential decrease of the forward bias of $T_2$. Less current flows through the latter and the voltage drop across $R_5$ declines an additional amount. This regenerative effect continues, and in a short time interval $T_1$ conducts fully and $T_2$ is cut off. When $T_2$ cuts off, the voltage drop across $R_4$ declines to zero and hence the collector potential of $T_2$ rises in amplitude to that of the power source potential. This rise in collector potential represents a *change* of amplitude which is transferred to the output by coupling capacitor $C_2$. The Schmitt trigger has now attained the second stable state and will remain in this state for the duration of the input pulse. When the input pulse drops to zero, the circuit reverts to its original state with $T_1$ nonconducting and $T_2$ operating at satuation. Once the input pulse has reached sufficient amplitude to trigger the circuit, the circuit produces an output pulse of constant amplitude regardless of any amplitude changes above the triggering level of the input pulses.

Thus, if the applied pulses have undesired transients above the pulse levels which cause triggering or if noise signals occur between incoming pulses (with noise amplitudes below the triggering level), such signals will be eliminated at the output of the Schmitt trigger circuit.

## Signal-shaping Circuits

Typical circuits employed for modifying signal waveforms are shown in Fig. 1-10. Such circuits are useful for removing noise

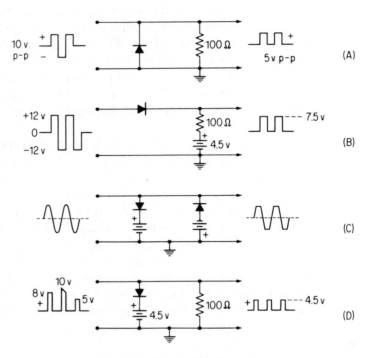

Fig. 1-10. Clipper and limiter circuits.

signals from waveforms, for clipping sinewaves to form square waves, and for converting square waves to pulse signals, as well as for maintaining a constant amplitude in a signal train of pulses or square waves.

The circuit shown in A of the figure utilizes a shunting diode across the output resistor and the purpose of the diode is to form pulse signals from an incoming square-wave type of signal as shown. When the first alternation of the input square wave has a positive polarity, the high reverse resistance offered by the diode prevents diode conduction and hence the signal current develops through the output resistor and the signal output voltage is produced as shown. For the second alternation (negative) the diode is forward biased and hence conducts. During conduction, the diode resistance is substantially lower than the output resistor value, and hence the signal is shunted around the output resistor and does not appear at the output. For the third alternation, the diode again is unable to conduct and an output waveform is produced as shown. Thus, for a square wave which has a peak-to-peak amplitude of 10 volts, a pulse train having a 5-volt peak is produced.

In B of Figure 1-10 is shown another clipper circuit which has the diode in series with the output resistance. Here, a positive bias is supplied to preset the output amplitude. In the absence of a signal, the diode does not conduct, since the battery potential applies a reverse bias to the diode. With a battery value of 4.5 volts as shown, no diode conduction occurs until a positive input signal appears which has an amplitude exceeding the bias value. Thus, if we apply a positive alternation having an amplitude of 12 volts as shown, the diode does not conduct until the pulse amplitude exceeds the 4.5 value of the bias battery and so applies the necessary forward bias to the diode. Therefore, the diode conducts for levels *above* the 4.5 value, and since the input positive alternation has a 12-volt peak value, the output pulse reaches an amplitude of 7.5 volts, as shown. Thus, the output signal has an amplitude proportional to the amplitude of the input signal which exceeds the bias potential value. During the negative alternations of the input signal, the diode is biased an additional amount into the reverse bias region, and hence the negative signals are clipped and do not appear at the output.

A shunt type of clipper using dual diodes is shown in Fig. 1-10 C. This circuit is sometimes referred to as a *slicer*. Such a circuit clips both positive and negative alternations of the sinewave to a predetermined level and thus produces an output signal which has square-wave characteristics. The degree of clipping is determined by the amplitude of the bias potentials utilized. For this circuit each diode has applied to it a battery potential opposite to that which causes conduction. Hence, neither diode conducts if no input signal is applied to the circuit. When an input signal is applied, the rising amplitude appears at the output until the level is reached where the bias value is overcome. At this time the diode conducts and clips that portion of the output signal which is above the conduction level of the diode.

A pulse-peak limiting circuit is shown in Fig. 1-10D. Here, with a bias of 4.5 volts, the amplitude of the output signals will be held at this value regardless of the signal amplitudes applied to the input which exceed the 4.5 critical value. Again, the diode is in reverse bias to the battery and will not conduct until the battery potential is exceeded. Once this value is reached by the amplitude of the incoming signal, all signals above this level will be shunted and the output signal will be limited to the 4.5 value as shown.

## Clamping Circuit

Because a pulse signal is a single-polarity type, the characteristics of a pulse are altered when a pulse is amplified in a conventional capacity-coupled transistor amplifier. Because the capacitor does not pass a d-c level, a square-wave type of waveform will be produced at the base input of the succeeding amplifier. Thus, the d-c component which characterizes the pulses to be amplified is lost. The d-c level which is lost by capacity coupling can be restored by a clamping diode as shown in Fig. 1-11. Such a circuit is often referred to as a *restorer* or

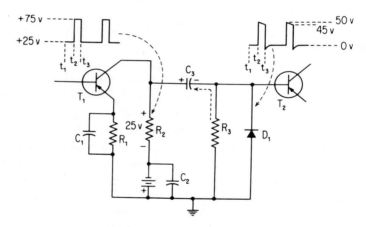

**Fig. 1-11. Clamping with diode.**

*clamper.* As shown, $RC$ coupling is utilized between transistors $T_1$ and $T_2$, and the coupling capacitor $C_3$ would upset the d-c level of the amplified pulse and hence the level is restored by the shunting diode $D_1$. In the absence of an input signal at time $t_1$, capacitor $C_3$ charges through the collector load resistor $R_2$ with a polarity as shown and in the direction indicated by the broken arrow. When the incoming pulse appears at the collector of $T_1$ at a time $t_2$, it causes the 25-volt drop across resistor $R_2$ to increase to a 75-volt value, representing a pulse amplitude of 50 volts. The rapid rise time of the leading edge of the pulse does not cause the capacitor to charge because of the long time constant. The time constant of $C_3$ and $R_3$ is long compared with the pulse duration; hence the capacitor charges only slightly more for the duration of the pulse over a time interval from $t_2$ to $t_3$. If the capacitor charge increases, for example, to a 30-volt potential from its normally charged 25-volt potential at the end of the pulse duration, the output pulse amplitude declines by 5 volts to a value of 45 volts as shown.

When the pulse developed in the collector drops to zero, the voltage drop across $R_2$ again drops to the 25-volt level (at time $t_3$) and the capacitor charge of 30 volts has a potential opposing that of the voltage drop across $R_2$. Hence the voltage across resistor $R_3$ now becomes $-30 + 25$ volts $= -5$ volts. Thus, at $t_3$, the output voltage drops to $-5$ volts as shown. This negative potential biases the diode forward and causes it to conduct. During conduction, diode $D_1$ has a low resistance and shunts $R_3$, changing the long time constant to a short time constant. Therefore, there is a rapid discharge of the additional $-5$-volt potential of the capacitor, and the original 25-volt charge now prevails across $C_3$. Thus, the interval between the output pulses is clamped to a zero level as shown.

## Differentiation

In digital computer design it is often desirable to use only the leading edge of a pulse (with its sharp-rise time) for triggering and switching. This avoids the comparatively long-duration flat top which maintains a steady-state voltage for a definite time interval. Such a flat top voltage is not only useless but affects the rapidity with which a circuit is changed from one electronic state to another. The production of a spiked waveform from a flat-topped pulse is accomplished by a circuit referred to as a *differentiating* circuit. As shown in A of Fig. 1-12, a capacitor is in series with the input, and the output is shunted by a resistor. The time constant $RC$ is *short* compared to the width of the applied pulse. Essentially it behaves as a high-pass filter by attenuating the lower-frequency signal components of the pulse while passing the high-frequency components. In sinewave signals, there is some attenuation but no alteration of the waveshape as in pulse signals.

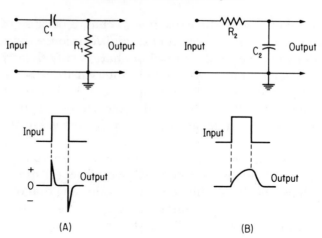

**Fig. 1-12. Differentiating and integrating.**

When voltage is applied to a capacitor, the resultant current flow is proportional to the time derivative of the voltage appearing across the capacitor

$$i = C \frac{de_c}{dt} \tag{1-1}$$

Because of the short time constant, lower-frequency signal components of the input pulse encounter a capacitive reactance greater than the resistance value. Hence, voltage across the output resistor is

$$e_R = iR = RC \frac{de}{dt} \tag{1-2}$$

Thus, when a pulse is applied at the input, the leading edge indicates a sharp rise in voltage, and maximum current flows in the circuit as the capacitor charges. Hence, there would be an immediate high current flow through resistor $R_1$, with the result that there would be a sharp rise in voltage across resistor $R_1$. If the capacitor is small in value and charges fully as the steady-state flat-top portion of the pulse arrives at the input, the current flow would decline to the capacitor and in consequence the voltage across the resistor would also decline, as shown below the circuit drawing in A of Fig. 1-12. During the trailing edge of the pulse (indicating a decline in the voltage input) the charged capacitor would suddenly discharge through resistor $R_1$, and current flow through the latter would be opposite to its direction during the charge of the capacitor. Thus, a negative voltage rise would occur. As soon as the capacitor discharged fully, the voltage drop across $R_1$ would fall to zero, as shown in the waveform drawing of A.

Thus, by differentiating a pulse, two spike type of signals are procured, one with a positive polarity and the other with a negative polarity. Either the positive or negative signal can be eliminated by appropriate clipper circuitry to obtain the desired signal polarity.

### Integration

A circuit having opposite characteristics to the differentiating circuit can be formed by a series resistor and a shunt capacitor, as shown in B of Fig. 1-12. Such a circuit is known as an *integrating* circuit, and the $RC$ is a *long* time constant compared to the pulse width. Essentially, the integrator circuit behaves as a low-pass filter by attenuating the higher-frequency signal components of the pulse but passing the lower-frequency signals. The circuit is used in analog computers and also, on occasion, in various other branches of electronics. (The differentiating circuit finds practical applications in digital computers.)

For the integrating circuit, higher-frequency signal components find the capacitive reactance of $C_2$ lower than the resistance value of $R_2$. Hence, the output signal voltage is proportional to the integral of the input signal. The input signal and resultant output waveform are shown in the lower drawings in Fig. 1-12B. With a long time constant, the capacitor charges slowly for the flat-top portion of the pulse and discharges slowly for the trailing edge. The result is a loss of both the steep leading and trailing pulse edges.

While there are occasions when integrating circuits are of considerable usefulness in specialized electronic circuitry, there are also occasions when undesired integrating effects may be present because of faulty circuit design. Also, capacitor $C_2$ in Fig. 1-12 may represent shunt capacitance between signal-carrying conductors and ground, or interelement capacitances in transistors. Such integrating effects will impair the waveshape of the signals (causing distortion). Signal modification and reamplification must then be undertaken to restore the proper waveshape and amplitude. (More information on integrating circuits is given in Chapter 11, Analog Computer Principles).

## Amplifiers and Buffers

Low signal amplitudes in a computer are brought to the desired level by conventional transistor amplifiers. The three basic methods for connecting a transistor to a circuit are shown in Fig. 1-13. These circuits could also utilize NPN transistors with appropriate battery polarity reversals.

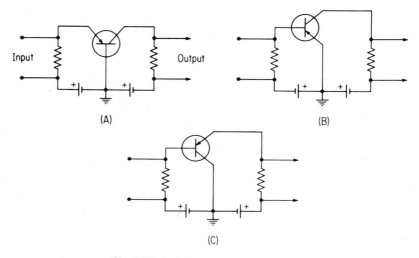

Fig. 1-13. Basic transistor circuit types.

The grounded-base circuit shown in A of the figure compares with the grounded-grid vacuum-tube circuit. There is no phase reversal of the signal between input and output circuits, and, because of the grounded base, the circuit finds wide application in the handling of *RF* signals, where triode amplifiers are susceptible to regeneration and oscillation. The use of a grounded-base circuit eliminates the need for neutralization of the regeneration. Because of the grounded base, there is effective isolation between the input and output circuits.

The grounded-emitter circuit shown in B of Fig. 1-13 compares with the grounded-cathode vacuum-tube type and is the most widely used amplifier circuit. There is a phase reversal of the signal between input and output. Because of this, it assumes a logic function and is discussed in greater detail in Chapter 3 with the other logic circuits.

The circuit shown in C is known as an *emitter follower* and has also been called a *grounded-collector* circuit. The circuit compares with the vacuum-tube cathode-follower circuit, and in each case the term in-dicates that the output signal *follows* the input signal in phase. Because there is no phase reversal between input and output, the circuit is of particular advantage in logic design, as described in Chapter 3. The collector is at signal ground, and the output is taken from the emitter.

For junction-transistor emitter-follower circuits the input imped-ance is high and can exceed 300,000 ohms. The output impedance is low and may be less than 100 ohms for some circuits. Thus it is useful as a step-down device for transferring signals to other circuits with a minimum attenuation of the high-frequency harmonic components of a pulse signal. As such, it is superior to a step-down transformer while essentially performing the same function of impedance matching between a high-impedance circuit output and a low-impedance input. In computers it is also useful for developing the higher signal current levels needed when coupling diode logic circuits to several other cir-cuits. In such circuit-isolation usage it is sometimes called a *buffer*. Signal *voltage* amplification is less than unity.

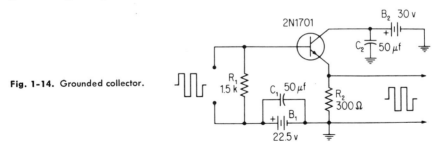

**Fig. 1-14. Grounded collector.**

A practical emitter-follower circuit is shown in Fig. 1-14. The collector is placed at *signal* ground by capacitor $C_2$, which provides a low reactance for the pulse signals. The necessary forward bias for the NPN transistor is supplied by $D_1$, which makes the emitter minus with respect to the base. The necessary reverse bias for the collector is supplied by $D_2$, which makes the collector plus with respect to the emitter. The input signal is applied between base and emitter and developed across the emitter resistor $R_2$ in phase with the input signal.

## Signal Delay Systems

Pulse-signal delay systems are used in computers for introducing a delay in a pulse (or a series of pulses) for a predetermined time interval equal to the duration of one or more arithmetical places. Such a delay is necessary in some calculation circuits and registers as is more fully explained in subsequent chapters.

One method for producing a signal delay is to employ the network shown in Fig. 1-15. A section of coaxial cable or other transmission

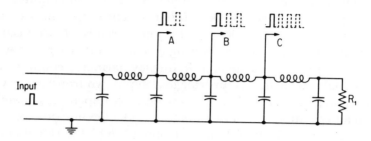

**Fig. 1-15.** Delay line.

line may also be employed with the inductor and capacitor components of Fig. 1-15 representing the lumped $L$ and $C$ constants of the line. The amount of delay obtained is determined by the time interval which prevails for a signal to travel through a given section. This time interval is found by

$$T_i = \sqrt{LC} \qquad (1\text{-}3)$$

where $T_i$ is the time interval in seconds,
$\quad\quad L$ is the inductance in henrys,
$\quad\quad C$ is the capacity in farads.

As shown in Fig. 1-15, the line may be tapped at various sections to obtain the precise degree of delay needed. For instance, if one pulse is applied to the input, it will appear at the output marked $A$ at a time interval equal to the distance between pulses. Thus, the pulse output at $A$ would represent a second place pulse shown by the solid line instead of the first place pulse indicated by the dotted line. The output from $B$ would represent a third place pulse instead of the first place pulse applied to the input, again shown by the solid line as compared with the dotted lines. The output at $C$ represents a three-place delay, with the dotted outlines showing the amount of delay encountered. Thus, with a single pulse representing the numeral 1 applied to the line, the output at $C$ would represent the number 1000. Similarly if 11 were entered, the output at $C$ would represent 11000. (The number representations are *binary* as explained in the next chapter.)

Delay lines are usually terminated by a load resistor equivalent to the surge impedance of the line. The surge impedance Z of the type of line illustrated is a function of the square root of the value of the inductance divided by the value of the capacitance

$$Z = \sqrt{L/C} \qquad (1\text{-}4)$$

The load resistor is necessary so that the energy which reaches the end of the line is absorbed and not reflected back as would be the case if the line were not terminated by a proper resistance. If no resistor were placed at the end of the line, the energy which reaches the end of the line would be reflected back again and would reappear, displaced in phase, at the various output terminals. This reflection process would produce undesired results, since there would be multiple pulse outputs for every pulse input at any given output terminal.

By using the circuits discussed earlier in this chapter, a delay system can be formed as shown in Fig. 1-16. Here a single-shot multivi-

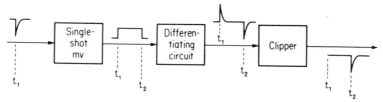

Fig. 1-16. Delay system.

brator is triggered by an input pulse which is to be delayed for a predetermined interval. The multivibrator output pulse has a duration equal to the delay desired, with its leading edge $t_1$ coinciding with the time of the input pulse. The multivibrator output pulse is differentiated, producing a positive spike $t_1$ for the leading edge and a negative spike $t_2$ for the trailing edge. The positive pulse is removed by a clipper circuit as shown, and the remaining $t_2$ pulse is the equivalent of the original pulse delayed by the required time interval.

## Direct-coupled (DC) Amplifier

A direct-coupled amplifier is a special-purpose type designed to offer a number of advantages over those using capacitive coupling or transformer coupling between stages. By eliminating such coupling components, the reactance effects on signals are nullified. Consequently signal frequency response is improved and the waveshape of pulse signals is retained. Signal-to-noise ratio is also improved, and low-frequency response is extended to the d-c level.

A direct-coupled amplifier, using dissimilar (complementing) transistors is shown in Fig 1-17 A. The first transistor has the collector

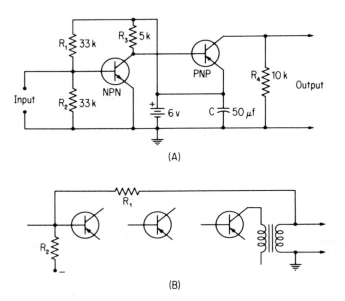

(A)

(B)

**Fig. 1-17. Direct coupling and feedback.**

directly coupled to the base of the second transistor. For the input transistor (NPN) the emitter obtains the necessary negative potential from the negative terminal of the battery through the common ground lead. The positive terminal of the battery is connected to the top of two series resistors $R_1$ and $R_2$, which form a voltage-divider circuit. Because these resistors have equal values, the base of the first transistor is positive with respect to the emitter by 3 volts. The collector is positive with respect to the emitter because of the coupling to the positive terminal of the battery by $R_3$.

The second transistor, a PNP type, has its emitter connected to the positive terminal of the battery for the required forward bias. Resistor $R_3$ plus the impedance of the first transistor are also across the battery and hence behave as a voltage divider. Thus, the junction of

$R_3$ and the collector of the first transistor are negative with respect to the positive terminal of the battery. This causes the base of the second transistor to be negative with respect to the positive emitter, providing forward bias. Resistor $R_4$ supplies the necessary negative potential for the collector (with respect to the emitter) for the second transistor, this providing the required reverse bias for the PNP transistor. Additional stages can be added without increasing source potentials beyond normal power-handling requirements in successive stages.

## Inverse Feedback

Inverse (negative) signal-voltage feedback is used for reduction of harmonic distortion, increased bandpass, and noise reduction. With inverse feedback, signal amplification is reduced in proportion to the amount of inverse feedback employed. In such a circuit, a portion of output signal voltage is applied to an earlier circuit. The signal which is fed back is out of phase with the signal at the place where the feedback signal is applied.

A typical inverse feedback system is shown in B of Fig. 1-17. Here, a portion of the output signal appearing across the secondary of the transformer is fed back to the base input circuit of the first-stage transistor. The amplitude of the feedback voltage is selected by the ohmic value of $R_1$. The feedback signal, introduced into the base of the first transistor, appears at the output of this transistor out of phase with the distortion developed internally. In consequence, cancellation of distortion (or noise signals) is obtained to the degree established by the level of the feedback voltage.

The amplitude of the voltage fed back is designated by the lower-case Greek beta, $\beta$, and it indicates the decimal equivalent of the percentage of output voltage fed back. Another symbol, $A'$, designates the signal-voltage amplification *with* feedback. The $A$ without the prime sign indicates signal-voltage amplification *without* feedback. The product $A\beta$ is sometimes used to indicate the *feedback factor*. Thus, $1 - A\beta$ is a measure of the feedback amplitude. In equation form, the signal-voltage amplification using inverse feedback is

$$A' = \frac{A}{1 - A\beta} \qquad (1\text{-}5)$$

where $A'$ is the signal-voltage amplification with feedback,

   $A$ is the signal-voltage amplification without feedback,

   $\beta$ is the decimal equivalent of percentage of output signal voltage fed back.

When the feedback factor $A\beta$ is much greater than 1, the signal-voltage gain is independent of the factor $A$ and the equation for signal-voltage amplification with feedback becomes

$$A' = -\frac{1}{\beta} \qquad (1\text{-}6)$$

The necessary $180°$-phase difference for inverse feedback can be obtained by using an odd number of stages or by reversing the leads of the output transformer when even-numbered stages are used. If the feedback is not negative, degeneration will not occur and the positive feedback will produce regeneration.

Inverse feedback, used with direct-coupled amplifiers, forms *operational amplifiers* for use in analog computers, as described more fully in Chapter 11.

### Clock-pulse Generation

In a digital computer, the pulse waveforms are used not only to represent numerical values but also to initiate certain processes, to gate signals in or out of certain circuitry as required, and to time the sequential steps in arithmetic operations or the processing of data. Thus, all pulses must have precise timing to obtain precision results and to synchronize the various steps which the computer must undertake to perform its functions properly.

In order to assure a stable pulse repetition rate, a crystal-controlled oscillator is used. If such an oscillator is of the resonant-circuit

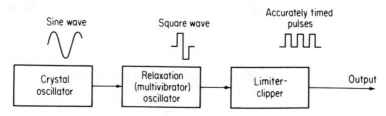

**Fig. 1-18. Clock-pulse generating system.**

type, the output will be in the form of sinewaves. Hence, to obtain the necessary pulse signals, the system shown in Fig. 1 18 may be employed. Here, the crystal oscillator is used to synchronize a relaxation type of oscillator. Thus, the latter becomes locked into the stable crystal-oscillator frequency and produces square waves under crystal control. The square waves, in turn, are clipped to produce the required pulses. If positive-polarity pulses represent logic-1 quantities, the nature of the clipping is as shown in Fig. 1-18. For negative pulses, the positive portions would be removed.

By incorporating a crystal in a multivibrator type of oscillator, one stage of the system can be eliminated, and this method has been used. Another method is to lock in the multivibrator or pulse-rate system by using the line-voltage frequency. Since this 60-cycle-per-second a-c is regulated for stable frequency at the generating plants, it provides a ready means for basic frequency control.

Regardless of the methods used, however, the system is referred to as the *clock* and the output signals are called *clock pulses*. They represent the shortest operational time interval of the computer, and, for longer pulse intervals, the clock pulses are used as the gating control signals for circuits which produce such longer pulse intervals, as detailed later.

## PROBLEMS

1. Briefly explain the basic differences between a digital computer and an analog computer.

2. Define the terms *accuracy* and *precision* in relation to computer systems.

3. Define the terms *storage*, *address*, *program*, *read-in*, and *read-out*.

4. Draw a series of positive pulses to indicate the following numbers: 101, 1101, 1011, and 11100111.

5. Explain the differences between serial-form and parallel-form computer signals.

6. Explain why a crystal oscillator maintains a stable signal frequency.

7. Prepare a schematic of an astable multivibrator using PNP type of transistors, and briefly explain its basic operation.

8. List some of the usages for a monostable multivibrator.

9. Prepare a schematic of a Schmitt trigger using PNP transistors, and explain its operation.

10. Explain the purpose of the circuit shown in Fig. 1-10D.

11. On what occasion is a *restorer* (clamper) necessary?

12. Explain in what manner a differentiation circuit alters a pulse waveshape.

13. In what manner may integration be an undesired factor in computer circuitry?

14. In what type computer is integration used deliberately?

15. Redraw the basic circuits shown in Fig. 1-13, using NPN transistors instead of PNP, showing correct polarities for both forward and reverse bias.

16. What advantages does a direct-coupled amplifier have over reactance-coupled types?

17. What are the advantages of inverse feedback?

18. What is meant by the *feedback factor* of an amplifier?

19. What is the purpose for a clock-pulse generating system?

20. How are clock pulses related to the operational time of a digital computer?

# COMPUTER

# ARITHMETIC

**2**

**Introduction.** In Chapter 1 the types of signals used in a digital computer were illustrated and discussed, and it was indicated that the presence of a pulse represents the numeral 1, whereas the absence of a pulse equals zero. This is a *base-2* (binary) system which, while limited to only two arithmetic symbols (0 and 1), can still be used to perform all the normal calculation operations of addition, subtraction, multiplication, division, and other numerical manipulations performed by the common base-10 system. The advantages of the binary system over the base 10 for computers include simplicity and reliability. Accuracy is obtained because circuit operation can be confined to two states: the *off* condition representative of *zero*, and the *on* state indicating the number *one*. Hence, changes in transistor (or tube) characteristics over extended usage have a negligible effect on operation as opposed to the variables which would accrue if an attempt were made to base numerical representations on the slope of the transistor's characteristic curve.

## The Binary System

The manner in which only two symbols (0 and 1) can be utilized in complex addition, subtraction, division, and multiplication processes can be more clearly understood by reviewing initially the manner in

**35**

which a simple desk type of adding machine functions. The basic principle can be illustrated by showing disks with equally spaced numbers on them from 0 to 9, as shown in Fig. 2-1. Assume that the disks are wheel devices with tripping-mechanism linkages between them.

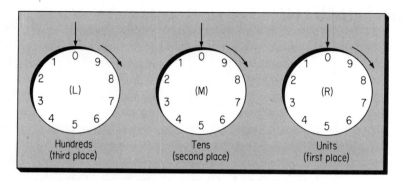

**Fig. 2—1.** Simple adding machine.

In such a simple adding machine, the wheel on the right designated as $R$ represents the units, or first-place digits. When this wheel is turned one-tenth rotation to the right, the number 1 appears below the arrow indicating that the machine has *stored* the numeral 1 and is ready to add another number to it. Successive turns will increase the number beneath the arrow until number 9 is reached. On the next one-tenth turn, the wheel returns to 0 but in doing so an internal trip lever turns the second wheel $M$ one-tenth turn. The middle wheel thus indicates the tens, and it would take another complete revolution of wheel $R$ to cause wheel $M$ to turn one-tenth turn to complete 20. A complete revolution of wheel $M$ will trip wheel $L$ one-tenth turn to register the numeral 1, which, in the third place from the right, represents hundreds. This is the basic decimal system we utilize, since we have only 10 digits (0 to 9), and the symbols used for these numbers are Arabic. As mentioned in Chapter 1 (in the section on Digital Development), the reason for only 10 digits in our decimal-system probably has its origin in the early days of civilization. At that time, when man first found it expedient to count, he used his fingers as the reference for indicating one, two, or more items up to 10. Since only 10 symbols are used, we exhaust our stock of identifying symbols after counting from 0 to 9. Thus, in order to indicate a larger number, initial symbols must be repeated by combining them.

Symbol systems other than the Arabic exist, however, such as the Roman numeral system, still used on some clocks as well as in some published works (such as in the preface numbering and appendix numbering of books). The Roman numeral system utilizes the letters of the alphabet of which the letter I represents 1, V equals 5, and X equals 10. In the Roman numeral system a representation of 2 involves placing an additional I beside the original I, and 3 is repre- by placing an additional I beside the two I's. Once the next highest order symbol is reached (V) an additional letter I is used to indicate 6, as VI, and for 7 an additional letter I is placed beside it, VII, etc.

The decimal system with a base 10 is not the only one which can be employed for arithmetical purposes. Systems with a base 5 or even a base 15 can, in principle, be employed. An extremely useful system for digital computers is one using the base 2, utilizing only the two symbols 0 and 1 and known as *binary* arithmetic. Each digit is called a *bit* and use of the 0 and 1 symbols is known as *binary notation*.

The number of digits employed in a numbering system is known as the *radix*. Thus, *radix* 10 (0 to 9) designates the decimal system commonly in use. A *radix two* refers to the binary number system which utilizes two numbers, 0 and 1. A radix eight and a radix sixteen have, on occasion, been used to a limited extent for some computers, but the radix two system is the most suitable for digital computer application.

The manner in which a system using only two identifying digits can be set up as an adding machine is shown in Fig. 2-2. Here again are three wheels, *R*, *M*, and *L*. As before, the progression is from right to left in *accumulating* the results of additive digits. In the case shown, however, each wheel has only a 0 and a 1 on it. Instead of each wheel

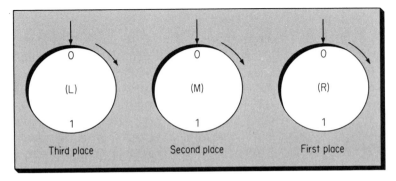

| Third place | Second place | First place |

rotating one-tenth turn to indicate the addition of the numeral 1, each wheel rotates *one-half turn* to indicate the insertion of the numeral 1. Thus, for the beginning of the addition, each wheel would be set as shown in Fig. 2-2 to represent 0. When 1 is to be added to another number, the $R$ wheel on the right is turned one-half turn and the numeral 1 appears below the arrow to indicate the *registering* of this number. The numeral 1 representation is similar to the base-10 adder previously mentioned, but the addition of other numbers changes the "answers" appearing under the arrows to a considerably greater

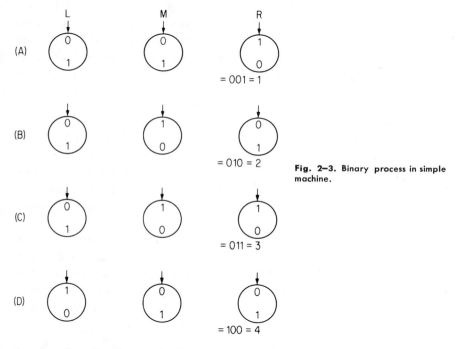

Fig. 2–3. Binary process in simple machine.

degree than in the decimal system. If, for instance, the $R$ wheel is turned another one-half turn to indicate the insertion of another digit, it will trip wheel $M$ and cause it to rotate one-half turn. The process is illustrated in A of Fig. 2-3 where the right wheel $R$ indicates the numeral 1 beneath the arrow, while the middle wheel $M$ and the left wheel $L$ indicate 0's. If another digit 1 is to be added to the 1 now stored in the machine, the right wheel will be rotated another one-half turn. This will cause the middle wheel to rotate one-half turn also and register 1. The right wheel, however, returns to 0 as shown in B of Fig. 2-3. Now, only the center wheel registers a 1, but in this device the sum under the arrows, 010, represents the decimal number 2.

If another digit is to be added to the sum now stored in the machine, the wheel at the right will be made to rotate another half turn, and the numeral 1 will appear under the arrow as shown in C. Since, however, it takes a full revolution of the $R$ wheel to turn the $M$ wheel one-half turn, the $M$ wheel is not tripped during this operation but remains with the numeral 1 beneath the arrow. Hence, the machine now registers 011, which represents 3 in our base-10 (decimal) system.

To carry the illustration further, assume that another digit is to be added to the stored number of the machine. In such an instance the right wheel will be rotated another one-half turn, which will bring the 0 of this wheel under the arrow, as shown in Fig. 2-3D. Now, however, the $R$ wheel will cause the $M$ wheel to rotate one-half turn bringing the 0 of the latter to the top. Since the $M$ wheel has now made a complete revolution, it trips the $L$ wheel at the left one-half turn and registers the number 1 of this wheel under the arrow. Now the machine indicates 100, and this represents 4 in our base-10 (decimal) system. The addition of another number will cause the right wheel to indicate 1, and hence the machine will register 101, which equals 5 in our decimal system. If such wheels are utilized, a large sum of numbers can be added just as is the case of the decimal type of adding machine shown in Fig. 2-1. The numbers represented by the wheels are binary numbers, and the process of utilizing such numbers is binary notation.

The chart shown below represents the decimal numbers indicated by the numerals appearing on the wheels. Five possible wheels are shown, and the wheel positions also indicate the *place* of the numerals from right to left in the binary system. The decimal count to 20 is given, though this is not the limit of a five-place counter. For practice, the binary notation should be completed by the reader up to the limit of the numbers which can be indicated by the five-place device.

You will note that in the first-place column the numeral 1 alternates with 0 for the entire vertical column. In the second-place column, two 0's alternate with two 1's in progression down this column. In the third-place column, four 0's alternate with four 1's for this entire column. If the binary numbers up to 100 or 200 were to be included, this same radix 2 factor would prevail for all the successive columns added to the left, following the 1, 2, 4, 8, 16, etc., characteristic pattern.

The method employed to identify by symbols the progressive value of numbers is the same in both the decimal and binary systems. In our decimal system we only have 10 different symbols (0 to 9). When

| Wheel Position: | 5 | 4 | 3 | 2 | 1 | | Decimal Sum |
|---|---|---|---|---|---|---|---|
| Wheel Registration: | 0 | 0 | 0 | 0 | 0 | = | 0 |
| | 0 | 0 | 0 | 0 | 1 | = | 1 |
| | 0 | 0 | 0 | 1 | 0 | = | 2 |
| | 0 | 0 | 0 | 1 | 1 | = | 3 |
| | 0 | 0 | 1 | 0 | 0 | = | 4 |
| | 0 | 0 | 1 | 0 | 1 | = | 5 |
| | 0 | 0 | 1 | 1 | 0 | = | 6 |
| | 0 | 0 | 1 | 1 | 1 | = | 7 |
| | 0 | 1 | 0 | 0 | 0 | = | 8 |
| | 0 | 1 | 0 | 0 | 1 | = | 9 |
| | 0 | 1 | 0 | 1 | 0 | = | 10 |
| | 0 | 1 | 0 | 1 | 1 | = | 11 |
| | 0 | 1 | 1 | 0 | 0 | = | 12 |
| | 0 | 1 | 1 | 0 | 1 | = | 13 |
| | 0 | 1 | 1 | 1 | 0 | = | 14 |
| | 0 | 1 | 1 | 1 | 1 | = | 15 |
| | 1 | 0 | 0 | 0 | 0 | = | 16 |
| | 1 | 0 | 0 | 0 | 1 | = | 17 |
| | 1 | 0 | 0 | 1 | 0 | = | 18 |
| | 1 | 0 | 0 | 1 | 1 | = | 19 |
| | 1 | 0 | 1 | 0 | 0 | = | 20 |

we reach the 9 count, we have exhausted our symbols and, to continue with the count, we place our second symbol (1) in *second* place and then reuse our original symbols in *first* place to produce 10, 11, 12, 13, etc. Similarly, in binary notation, when we have exhausted our symbols (which occurs at the binary count of 1), we place our second symbol (1) in second place, and repeat our original symbols in first place to produce 10, followed by 11 (which now represents 3 in decimal notation). Now in the binary system we have exhausted the symbols in the first two places, just as we have in the decimal system when we have reached 99.

When 99 is reached in the decimal system, we place the second symbol (1) in *third* place and reuse our original symbols in *first* and *second* place to produce 100, 101, 102 103, etc. Similarly, in binary notation, when we have exhausted our symbols in the first and second place (which occurs at the binary count of 11), we place our second symbol (1) in third place, and repeat our original symbols in the first and second places to produce 100, (which equals 4), followed by

101, 110, and 111 to represent 5, 6, and 7. The same method is followed throughout the entire progression of counts.

The binary system is based on the powers of 2 and each power of 2 which a place represents can be set down, as follows:

| | 8 | 7 | 6 | 5 | 4 | 3 | 2 | 1 | ←*Place* |
|---|---|---|---|---|---|---|---|---|---|
| etc., | $2^7$ | $2^6$ | $2^5$ | $2^4$ | $2^3$ | $2^2$ | $2^1$ | $2^0$ | ←*Power* |
| | 128 | 64 | 32 | 16 | 8 | 4 | 2 | 1 | ←*Value* |

The foregoing table is useful for ascertaining the decimal equivalent of a binary sum. If, for instance, the decimal equivalent of the binary number 111 is desired, reference to the foregoing table indicates the first digit has a value of 1, the second digit a value of 2, and the third digit a value of 4. The decimal sum is then equivalent to

$$\begin{matrix} 1 & 1 & 1 \\ 4 + & 2 + & 1 = 7 \end{matrix}$$

In utilizing this method, however, it must be remembered that 0's in *any* place cancel out the value such a place would have. Thus, if the decimal equivalent of the binary number 1010 is needed, reference to the table indicates that the fourth-place digit represents 8 and the second-place digit represents 2. Hence, the resultant decimal sum is indicated as follows:

$$\begin{matrix} 1 & 0 & 1 & 0 \\ 8 + & & 2 & = 10 \end{matrix}$$

In this manner, any sum in binary notation can be converted to its base-10 (decimal) equivalent by reference to the powers of 2 table shown above. Another example will help in understanding the process involved:

$$\begin{matrix} \text{Binary sum:} & 1 & 0 & 1 & 0 & 1 & 0 & 0 \\ \text{Value:} & 64 & + & 16 & + & 4 & & = 84 \end{matrix}$$

A decimal number can be converted to binary by dividing successively by two and writing down each remainder. The sequence of remainders forms the binary equivalent of the base-10 number. (The remainder will always be either a 0 or a 1.) As an example, assume we wish to find the binary number equivalent of 86.

|  | | Quotient | Remainder |
|---|---|---|---|
| $\frac{86}{2}$ | = | 43 | 0 |
| $\frac{43}{2}$ | = | 21 | 1 |
| $\frac{21}{2}$ | = | 10 | 1 |
| $\frac{10}{2}$ | = | 5 | 0 |
| $\frac{5}{2}$ | = | 2 | 1 |
| $\frac{2}{2}$ | = | 1 | 0 |
| $\frac{1}{2}$ | = | 0 | 1 |

Thus, writing down the remainders with the uppermost bit at the right produces

$$1010110 = 86 \quad (64 + 16 + 4 + 2)$$

For the last step, since 1 divided by 2 does not yield a whole number, the 1 is set down as a final remainder, as shown.

As an additional illustration of this process, assume we wish to find the binary equivalent of 95. The sequential steps are

|  | | | Remainder |
|---|---|---|---|
| $\frac{95}{2}$ | = | 47 | 1 |
| $\frac{47}{2}$ | = | 23 | 1 |
| $\frac{23}{2}$ | = | 11 | 1 |
| $\frac{11}{2}$ | = | 5 | 1 |
| $\frac{5}{2}$ | = | 2 | 1 |
| $\frac{2}{2}$ | = | 1 | 0 |
| $\frac{1}{2}$ | = | 0 | 1 |

Thus, setting the upper remainder numbers at the right, we get

$$1011111 = 95 \quad (64 + 16 + 8 + 4 + 2 + 1)$$

## Binary Addition

Binary numbers can be added in similar fashion to the addition employed in the decimal system. If, for instance, the binary number 11 (3) is to be added to the binary number 100 (4), the numbers will be added together in simple fashion as shown below to give the binary sum of 111. Reference to the table given earlier indicates that this binary number equals 7 and thus proves the addition.

$$
\begin{array}{ll}
\phantom{+}11 & (3) \quad \text{addend} \\
+100 & (4) \quad \text{augend} \\
\hline
111 & (7) \quad \text{sum}
\end{array}
$$

In binary arithmetic, however, the addition process requires the "carrying" of a number just as it does with the decimal system addition. If, for instance, we added 01 to 101, it would be set down as follows:

$$
\begin{array}{l}
\phantom{+}01 \\
+101 \\
\hline
\end{array}
$$

The addition of the two digits in the first-place column would represent the decimal number 2; but, since the numeral 1 is our highest number in the binary system, we must set down a 0 for the *sum* of 1 and 1, just as we set down a 0 in the first place if we have reached the highest order of our decimal numbers, 9, and are adding another 1 to it. After setting down the 0 we carry 1 to the second place, and therefore the binary sum would be 110 as shown below.

$$
\begin{array}{l}
{}^{1}01 \\
+101 \\
\hline
110
\end{array}
$$

Proof of this addition can be obtained by reference to the table, since 01 equals 1 and 101 equals 5 and the sum of these equals 6 (110). (The rule to remember is that $1 + 1 = 0$ with 1 to carry.)

Sometimes it is necessary to carry more than a single digit, as represented by the following example:

$$
\begin{array}{lllll}
 & & {}^{1}1_{0} & 1 \\
 & & 1 & 1_{0} \\
{}^{1} & {}^{1}1 & 0 & 1 \\
\hline
1 & 0 & 1 & 1
\end{array}
$$

Here, we should start with the top first-place digit and add this to the next column first-place digit, which gives us 0 and 1 to carry. The remaining 1 in the bottom row plus the 0 resulting from the addition of the first place digits equals 1, and hence the numeral 1 is placed below the first-place column as shown. In the second-place column the 1 which carried plus the top 1 equals 0 with 1 to carry. Zero plus 1 in the second column equals 1, and this is set down below as shown. In the third-place vertical column the 1 which was carried plus the 1 in the column equals 0 with 1 to carry. When the 1 which is carried is placed in the answer, the resultant binary sum equals 1011, which represents 11 in the decimal system. Since the binary numbers which were added are represented in decimal system addition as 3 plus 3 plus 5, the true sum has been obtained by the addition of the binary numbers.

## Binary Subtraction

Binary numbers can also be subtracted from other binary numbers in a fashion similar to that employed in the decimal system. If, for instance, the binary number 11 is to be subtracted from 111 the operation will be as follows:

$$
\begin{array}{rll}
111 & (7) & \text{minuend} \\
-11 & (3) & \text{subtrahend} \\
\hline
100 & (4) & \text{remainder}
\end{array}
$$

The foregoing is a simple illustration, since the digit 1 is subtracted from another digit just as in the decimal system. As in the latter, however, it is necessary to "borrow" a number from the next place when the number in the minuend is smaller than the number in the subtrahend. This is shown in the following example where the binary number 01 is to be subtracted from the binary number 110:

$$
\begin{array}{rl}
110 & (6) \\
-01 & (1) \\
\hline
101 & (5)
\end{array}
$$

Since the numeral 1 in the subtrahend is a larger number than the 0 in the minuend above it, one numeral is borrowed from the second place. (The second-place numeral 1 plus the 0 in first place represent 2.) The subtraction of the first-place numeral 1 from the minuend therefore equals 1. The second-place subtraction indicates a 0 which is to be subtracted from the minuend number. Since the second-place minuend was borrowed, however, it represents 0, and hence the subtraction gives the remainder as the binary number 101 as shown above. As in the decimal system, borrowing from second and third place is also necessary, as shown below:

$$
\begin{array}{ll}
1000 \quad (8) & 1000 \quad (8) \\
-11 \quad (3) & -111 \quad (7) \\
\hline
101 \quad (5) & \overline{0001} \quad (1)
\end{array}
$$

## *Binary Multiplication*

Multiplication with binary numbers can also be performed as with the decimal system. If, for instance, the binary number 101 (5) is to be multiplied by 11 (3), the multiplicand is set down once to represent the first-order multiplier and then is set down again but displaced to the left by one place to indicate the second-place multiplier function. Addition of these two (known as *partial products*) is then performed as in regular multiplication problems. The result is the binary number 1111, representing the decimal equivalent 15 as shown below:

$$
\begin{array}{ll}
101 & (5) \quad \text{multiplicand} \\
\times 11 & (3) \quad \text{multiplier} \\
\hline
\left.\begin{array}{l} 101 \\ 101 \end{array}\right\} & \qquad \text{partial products} \\
\hline
1111 & (15) \quad \text{product}
\end{array}
$$

If the multiplier has a 0 in it, the 0's may be set down as in the example shown below. The same problem given above is used for the example, except that the multplicand and multiplier numbers have been interchanged.

$$
\begin{array}{r}
11 \\
\times 101 \\
\hline
11 \\
00 \\
11 \\
\hline
1111
\end{array}
$$

As the following example indicates, in some instances it will be necessary to employ the carry principle in the addition process just as would be the case in high numbers involving the decimal system. In

the following multiplication of 111 (7) by 11 (3), the decimal sum of 21
is indicated by the binary sum 10101 as shown.

$$
\begin{array}{r}
1\ 1\ 1 \\
\times 1\ 1 \\
\hline
{}^1 1_0\ 1\ 1 \\
{}^1 1\ \ 1\ \ 1 \\
\hline
1\ 0\ 1\ 0\ 1 = 16 + 4 + 1 = 21
\end{array}
$$

## Binary Division

Division can also be employed, and the problem becomes quite
simple when first- or second-place 0's are involved, since such 0's can
be canceled just as in the decimal system. A simple example is shown
below, where the binary number 1100 is to be divided by 100. Cross-
ing off the end 0's indicates the quotient to be 11 (3), which is the
correct answer.

$$
\begin{array}{ll}
\text{Dividend} & \dfrac{1100}{100} \quad \dfrac{(12)}{(\ 4)} = 11 \quad (3) \quad \text{quotient} \\
\text{Divisor} &
\end{array}
$$

A more complex type of division occurs when the binary number
1110 is to be divided by 11, or the binary number 10010 is to be
divided by 110. Both examples are shown below:

$$
\begin{array}{cc}
\begin{array}{r}
10 \\
111\,\overline{)\,1110} \\
111 \\
\hline
0
\end{array}
&
\begin{array}{r}
11 \\
110\,\overline{)\,10010} \\
110 \\
\hline
110 \\
110 \\
\hline
\end{array}
\end{array}
$$

In the second example shown above, the binary number 110 is
larger than the first three digits in the dividend, 100; hence the division process must embrace that portion of the dividend represented by
1001, which follows the general rule in decimal divisions.

The divisor 110 "goes into" the 1001 portion of the dividend and
hence is set below it as shown. When 110 is subtracted from 1001 by
binary subtraction, the resultant is 11. When the last 0 in the dividend
is then brought down, the result is 110, which means that the divisor
can go into this number once, and, when this is indicated in the quotient, the proper answer 11 is derived. The latter problem converted to

the decimal system involves dividing 18 by 6 to provide a quotient of 3, as reference to the previous table will indicate.

## *Fractional Values*

In the base-10 system the place representation to the *left* of the decimal point is in the order of units, tens, hundreds, thousands, tens of thousands, etc. In the binary system the order is units, twos, fours, eights, sixteens, etc. In the base-10 system the place representation to the *right* of the decimal point is in the order of tenths, hundredths, thousandths, etc. In the binary system the order to the right is halves, fourths, eighths, sixteenths, etc. Thus, while in the base-10 system 5.1 represents five and one-tenth, in the binary system 101.1 equals *five and one-half*. Similarly, 0.01 equals one-fourth and 0.001 equals one-eighth. (Since the term *decimal point* refers to base-10 notation, the term *binary point* is used instead in binary notation.)

In the base-10 system the number 0.11 equals eleven-hundredths, but in the binary system the number 0.11 represents three-fourths. This occurs because two places to the right of the binary point indicates fourths and the number 11 in binary notation is *three*. Similarly, 0.011 in binary equals three-eighths, and 0.0011 equals three-sixteenths. The number 0.111 in binary represents *seven-eighths* (the binary number 111 equals 7, and three places to the right of the binary point equals eighths). Some random numbers are given below for additional reference:

$$
\begin{array}{rl}
110.1 & = \text{six and one-half} \\
111.11 & = \text{seven and three-fourths} \\
1010.101 & = \text{ten and five-eighths} \\
11.1001 & = \text{three and nine-sixteenths} \\
101.00101 & = \text{five and five thirty-seconds}
\end{array}
$$

In binary fractional values the limitations are no different than in the base-10 system. In base 10, for instance, we should have to represent three-quarters as 0.75. This value is *equal* to three-quarters. In binary, however, we can get an exact representation, 0.11. In binary we should have to indicate twenty-five hundredths as 0.01, which is equal to that sum. In decimal notation, however, we can indicate the precise value by 0.25. If it were necessary to show the true three-quarters in base 10, we should have to show it as 3/4. Similarly, to represent a number such as 0.3 in binary, we must resort to 11/1010 (3/10).

### Complement Numbers

By employing the complementing principle in arithmetic operations it is possible to perform subtraction processes by *addition*. This method simplifies the subtraction procedures in computers because it permits both addition and subtraction to be performed by common circuitry. In order to understand how this principle is applied to binary notation, it is necessary to examine first the nines complement process as applied to decimal notation. The process involved consists of changing the subtrahend (the number to be subtracted) and then employing an addition process. This can be better understood by analyzing a typical example. For instance, assume that 2341 is to be subtracted from 7465 to produce a remainder of 5124 as follows:

$$\begin{array}{r} 7465 \\ -2341 \\ \hline 5124 \end{array}$$

The subtrahend is now changed by subtracting each digit from 9. Thus, 2341 becomes 7658 because 2 from 9 is 7, 3 from 9 is 6, etc. This changed subtrahend is now *added* to the minuend as follows:

$$\begin{array}{r} 7465 \\ +7658 \\ \hline 15123 \end{array}$$

The leading digit in the remainder shown above (the digit 1) is now shifted to the units position and added, getting the correct answer as shown below:

$$\begin{array}{r} 7465 \\ +7658 \\ \hline 1\ 5123 \\ +1 \\ \hline 5124 \end{array}$$

In the foregoing, the process of shifting the leading 1 to the units position is known as *end-around carry*. The following is another example of the entire process:

```
  53682          53682
 -52620         +47379
 ------         -------
   1062         1 01061
                    +1
                -------
                   1062
```

The foregoing, which involves nines complementing, can also be applied to binary notation in terms of *ones complementing*. Here, the process is much more simple because the subtrahend need not be subtracted from 9, since the base-2 system is employed. Instead, the subtrahend is simply inverted; that is, each 0 is changed to 1 and each 1 is changed to 0. For instance, if the number 101(5) is to be subtracted from 1101 (13), the remainder will be 1000 (8). The following shows the ones complementing process with the end-around carry:

```
  1101          1101
 -0101         +1010
 -----         ------
  1000         1 0111
                  +1
               ------
                 1000
```

When subtracting, the subtrahend must have as many binary digits (0 and 1) as are in the minuend, or an error will result during the ones complementing process. Even though in normal binary subtraction both answers would be the same if the subtrahend were not filled out, an error would result in the ones complementing process. This can be proved by subjecting the two examples shown below to the ones complementing process:

```
   Incorrect      Correct

     11110         11110
    -1011          01011
    ------         ------
    10011          10011
```

The following is an additional example to help illustrate the ones complementing process:

```
  10110  (22)            10110
 -01011  (11)    =      +10100
 ------  ----           -------
   1011  (11)           1 01010
                            +1
                        -------
                           1011
```

While the process may appear complex for applications to computers, it is actually simpler to convert a digit 1 to 0 and vice versa in terms of the electronic circuitry in computers than to employ circuit combinations which must have the ability to borrow numbers. Binary numbers can be inverted (complemented) by utilizing conventional inverting circuits as described in subsequent chapters. Instead of end-around carry, the carry digit is dropped and a one digit added to the sum automatically.

## Negative Numbers

Generally, negative numbers in a computer are identified by preceding the number by a *sign bit* consisting of another 1 bit. Thus, if the magnitude of a number consists of four significant digits such as 1001, this will be indicated as a positive number if it is preceded with a zero, such as 01001. If the representation were 11001, the computer circuitry would recognize the 1001 as the actual binary number (since the magnitude of four bits has been set as a limit by circuit switching) and the additional 1 to the left would be the sign bit identifying the 1001 as a negative number. (Additional information on the sign bit is given in Chapter 10.)

The *complement* principle lends itself to the representation of negative numbers in computers and permits the execution of arithmetical processes in binary form. Thus, the binary positive number 101 (5) becomes 010 when it is a binary −5. Identified by a sign bit, the complete representation is 1010. Similarly, the binary 011 (3) becomes 100 in complement form to represent −3.

When using such binary negative numbers in addition, the usual end-around-carry method is employed. Assume, for instance, that the computer is to add a negative number to a positive one:

$$7 + (-3) = 4$$

In binary form the 7 is 111 and the negative representation of 3 is the complement 100. Adding these produces

$$
\begin{array}{r}
111 \\
+\ 100 \\
\hline
1\ 011 \\
+\quad 1 \\
\hline
100
\end{array}
$$

$\phantom{}$(3 complement)

$\phantom{}$(end-around carry)

$100 = +4$

If two negative numbers are to be added, such as $-3$ to $-3$ to produce a sum of $-6$, both complement numbers are added and the end-around-carry method is again used:

$$
\begin{array}{rl}
100 & \text{(3 complement)} \\
+\ 100 & \\
\hline
1\ 000 & \\
+\quad 1 & \text{(end-around carry)} \\
\hline
001 = -6 & \text{(the complement of +6, 110)}
\end{array}
$$

The *magnitude of the sum* determines the magnitude (number of bits) of the addend and the augend. Thus, if $-8$ is to be added to $-9$, the four-bit complements 0111 (for $-8$) and 0110 (for $-9$) cannot be used. Instead, five-bit complements of $-8$ and $-9$ are used

$$
\begin{array}{ll}
\text{Five-bit 8 in binary:} & 01000 = 10111 \quad \text{for } -8 \\
\text{Five-bit 9 in binary:} & 01001 = 10110 \quad \text{for } -9
\end{array}
$$

Hence, when these two five-bit binary numbers are used for the addition of $-8$ and $-9$, they yield the true sum

$$
\begin{array}{rl}
10111 & \\
+\ 10110 & \\
\hline
1\ 01101 & \\
+\quad\ 1 & \text{(end-around carry)} \\
\hline
01110 = -17 & \text{(the complement of +17, 10001)}
\end{array}
$$

In the foregoing, if 0111 had been used for $-8$ and 0110 for $-9$, the addition with end-around carry would have produced the sum 0110, which equals $-9$ and is incorrect. Similarly, if $-6$ is to be added to $-4$, the four-bit sum establishes the magnitude of the complement form of $-6$ and $-4$:

$$
\begin{array}{rl}
1001 & (-6, \text{ complement of } 0110) \\
+\ 1011 & (-4, \text{ complement of } 0100) \\
\hline
1\ 0100 & \\
+\quad 1 & \text{(end-around carry)} \\
\hline
0101 = -10 & \text{(complement of 1010)}
\end{array}
$$

When subtracting a negative number from a positive one, the same arithmetical principles which apply to base-10 numbers are employed. For instance, assume the following subtraction is to be done:

$$
7 - (-3) = 10
$$

Here the sign of the negative number is changed, and an addition is performed:

$$7 + 3 = 10$$

In binary form, the process then becomes one of simple *addition*, with the binary complement number 100 (−3) converted to the positive binary number 011. Since no complement number is now involved in the addition, no end-around carry is used:

$$
\begin{array}{l}
111 \\
011 \\
\hline
1010
\end{array} = 10 \quad \text{(in base-10 form)}
$$

The necessity for the sign bit is indicated when we consider that the complement of 111 (with a three-bit magnitude) is 000. To subtract a +7 from 0, for instance, yields a −7. Without sign bits this is notated as

$$
\begin{array}{ll}
000 & \text{(three-bit zero)} \\
000 & \text{(7 complement)} \\
\hline
000 & = -7
\end{array}
$$

With sign bits,

$$
\begin{array}{ll}
0000 & \\
1000 & \text{(sign bit indicates a negative 7)} \\
\hline
1000 & = -7
\end{array}
$$

The subtraction of a positive number from one having a lower value again employs the complement method for the larger number:

$$
\begin{array}{lll}
(+)3 & \text{With sign bit} & 0011 \\
-(+)5 & \text{and adding:} & 1010 \\
\hline
-2 & & 1101
\end{array}
$$

The subtraction of a negative number such as −7 from 0 (to yield a positive 7) again employs binary addition, with the −7 converted to a positive binary representation:

$$
\begin{array}{l}
000 \\
+111 \\
\hline
111
\end{array} = +7
$$

In normal base-10 arithmetic operations we encounter only the basic 0 representation. In computers, however, where the complement numbers in binary form are involved, we occasionally must recognize two types of zeros, the positive zero and the negative zero. Consider, for instance, the subtraction of 7 from 7 by the complement-addition method:

$$
\begin{array}{lll}
0 & 111 & (+7) \\
1 & +000 & (-7 \text{ complement}) \\
\hline
\overline{1} & \overline{111} & (\text{negative zero})
\end{array}
$$

As shown by the sign-bit representation at the left, the addition of a positive 111 and a negative 000 yields 111. When preceded by the negative sign bit, it indicates a negative zero to distinguish it from the positive zero 0 000.

In multiplication and division, the basic rules of base-10 numbers are followed, where like signs produce a positive answer and unlike signs produce a negative answer. In multiplication or division, however, additional steps are involved during calculation by computer, since the negative number must be changed to its positive equivalent and the answer restored to its proper sign. Multiplying 4 by $-3$, for instance, yields $-12$, but this would not be the product if the $-3$ were a complement number 100, because $100 \times 100 = 10000$. Thus, 100 is multiplied by the positive number 11 to produce 1100 (decimal 12) and complemented to produce 0011 (the binary complement = $-12$).

Similarly, in division, if 12 is the positive-number dividend and $-3$ is the negative-number divisor, the quotient will be $-4$. In binary division the $-3$ number is converted to its positive equivalent (0011) with its magnitude set by the magnitude (number of bits) of the dividend (1100). Now the positive dividend 1100 is divided by the positive divisor 0011 to produce a quotient of 0100. This is then converted to the complement form 1011 to represent the negative number $-4$.

## Other Codes

The binary code is the fundamental number system employed in all digital computers. The actual calculations involving such binary numbers are, of course, performed by the computer electronically during time intervals incredibly short compared with the time it would take for similar calculations to be performed by the most proficient team of mathematicians. Despite such automatic handling of mathematical process by the computer circuitry, a thorough understanding of binary processes aids in comprehending the actual calculation processes performed by the computer and enables the reader to grasp the manner in which circuit combinations perform the various functions of multiplication, addition, division, etc.

Other codes are, however, also employed as the occasion demands, and these are fully discussed in Chapter 5. Such codes are still related to the pure binary code; hence the necessity for comprehending the fundamental principles of the basic binary system.


# PROBLEMS

**1.** Define the term *radix two*.

**2.** Show, by a simple table, how the identity of any binary number up to 111111111 can be found.

**3.** What is the binary sum when 1010 is added to 1100?

**4.** In problem 3, what is the base-10 equivalent of the answer?

**5.** (a) What is the binary sum of the numbers 101, 011, 100, and 111?
   (b) What is the base-10 equivalent of the answer to (a)?

**6.** What is the binary remainder when 1010 is subtracted from 1110?

**7.** What is the *base-10* answer when 101 (binary) is subtracted from the binary number 1010?

**8.** (a) What product (binary) is formed when the binary number 1111 is multiplied by 101?
   (b) In (a) above, what is the base-10 equivalent of the binary product?

**9.** What is the binary product when the binary numbers 101 and 111 are multiplied?

**10.** What is the binary quotient when 101000 is divided by 101?

**11.** What base-10 number does the binary number 11.1111 represent?

**12.** (a) What is the binary sum of the binary numbers 101.01 and 10.01?
   (b) In (a) above, what is the base-10 equivalent of the answer?

**13** (a) Subtract the number 1101 from 10101 by the standard subtraction process; then repeat, using the complementing principle and end-around carry.

(b) Subtract the number 1 (binary) from 11001 by the standard process; then repeat, using complementing and end-around carry.

**14.** Using binary numbers, perform the following addition: $8 + (-2) = ?$

**15.** Using binary numbers, perform the following addition: $(-4) + (-5) = ?$

**16.** Using binary numbers, subtract $-8$ from 0, and show sign bits.

# LOGIC GATES
# AND BOOLEAN
# ALGEBRA

**3**

**Introduction.** In addition to the circuits described in Chapter 1, a digital computer also uses a number of bistable multivibrators (flip-flops) and logic switching (gating) circuits. The bistable circuits are combined to form counters and other calculating circuits as described in the next chapter, while the gating and switching circuits perform logic functions and act as links between the various calculating, storage, and other computer sections. While there are less than a half-dozen different *types* of logic gates found in a computer, such circuits are used over and over again and form the bulk of the many making up the total computer.

Thus, as in our modern telephone systems, the switching, routing, and other interconnections necessary to perform the various functions required, makes for a complex linkage system. Hence, though there are only a few circuits involved, the manner in which certain ones are switched for linkage with others at specific times becomes an important aspect of computer technology.

Because the switching, gating, and linkage of signals through numerous circuits must be based on logical demands, it follows that a logical approach must be used in the design of such systems. Conversely, the analysis and understanding of an existing system is expedited by applying certain rules of logic.

Of immeasurable value to the design of telephone switching systems and computers were the noteworthy contributions made over the years by such men as De Morgan, Boole, Shannon, and others. Augustus De Morgan (1806–1871) was an English mathematician and logician, who published numerous works on mathematics, including several on logic. George Boole (1815–1864), also an English mathematician and logician, made the most outstanding contribution to a logic-associated algebra by the publication in 1854 of his text, *An Investigation of the Laws of Thought on Which Are Founded the Mathematical Theories of Logic and Probabilites*. In this treatise Boole proposed mathematical rules for producing logical conclusions by combining certain algebraic statements or propositions. His proposition for transforming statements into symbols and employing specific rules for manipulating such symbols to procure logically valid answers is now referred to as *Boolean algebra*.

The symbolic logic concepts were stimulated by two other English mathematicians and writers, Alfred North Whitehead and Bertrand Russell. The latter, in 1910, published an outstanding text in this field, *Principia Mathematica*. In this book the interrelationships between basic mathematics and formal logic are emphasized and deductions performed along strict symbolic principles. As such, it covered new areas in the study of philosophy, particularly in semanics (the science of the meanings of words and word forms in language). Over 25 years were to elapse, however, before the full significance and value of symbolic logic in electric and electronic switching systems were to be recognized.

The true stature of symbolic logic was attained when Claude E. Shannon wrote his thesis for a Master of Science degree at Massachusetts Institute of Technology. An abstract of this thesis was published in the *Transactions of the American Institute of Electrical Engineers* (1938) under the title, *A Symbolic Analysis of Relay and Switching Circuits*. In this thesis Shannon investigated the methodology for finding the most simple and effective switch and/or relay combinations for obtaining a desired end result. The basic technique consisted of representing multiple-switch circuitry by prescribed mathematical expressions and providing the necessary arithmetical means for manipulating them, based on the symbolic logic indicated by Boolean algebra. Thus, the seemingly abstract symbolic logic was unified with the practical applications found in digital computer design as well as in other electric and electronic switching systems. Since then, the applications of Boolean algebra to switching and gating as described by Shannon have been widely used in switching-circuit analysis and design and, in particular, in the design of logic circuitry of digital computers.

In this chapter, the basic aspects of Boolean algebra are first covered in relation to the basic logic circuits of switching and gating and then covered in greater detail with respect to multiple-level logic circuitry.

## *Basic Logic Gates*

As detailed in Chapter 2, arithmetic operations in a digital computer are undertaken by using the binary code, which has only two symbols, 1 and 0. Thus, a digital computer operates with what is known as a *two-level logic*, since only two states are used. As described in later chapters, these two states also encroach on the other units associated with a computer, such as punched cards (the absence or presence of a hole punch), magnetic tape (the absence or presence of a magnetized area), and optical scanning (the absence or presence of a segment of print). In Boolean algebra, the 1 and 0 states may be designated as *true* and *false* (T and F) or related to *yes* and *no* con-

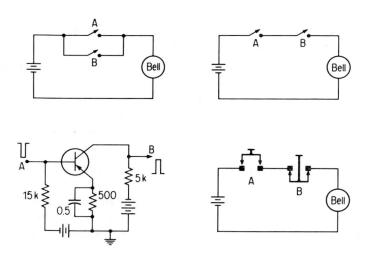

**Fig. 3–1.** Basic logic circuit functions.

ditions. From these 1 and 0 (or T and F) states, certain logic statements are evolved for the switching and gating circuits used in digital computers.

For one unfamiliar with computer terminology, the special logical circuits used have unique names such as *and gates, or gates, not circuits,* and *inhibitors.* The *and* and *or* circuits, in conjunction with the *not* and *inhibitor* types perform a variety of useful tasks in a computer, including addition, subtraction, gating specific signals in or out of other circuits, and routing numbers to sections as required.

The reader is already familiar with some of these logic circuits used in ordinary walks of life. A doorbell, for instance, which can be rung from either the front door or the back door employs an *or* circuit as shown in the upper left drawing of Fig. 3-1. Here, switch *A* is in parallel with switch *B*; hence either *A or B* rings the bell, *or* both (if pushed simultaneously).

If two switches are wired in series as shown at the upper right, an *and*-circuit system is formed. Here, both the *A* switch *and* the *B* switch must be depressed simultaneously for the bell to ring. A *not* circuit is shown at the lower left of Fig. 3-1 and consists of a conventional transistor amplifier such as discussed in Chapter 1. Since the phase of the signal is inverted from input to output, the phase of the output is *not* the same as the input; hence the term *not* circuit. A *not* circuit need not have amplifying characteristics and may consist of a transformer, as shown later. As long as it inverts signal phase, it has the logic-circuit designation of *not.*

An *inhibitor* circuit is shown at the lower right of Fig. 3-1. Here, switch *B* is a push-button, *normally closed* type as shown. If the *normally open* switch *A* is depressed, the bell will ring. If, however, switch *B* is depressed, it opens the circuit and the bell is inoperative even though switch *A* is depressed at the same time as switch *B*. Thus, switch *B* has an *inhibiting* function, since its use inhibits the function of the *A* switch.

The electronic logic-gate circuits employed in computers are not, of course, composed of the mechanical switches shown in Fig. 3-1. These are only shown to illustrate the basic logic aspects of the *and, or, not,* and *inhibiting* functions. An understanding of the foregoing factors, however, will be of considerable help in applying Boolean algebra to the solid-state logic circuitry so extensively employed in modern digital computers.

## Diode And-Gate Circuits

In practical logic-gate circuitry, design factors are related to the nature of the signals used. In some applications a negative signal is considered logic 1, and the absence of a signal logic 0. On the other hand, some computers may recognize a positive signal as logic 1 and the absence of a signal as 0. The basic *and* gate identified by a small capital letter in Fig. 3-2A functions properly with the application of positive voltages or pulses to the input. This circuit uses to advantage the high reverse resistance characteristics of the diode in one direction, and the low forward resistance in the other direction. For analysis, the inputs may be identified by the letters $A$ and $B$, as shown, with the output designated by $C$.

With a positive voltage applied to the load resistance $R_L$, the negative potential of the supply is present at each input as shown in Fig. 3-2B. In such an instance, both diodes conduct because of their low forward resistance. Electron flow is from the minus voltage source

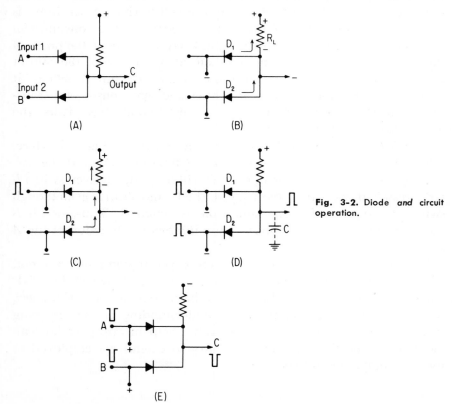

**Fig. 3-2.** Diode *and* circuit operation.

through the diodes in parallel and up through the load resistor as shown by the arrows. Because of the low forward resistance of the two diodes, virtually all of the voltage drop will occur across the load resistance. Under this condition the output is a steady-state low voltage (near the negative level) and hence represents 0. In C is shown the condition in which a positive pulse is applied at input no. 1. This positive polarity overcomes the negative potential applied to diode $D_1$, and conduction drops to a negligible level because of the high reverse resistance. The output circuit is, however, still effectively connected to the negative potential level at the input through the low forward resistance of diode $D_2$. Hence, the output level is still toward the negative potential.

In D of Fig. 3-2, the circuit is shown with a positive pulse applied at the first input and another positive pulse applied to the second input. Now neither diode conducts to any appreciable degree, and hence current flow drops to a zero (or virtually negligible) level. With no current flow, there is no voltage drop across the load resistor and the output voltage level rises to the maximum voltage-supply amplitude. When the input pulses drop to zero amplitude, current again flows through both diodes and the large voltage drop across the load resistor again drops the output voltage level to a steady-state value near the negative battery potential. Thus, during the time that pulses appeared at the input, a *positive-voltage change* occurred at the output, representing a logic 1 output pulse.

The capacitor $C$ shown in the dotted connections at the output represents the input capacitance of the following circuit, as well as stray wiring capacitances and the inherent capacitances of the solid-state diodes. The shunting effect which results causes a slight integration of the output pulse waveform and modifies somewhat the leading edge (see Chapter 1). Such capacitances affect triggering time and must be taken into consideration in design.

From the foregoing, it is evident the *and* circuit produces no output signal unless proper polarity signals are applied at both inputs simultaneously. Since both input signals must coincide, the circuit is sometimes called a *coincidence circuit*. Thus, only an input *A and B* produces a *C* output. If negative pulses represent logic 1's, the diodes are reversed as shown in Fig. 3-2E and the polarity of the potentials applied are also changed as shown.

The term *gate* is applicable to the *and* circuit since either *A* or *B* can be considered a gating signal for the other. Thus, if an *A* input is applied, no output results. With an applied *A* signal, a coinciding signal at $B$ opens the circuit gate and an output signal is produced. The term *switch* also applies, since $A$ can be considered as a switch function for $B$ (or vice-versa) to close (theoretically) the circuit and produce an output signal. The letters DCL are often used to indicate *diode circuit logic*.

### Boolean Logic and Truth Tables

In expressing the *and* function in Boolean statements, the multiplication sign is used as the logical connective. Thus, $A \cdot B$ indicates $A$ *and $B$*, but does not mean multiplication of one by the other. This logical connective could be omitted and the algebraic multiplication indicated by placing the letters close together, as $AB$. Thus, for the two-input *and* circuit shown in Fig. 3-2, the logic expressions for every possible input combination could be shown as

$$0 \cdot 0 = 0$$
$$A \cdot 0 = 0$$
$$0 \cdot B = 0$$
$$A \cdot B = C$$

A so-called *truth table* can also represent the *and* function by designating the logic 1 by T and the logic 0 by F (for true and false):

$$F \cdot F = F$$
$$T \cdot F = F$$
$$F \cdot T = F$$
$$T \cdot T = T$$

Still another form which the truth table can assume is the use of a 1 for an input signal and a 0 for no input:

$$0 \cdot 0 = 0$$
$$1 \cdot 0 = 0$$
$$0 \cdot 1 = 0$$
$$1 \cdot 1 = 1$$

Some logicians prefer the symbol $\cap$ or $\wedge$ for the logical *and* function connective. Because of the widespread use of the multiplication sign for the *and* connective, however, it will be used in this text.

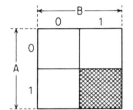

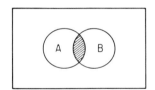

**Fig. 3-3.** Logic diagrams for *and-gate* circuit.

Diagrams can also be employed to illustrate the truth table graphically, as shown in Fig. 3-3. In the square representation shown, the *and*-circuit function is illustrated, with the horizontal rows representing 1 or 0 input for $A$ and the vertical rows representing 1 or 0 input for $B$. The *intersection* of the horizontal and vertical rows represents the logic statement for the selected input logic. The intersecting square *is shaded if true, and blank if false*. Thus, if the vertical 0 for $B$ is taken as against the horizontal 1 for $A$, the intersection is at the lower left. Since this is a blank square, the answer is false. If the vertical 1 is selected for $B$ and the horizontal 1 for $A$, the intersection of the two rows is at the lower right. Since this is a shaded area, the statement is true and represents the *and*-gate function.

Such truth diagrams are sometimes called *logic maps*. An early use of such map diagrams to express logic statements was made by Charles L. Dodgson (1832–1898), English mathematician and author. They were described in his books *The Games of Logic* and *Symbolic Logic*. (Dodgson's pen name was Lewis Carroll and under this pseudonym he wrote *Alice in Wonderland*, etc.) These truth diagrams are also called *Karnaugh maps*. Edward Veitch of Burroughs Corporation in 1952 presented certain chart methods to indicate logic statements relating to computer circuitry. In 1953 Maurice Karnaugh suggested a variation of this process, and hence his name has been associated with the modern usage of these truth maps.

A Venn diagram (named after the 19th century mathematican John Venn) is also shown in Fig. 3-3. Here, the $A \cdot B$ functions are represented by circles, with the overlapping (shaded) area representing $C$ = true, since both $A$ *and* $B$ are true.

## Multiple-input Diode And Gate

On occasion *and* circuits with more than two inputs are used. A three-input *and* circuit is shown in A of Fig. 3-4, and the Venn dia-

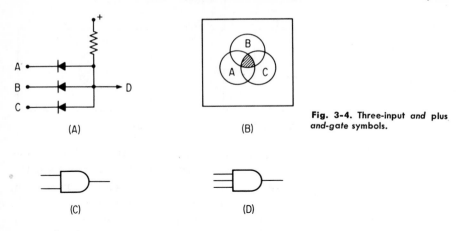

Fig. 3-4. Three-input *and* plus *and*-gate symbols.

gram for it is shown in B. For this circuit, there must be an input voltage applied to each terminal simultaneously to produce an output signal. For only two-signal input voltages, no output signal is obtained. Hence, the truth table for this circuit is

$$0 \cdot 0 \cdot 0 = 0$$
$$A \cdot 0 \cdot 0 = 0$$
$$0 \cdot B \cdot 0 = 0$$
$$0 \cdot 0 \cdot C = 0$$
$$A \cdot B \cdot 0 = 0$$
$$0 \cdot B \cdot C = 0$$
$$A \cdot 0 \cdot C = 0$$
$$A \cdot B \cdot C = D$$

A truth table using 1's and 0's would be similar, with $1 \cdot 0 \cdot 0 = 0$, $0 \cdot 1 \cdot 0 = 0$, etc. Only when coincidence occurs is an output produced, $1 \cdot 1 \cdot 1 = 1$.

The Venn diagram shows the logic which applies, with the shaded area indicating a *true* condition. Only the area where the three circles overlap is shaded, which shows that all three inputs must be present to obtain an output.

Symbols for *and* circuits are also shown in Fig. 3-4. The two input *and*-circuit symbol is shown in C, and the three-input *and*-circuit symbol is illustrated in D.

## Diode Or Circuits

A two-input diode *or* circuit is shown in A of Fig. 3-5. In this circuit no supply potential is needed; hence in the absence of an input

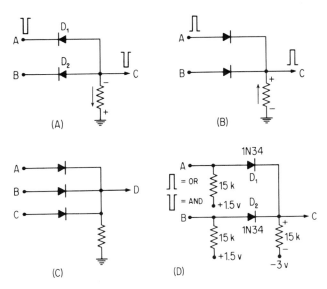

**Fig. 3-5.** Or circuits.

signal there is no voltage drop across the output resistor. If a negative voltage or pulse is applied to the *A* input as shown (in relation to ground), diode $D_1$ conducts and electrons flow in the direction shown by the arrow. In consequence a voltage drop appears across the output resistor, with a polarity shown, producing signal *C*. Similarly, if a negative signal is applied to *B*, current again will flow and produce an output signal. If signal voltages are applied to both *A* and *B* simultaneously, conduction again occurs and an output signal *C* is produced. Thus, an output signal is provided for an input signal at *A or B or* both. If a positive signal represents logic 1, the circuit shown at *B* is used. The only change is the reversal of the diodes.

The circuits shown at *A* and *B* are sometimes called *inclusive or* circuits, because the *true* statements not only consist of *A or B* but also *include* both at the same time. Another circuit, called the *exclusive or*, provides an output for either *A or B* but *not* both. The exclusive *or* circuit takes the form of the binary addition of $1 + 1 = 0$ (without carry). Hence, this circuit is also called a *half adder* and is discussed fully in Chapter 6, Calculation Circuits.

In Boolean algebra, the $+$ sign is used as the logical connective to denote the *or* function. Thus, $A + B$ actually denotes *A or B* and does not indicate arithmetical addition. Other symbols which have been used include $\cup$ as well as $\vee$. For our discussions, however, the $+$ signal will be employed throughout this text.

Truth tables for the two-input and three-input *or* circuits are

| A | B | C |
|---|---|---|
| 0 | + 0 | = 0 |
| 0 | + 1 | = 1 |
| 1 | + 0 | = 1 |
| 1 | + 1 | = 1 |

| A | B | C | D |
|---|---|---|---|
| 0 | + 0 | + 0 | = 0 |
| 1 | + 0 | + 0 | = 1 |
| 0 | + 1 | + 0 | = 1 |
| 0 | + 0 | + 1 | = 1 |
| 1 | + 1 | + 0 | = 1 |
| 0 | + 1 | + 1 | = 1 |
| 1 | + 1 | + 1 | = 1 |

The truth and Venn diagrams for the two-input *or* circuit are shown in A and B of Fig. 3-6. Since *A or B or* both produces a true condition, the 1 states as well as the intersecting areas are shaded in both diagrams. The symbol for the two-input *or* circuit is shown in *C*, and the three-input gate is shown in *D*. On occasion the symbol shown in *E* will be encountered for the *or* circuit. The symbols shown in *C* and *D*, however, will be used throughout this text.

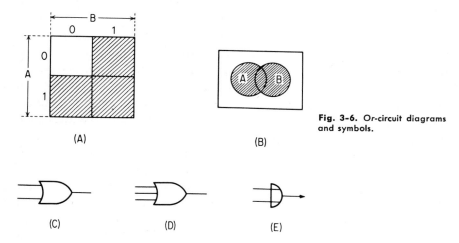

**Fig. 3-6.** Or-circuit diagrams and symbols.

The three-input *or* circuit shown in Fig. 3-5C is designed for an input signal having a positive polarity for representing the logic 1. With reversal of the diodes, negative input signals can be used to represent logic 1. In D of that figure a two-input *or* circuit is shown with a bias supply. Because positive potentials are applied to the diode input circuits and a negative potential is present at the bottom of the output resistor, current flows in the absence of input signals. Thus, a steady-state voltage drop occurs across the output resistor with a polarity as shown, representing logic 0. For a positive-polarity signal input at either A *or* B *or* at both, conduction is increased and the voltage drop across the output resistor rises, which produces an output signal.

The circuit shown in Fig. 3-5D will operate as an *and* circuit if negative signals are used to represent logic 1 inputs. If, for instance, a negative signal of sufficient amplitude is applied at $A$ alone, diode $D_1$ stops conducting and current no longer flows in the $A$ circuit. The diode in the $B$ input line still conducts, however, and the output polarity remains plus (logic 0). The same condition prevails for a negative input at $B$. When, however, negative signals are applied to both $A$ *and* $B$, both diodes stop conducting and current flow through the output resistor drops to zero. As a result, there is no longer a voltage drop across the output resistor, and the voltage at the output line $C$ drops to the $-3$-volt level, producing a negative output signal representing logic 1.

## Two-level Diode Logic

In digital computers the occasion often arises when combinations of *and* and *or* circuits must be used to perform more complex logic than that of the individual circuits. Thus, one or more *or* circuits may feed an *and* gate, or several *and* circuits may be applied to an *or* circuit. Such combinations are known as *two-level* logic circuits. The practical applications of these (and higher-level logic) is covered more fully in Chapter 6.

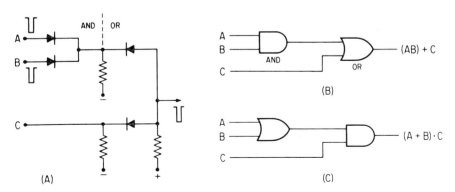

**Fig. 3-7.** Two-level diode logic circuit (DLC) with three inputs.

A two-level diode logic circuit with three input lines is shown in Fig. 3-7. Here, a two-input *and* circuit is applied to one of the input lines of an *or* circuit, as shown in A. The equivalent symbolic representation is shown in B. The *and* gate is the same as shown earlier in E of Fig. 3-2, where negative-polarity input signals were used. If positive input signals are to represent logic 1 values, all diodes will be reversed (as will supply-voltage polarities). In such an instance the *and* circuit will be as shown in D of Fig. 3-2, and the *or* circuit will be similar to that shown in D of Fig. 3-5.

The Boolean expression for the two-level circuit shown in Fig. 3-7A is given at the output of the symbolic representation in B. Since the $A$ and $B$ inputs must be in coincidence, they are expressed as $AB$, or as $A \cdot B$. Because the output from the *and* gate would produce an output signal from the *or* circuit, or an input at $C$ alone would produce an output, the expression is $(A \cdot B) + C$.

The truth table for this circuit, based on the Boolean expression $(A \cdot B) + C$, is

| $(A \cdot B)$ | | $+\ C$ | *Output* |
|---|---|---|---|
| 0 | 0 | 0 | 0 |
| 1 | 0 | 0 | 0 |
| 0 | 1 | 0 | 0 |
| 0 | 0 | 1 | 1 |
| 0 | 1 | 1 | 1 |
| 1 | 1 | 0 | 1 |
| 1 | 0 | 1 | 1 |
| 1 | 1 | 1 | 1 |

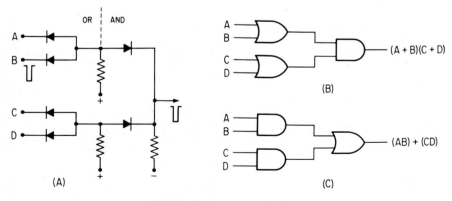

**Fig. 3-8. Four-input two-level DLC.**

If the diodes and the supply voltage polarities are reversed for the circuit shown in A of Fig. 3-7 but *negative signals are still used for the input,* the *and* circuit becomes an *or* circuit and the *or* circuit changes to an *and* circuit. Thus, the symbolic representation would be as shown in C, and the Boolean expression is $(A + B) \cdot C$, since either (or both) the $A$ and $B$ inputs must be used with $C$ to produce an output. A four-input circuit of this type is shown in A of Fig. 3-8. Here, two *or* circuits feed an *and* gate. An output will be provided by $A$ *or* $B$ *or* both, *and* by $C$ *or* $D$ *or* both. Thus, the Boolean statement is $(A + B)(C + D)$. The symbolic representation for this four-input two-level logic circuit is shown in B of Fig. 3-8.

A four-input two-level DCL is shown in C, using two *and*-circuit inputs. The circuits are the same as shown earlier in Fig. 3-7A. The Boolean expression for the two *and* circuits feeding an *or* circuit is shown at the output of the symbolic representation in C of Fig. 3-8, and is $(A \cdot B) + (C \cdot D)$. This indicates that both $A$ *and* $B$ must be present for an output, *or* $C$ *and* $D$.

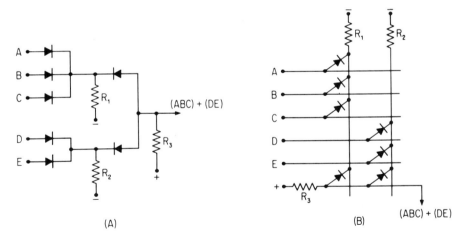

**Fig. 3-9. Five-input DLC and matrix.**

A five-input two-level circuit is shown in Fig. 3-9A. Here, a three-input *and* circuit as well as a two-input *and* circuit are applied to an *or*-circuit input. As shown, the Boolean expression for this circuit is $(A \cdot B \cdot C) + (D \cdot E)$. Such a circuit can also be represented schematically as shown in B. Here the circuit is arranged in the form of a *matrix* for clarity in circuit layout, both schematically and physically.

The term *matrix* originated with the English mathematician James J. Sylvester (1814–1897), who so designated an array of numbers in rectangular form and applied appropriate calculation procedures to their formation. In electronics it has been used to indicate the symmetrical arrangement of resistors, diodes, or other components. The matrix configuration is used for memory-cell layout, as discussed in Chapter 7, and for input and output encoders and decoders, as covered in Chapter 8.

### Not (Inverter) Circuits

The derivation for the term *not* circuit as it applies to a signal inversion was discussed earlier in this chapter, and a typical transistor circuit of this type was shown in Fig. 3-1. In Boolean algebra the *not* function is indicated by a line over the symbol. Thus, $\bar{A}$ means *not A* and, if $A$ represents 1, the expression $\bar{A}$ indicates 0. ($\bar{1} = 0$ and $\bar{0} = 1$.) The following logical statements apply:

$(A \cdot B)$      means    $A$ *and* $B$

$(A \cdot \bar{B})$      means    $A$ and *not* $B$

$(\bar{A} \cdot B)$      means    $B$ and *not* $A$

$(\bar{A} \cdot B) + C$    means    $(B$ and *not* $A)$ *or* $C$

$A + (B \cdot \bar{C})$    means    $A$ or $(B$ and *not* $C)$

A prime sign placed after a symbol has also been used to identify the *not* function, $A'$ (not $A$), $A \cdot B'$ ($A$ and *not* $B$), etc. In this text the line over the symbol will be used.

A transformer also has signal-inverting characteristics and hence is used on occasion to perform the *not* function. A *dot notation* is some-

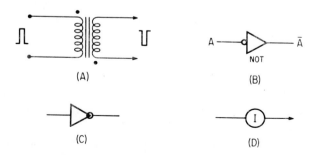

**Fig. 3-10.** *Not circuit symbols.*

times used, as shown in A of Fig. 3-10. Here, the dot at the top of the primary signifies a positive-polarity signal input, and the lower dot at the secondary shows a negative-polarity signal output. The inverting characteristics of a transformer depend on the phasing of the secondary winding versus the primary. If the secondary leads are reversed, the input and output signals will be in phase.

The triangle symbol for the *not* circuit is shown in B and will be used hereafter in this text. Other symbols which have been used for the *not* circuit are shown in C and D. The letter I in the circle in D indicates *inverter*. Regardless of the symbol used, the *not* characteristic indicates an $\bar{A}$ output for an $A$ input, or an $A$ output for an $\bar{A}$ input.

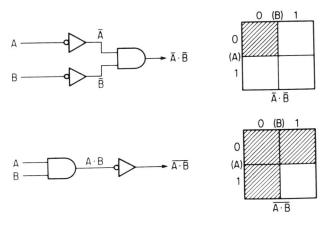

Fig. 3-11. Logic expressions of *not* function.

The *not* circuit can precede or follow logic gate circuits and thus perform a negation of the logic function. There is a difference, however, in the Boolean statement which results for an input use of the *not* circuit compared with a *not* circuit following a logic gate. This is shown in Fig. 3-11 which shows the two conditions applied to an *and* gate. When the *not* circuits are in series with the input of the *and* gate as shown, the $A$ and $B$ quantities are inverted before application to the *and* gate and hence $\bar{A}$ and $\bar{B}$ values are applied to the inputs. The resultant output is then $\bar{A} \cdot \bar{B}$. If, however, the *not* circuit is in series with the output, the $A \cdot B$ value is inverted and the output expression becomes $\overline{A \cdot B}$ as shown. The difference between the two is exemplified by the accompanying truth diagrams shown in Fig. 3-11.

## De Morgan's Theorem

If a *not* circuit follows an *and* gate, the results are equivalent to inverting the $A + B$ inputs to an *or* gate, as shown in Fig. 3-12. Similarly, if a *not* circuit follows an *or* gate, it is comparable to the circuitry obtained if the $A \cdot B$ inputs to an *and* gate are inverted. These logic functions are given by the two De Morgan rules:

$$\overline{A \cdot B} = \bar{A} + \bar{B}$$
$$\overline{A + B} = \bar{A} \cdot \bar{B}$$

De Morgan's theorem can be used to ascertain the complement of any Boolean expression. This can be more clearly understood by examining the logic circuits shown in C and D of Fig. 3-12. The principles expressed here were discussed earlier in this chapter and illustrated in D of Fig. 3-5. The logic functions of a particular circuit depend solely upon whether a positive-polarity signal represents logic 1 or whether a negative-polarity signal is used to indicate logic 1.

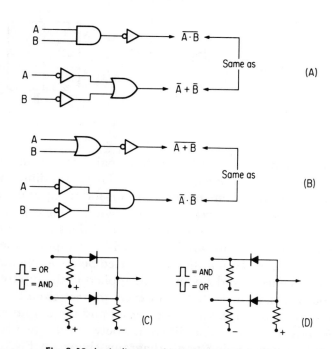

**Fig. 3-12.** Logic diagrams for De Morgan's theorem.

For the circuit shown in C of Fig. 3-12, an *or*-gate function prevails if the input signals are of positive polarity. If positive-polarity signals represent 1, the logic 0 is either at ground level or of negative polarity and *represents the complement*. If, however, the logic 1 is represented by a negative-polarity signal, as in C of Fig. 3-12, an *and*-gate function results. The logic 0 (complement) would then be represented by a positive polarity. If the diodes and supply-voltage potentials are reversed as shown in D, opposite conditions prevail in comparison with the circuit in C. Now, a positive-polarity signal representative of 1 forms an *and* gate as shown, with a ground-level or a negative voltage indicating 0. If, however, the logic 1 is a negative-polarity signal the circuit is an *or* gate, and a positive signal is the complement of 1 and hence is 0. This dual logic function for such circuits forms the basis for De Morgan's theorems.

In A of Fig. 3-12, the negation of the *and* $(\overline{A \cdot B})$ function (*not-and*) is equal to the alternate denial $(\bar{A} + \bar{B})$, which expresses, in essense, that *not-A or not-B* is true. Similarly, in B of Fig. 3-12, the negation of the *or* $(\overline{A + B})$ function (*not-or*), is equal to the joint denial $(\bar{A} \cdot \bar{B})$, which states that *not-A and not-B* is true.

The *not-and* circuits are also called *nand* circuits, and the *not-or* circuits are also termed *nor* circuits. The dual functions are realized in a single circuit when transistors are used to form logic systems, as discussed more fully later in this chapter.

## Transistorized *Or* and *And* Circuits

Transistors are also used to form logic *or* and *and* gates, providing higher-speed switching than diodes as well as furnishing signal-voltage or signal-current amplification. Both the transistorized grounded emitter and emitter follower are used in series and parallel circuitry to form logic switching and amplification and to combine the *not* function with the logic-gate operation in a single circuit.

The value of emitter followers in computer design has already been discussed in Chapter 1. Since there is no phase reversal between input and output, emitter followers can be used to form logic-gate circuits performing the identical logic functions that diodes do but with superior switching characteristics. A transistorized *or* gate formed by parallel emitter followers is shown in A of Fig. 3-13. Here, the necessary *reverse* bias is furnished for the collector-emitter circuits, but

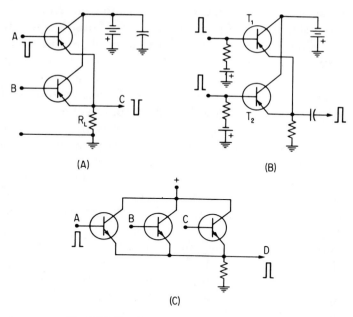

(A)                                                    (B)

(C)

**Fig. 3-13.** Transistorized *or* and *and* circuits.

no *forward* bias is applied to the base-emitter sections. When a negative voltage (or a pulse signal) is applied to either *A or B, or* both, it
establishes a forward bias and permits either or both transistors to
conduct. During conduction, the current flow through the load resistor $R_L$ produces a voltage drop having a negative polarity with respect
to ground to provide the output signal as shown. For this circuit, the
absence of an input signal represents logic 0, and a negative voltage or
pulse indicates logic 1.

As with the diode logic circuits discussed earlier in this chapter, the
transistorized circuit can be arranged to function as an *and* gate also.
If steady-state voltages are applied to both base-emitter circuits to
supply forward bias, both transistors will conduct and the resultant
voltage drop across the output resistor will be a steady-state negative
potential in the absence of an input signal. The circuit for forming the
*and* gate is shown in B of Fig. 3-13, and positive input pulses (or
voltages) applied to *A and B* simultaneously will produce an output
signal. If only the *A* signal is applied, the positive polarity overcomes
the forward bias and the $T_1$ transistor stops conducting. Since transistor $T_2$ still conducts, however, a voltage drop still occurs across the

output resistor. Similarly, conduction for $T_1$ still occurs if a signal is applied to the $B$ input to cut off transistor $T_2$. When both *A and B* are applied, however, both transistors stop conducting and the negative steady-state output voltage changes to the positive (ground) level because no voltage drop occurs across the output resistor. Thus, a positive-polarity output signal is produced and the expression $A \cdot B = C$ is satisfied.

A three-input *or* gate is shown in C, using NPN transistors instead of the PNP shown in diagrams A and B. Here, a positive-polarity voltage is applied to all collectors to satisfy the reverse-bias requirements. Now, any positive-signal input will furnish the necessary forward bias and cause transistor conduction. Thus a three-input *or* gate is formed $(A + B + C = D)$. The truth tables and diagrams given earlier in this chapter for the DLC (diode logic circuits) apply also to the transistor logic circuits (TLC).

## Transistorized *Nor* and *Nand* Circuits

Because the *grounded-emitter* circuit has a phase reversal of signal between input and output, it functions as a logic *not* circuit, as discussed earlier in this chapter. Hence, if two or more such circuits are combined to form logic gates, an inverted output will be produced for a given input-signal polarity. Thus, such circuits combine the *not-or* functions and are called *nor* circuits, or they combine the *not-and* functions to produce a *nand* circuit.

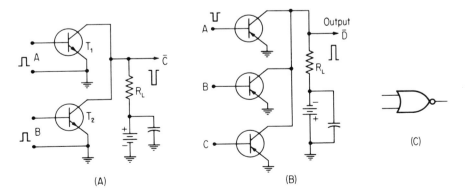

**Fig. 3-14.** *Nor* circuits.

Typical transistorized *nor* circuits are shown in Fig. 3-14. In A is shown a two-input *nor* circuit using NPN transistors. In the absence of forward bias, the operational characteristics are similar to those discussed for the emitter-follower *or* circuit. There is no conduction unless an input signal is applied at either *A or B* or at both. Since, however, each transist r operates as an individual *not* circuit, the output signal will have an opposite polarity to that applied to the input, as shown. Thus, $A + 0 = \bar{C}$; $0 + B = \bar{C}$; and $A + B = \bar{C}$. For PNP transistors the reverse-bias supply potential and the input polarity are changed as shown in B, where a three-input *nor* circuit is illustrated. The *nor* symbol is shown in C.

The circuits shown in A and B of Fig. 3-14 can also operate as *nand* gates by reversing the input symbology and applying forward bias potentials as was done for the emitter-follower *or* circuit. For *nand* function the pulse polarities at both inputs in A of Fig. 3-14 would be negative. For the circuit in B, however, positive input polarities are necessary for performing the *nand* function.

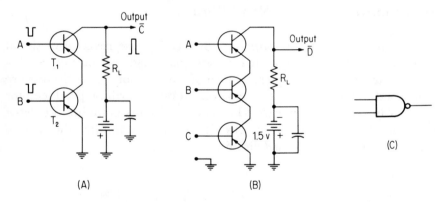

**Fig. 3-15. Transistorized *nand* circuits.**

In Fig. 3-15, *nand* circuits are shown using transistors in series. For the two-input circuit shown in A, the normal reverse bias is applied, but the forward bias is omitted. A negative-polarity signal applied at *A* would normally cause conduction of transistor $T_1$. Since, however, the emitter of $T_1$ is connected in series with the collector of $T_2$, no current will flow in the circuit. The same nonconduction prevails for a signal applied only to the *B* input. With both signals applied, however, conduction occurs and an output signal is developed having a polarity opposite to that of the input signal.

A three-input *nand* circuit, shown in illustration B, functions in similar fashion to that shown in A, since a signal must be present at all inputs to produce an output. Since all three transistors are in series, conduction will not occur upon the application of a signal to only two inputs because the transistor which is not receiving a signal will have no forward bias and will be unable to conduct. Since the nonconducting transistor is in series with the others, an output is produced only when $A \cdot B \cdot C$ are present. The resultant output then will be a *not D*, $\bar{D}$. The symbol for the *nand* circuit is shown in C of the figure.

A *nor* gate can be formed from the circuits shown in Fig. 3-15 by applying steady-state negative voltages to the base-emitter circuits to supply the forward bias necessary to cause conduction. If positive signals are now applied to $A$ *or* $B$ *or* $C$ *or* all, an output signal will be produced because a positive signal will overcome the bias between base and emitter and cutoff the transistor. With one or more transistors gated into the nonconducting state, the series arrangement causes the current to drop to zero. The current change which occurs at an input signal reduces the voltage across the load resistor $R_L$, and the voltage drops to the minus supply potential, producing a negative-signal output $(A + B + C = \bar{D})$.

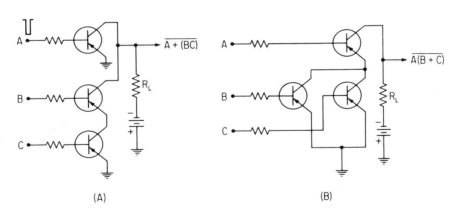

**Fig. 3-16. Series-parallel gate combinations.**

Transistors can also be connected in series or in series parallel to form combinations of logic functions. A typical circuit of this type is shown in A of Fig. 3-16, where *or* and *and* functions are combined and inverted to form an output $\overline{A + (B \cdot C)}$. Since no forward bias is applied to the transistors, there is no conduction and the output level is a negative value equal to the supply potential. When conduction occurs, a voltage drop appears across the load resistor $R_L$ and the output drops from a high negative value to near ground (zero).

If a negative signal is applied to the $A$ input, it will provide the necessary forward bias and conduction will occur, producing an output signal. When a signal is applied to the $B$ (or $C$) input only, no conduction can occur because of the series transistor connection. Thus, either $A$ alone will produce an output, or $B$ *and* $C$ will, or all three inputs simultaneously.

In B of Fig. 3-16 is shown a parallel *or* circuit combined with an *and* gate. As in the circuit in A, there is no conduction in the absence of input signals because no forward bias is applied to the base-emitter circuits. Input $A$ or $B$ alone will not cause conduction since the parallel *or* circuit is in series with one section of the *and* circuit. Thus, there must be an $A$ input as well as a $B$ or $C$ to produce an output.

Because of the inverting properties of the transistors, the output logic is $\overline{A \cdot (B + C)}$.

### Inhibitor Circuit

Another logic circuit often used in digital computers is the *inhibitor* circuit. In such a circuit, one input suppresses any output to perform the logic function $A \cdot \bar{B}$. A basic circuit of this type is shown in A of Fig. 3-17. The transistor has the normal reverse bias applied between collector and emitter as shown, but no forward bias is present between base and emitter. Instead, a reverse bias also exists between base and emitter because of battery $B_1$. Thus the transistor is driven into the cut-off region. If a negative signal of sufficient amplitude is applied to the $A$ input, it will overcome the reverse bias of $B_1$ and the transistor will conduct, producing an output signal voltage. If a negative signal is applied to the $B$ input alone, it will develop a positive signal at the secondary of the input transformer. The resultant voltage drop will be of correct polarity to add its value to that of the bias of battery $B_1$, which will drive the transistor more into the nonconduction region. Thus, a $B$ input alone will not produce an output. If $A$ and $B$ inputs are applied, the negative voltage at $A$ will be insufficient to overcome the increased reverse bias supplied by the positive pulse and the $B_1$ potential. Thus, the output is $A$ *but not* $B$. Since there is a phase inversion of signal, the output becomes $\overline{A \cdot \bar{B}}$, with a double negation sign over the $B$.

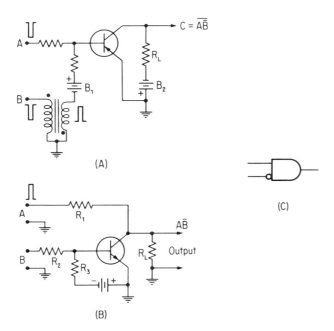

$$C = \overline{\overline{AB}}$$

(A)

(C)

$A\overline{B}$

Output

(B)

**Fig. 3-17.** Inhibitor circuits.

An inhibitor which dispenses with the transformer is shown in *B* of Fig. 3-17. Here, an NPN junction transistor is used in a grounded-emitter circuit. Here, again, a reverse bias is applied between base and emitter, as was the case with the circuit in A. In addition, no reverse bias is applied between collector and emitter; hence neither the base nor the collector circuits have the proper voltage or polarity for conduction.

If a positive signal is applied to the *A* input, it has the effect of supplying the required reverse bias for the collector and the (grounded) emitter. Since, however, there is no *forward* bias between base and emitter, the transistor does not conduct. Thus, the transistor is in effect an open circuit, and the signal applied to *A* appears across the load resistor at the output. Therefore, for an *A* input, the transistor is effectively out of the circuit. If a positive pulse of sufficient amplitude is applied to the *B* input alone, it will overcome the reverse bias. With proper polarity input bias the transistor would normally conduct, but since there is no reverse bias between collector and emitter, conduction does not occur and the *B* signal does not appear at the output.

If negative-polarity signals are applied simultaneously to the $A$ and $B$ inputs, the proper bias polarities will exist for both input and output circuits and the transistor will conduct at high level. When the transistor conducts at or near the saturation level, it has a low resistance between collector and emitter and hence places a virtual short-circuit shunt across the relatively higher resistance $R_L$. The signal from the $A$ input is thus effectively shorted to ground and inhibited from appearing at the output.

The symbolic representation of the *inhibitor* circuit is shown in C of Fig. 3-17. The input line with the small circle is the *inhibiting* input. The truth table for the logic of the inhibitor is

| $A$ | | $B$ | | $C$ |
|---|---|---|---|---|
| 0 | · | 0 | = | 0 |
| 1 | · | 0 | = | 1 |
| 0 | · | 1 | = | 0 |
| 1 | · | 1 | = | 0 |

## *Resistor-transistor Logic (RTL)*

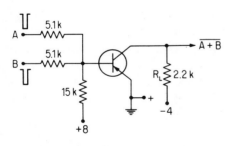

**Fig. 3-18. Resistor-transistor gate.**

Single transistor logic gates can be formed by using input resistors in a voltage-divider arrangement, as shown in Fig. 3-18. A multiple-input circuit of this type can also be constructed. For the circuit shown, an inverted gate function (*nor*) is procured, though *and* gates with multiple-resistor input lines can also be assembled. In the circuit shown, reverse bias is present at both the base emitter and the collector emitter; thus the transistor does not conduct. If a negative voltage of sufficient amplitude is applied to either *or* both the $A$ and $B$ inputs, the reverse bias between base and emitter is overcome and the transistor conducts, producing an inverted *nor* output $\overline{A + B}$. If this circuit is followed by a *not* circuit, the *or* function is obtained.

## Diode-transistor Logic (DTL)

The various diode logic circuits discussed earlier in this chapter provide simplicity and low-cost components. The disadvantages, however, include low signal voltages and signal currents and lack of amplification. Thus, where signal levels must be maintained or amplified, transistors are used with the diode logic circuits to achieve the performance levels required.

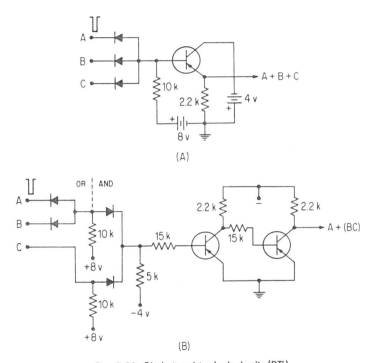

Fig. 3-19. Diode-transistor logic circuits (DTL).

A three-input diode-transistor logic *or* is shown in *A* of Fig. 3-19. Here an emitter-follower transistor circuit is used, though an amplifier of the grounded-emitter type could also be used if signal voltage gain is desired. In the circuit shown, a reverse bias potential of 8 volts is applied between the base and emitter, which results in operation beyond the transistor cut-off point. For any input signal having a negative potential sufficiently high to overcome the reverse bias, conduction will occur and an output signal will be produced, following in phase that of the input. Thus, the $A + B + C$ logic is obtained with this circuit. For an NPN transistor, both the signal and supply potential polarities would be reversed. In similar fashion, *and*-gate circuits using diode-transistor combinations can be formed.

Two-level diode-transistor combinations are also employed for signal amplification and for obtaining the proper logic expression for the output signal. A circuit of this type shown in B of Fig. 3-19, consists of the two-level *or-and* gate circuitry discussed earlier in this chapter. Two transistors are used, the second one inverting the signal to obtain an output logic level equal to the input at the diodes.

### Boolean Algebra Factors

Facility in the use of Boolean expressions, logic, and associated algebra can only be achieved by understanding the basic functions of the logic gates and circuits. For simplicity in diagramming, the

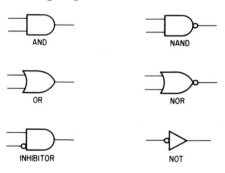

various symbols illustrated earlier in this chapter should be committed to memory. The basic logic-gate symbols used throughout this text are grouped together in Fig. 3-20 for easy reference.

One area of possible confusion in handling Boolean expressions is the relation of logic 1 or logic 0 to signal-voltage polarity. One common usage is to assign a positive voltage to represent logic 1 and a

**Fig. 3-20. Logic-circuit symbols.**

negative voltage to represent logic 0. In such an instance the positive and negative states are *relative to each other* and not necessarily positive or negative with respect to ground. This factor was shown in the diode logic gates discussed in this chapter, where a positive voltage may represent 1 and a less positive voltage indicate 0. Since the 0 voltage is less positive, it is *negative with respect* to the logic 1 signal.

When a positive signal represents 1, it is sometimes called the *up-state* signal and the negative signal for 0 is termed the *down state*. Alternative terms for these are *up level* and *down level*. When a negative signal is used to represent logic 1, a less negative signal (or a zero signal) indicates logic 0. Again, a less negative signal for 0 is an equivalent *positive signal* with respect to that for logic 1.

The basic *not* function must also be understood, since it is an important aspect of Boolean algebra and has no equivalent in ordinary algebra. As discussed earlier in this chapter, $\bar{A}$ means *not A*, and $\bar{1}$ means *not* 1. Since $\bar{1}$ means *not* 1, it must have a vaule of 0, since we have only two variables in our binary language. Similarly, $\bar{0}$ has a value of 1, and, if $A$ is 1, then $\bar{A}$ (*not A*) must represent 0. If, however, $A$ is assigned a value of 0, then $\bar{A}$ is 1. The letter symbols assigned to the input lines of logic systems are not confined to $A$ and $B$ only but depend on the logic involved and the particular design representation to be indicated. A typical example is shown in Fig. 3-21, where a multilevel logic system is shown with five inputs. The resultant logic expression for each circuit is shown to summarize the basic concepts covered earlier in this chapter.

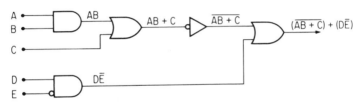

**Fig. 3-21. Multilevel logic.**

A double negation converts an expression back to its original form: $\bar{\bar{A}} = A$. A statement such as $\bar{A} + A$ is a true statement, since it indicates either one *or* the other is to be considered. The statement $\bar{A} \cdot A$, however, is a false statement, since the combination of $\bar{A}$ *and* $A$ (a negative and positive value) cancel out. The following should also be noted:

$$A + A = A$$
$$A \cdot A = A$$
$$A + (A \cdot B) = A$$
$$A + (\bar{A} \cdot B) = A + B$$

In Boolean algebra there are three basic laws which aid in the simplification of lengthy logic statements. By using the principles indicated by these rules, the designer of computer logic circuitry can substitute symbols and letters to represent circuits without having to draw them and can reduce the number of circuits to the minimum required to perform certain stated functions. Also, certain circuit variations are indicated to perform specific gating functions. The three Boolean algebra laws follow.

## Commutative Law

The commutative law states that the end results of the *or* and *and* connectives are not altered by the sequence which makes up the logical statements. Included in the commutative law are the De Morgan theorems discussed earlier in this chapter.

$$A + B = B + A$$
$$A \cdot B = B \cdot A$$
$$\left. \begin{array}{l} \overline{A \cdot B} = \bar{A} + \bar{B} \\ \overline{A + B} = \bar{A} \cdot \bar{B} \end{array} \right\} \quad \text{De Morgan's laws}$$

Thus, according to the commutative law, it is evident that the order in which addition or multiplication is sequenced has no effect on the sum or product.

## Associative Law

The associative law states that the elements of a Boolean expression may be grouped as desired so long as they are connected by the same sign.

$$(A + B) + C = A + (B + C) = A + B + C$$
$$(A \cdot B) \cdot C = A \cdot (B \cdot C) = A \cdot B \cdot C$$

## Distributive Law

The distributive law relates to the functional characteristics of the logic connectives. Proof is obtained by the use of ordinary algebraic manipulations.

$$A \cdot (B + C) = (A \cdot B) + (A \cdot C)$$
$$A + (B \cdot C) = (A + B) \cdot (A + C)$$

## *Circuit Simplification*

An example of how logic circuitry can be simplified and still perform the same functions is shown in Fig. 3-22. Here, two *or* gates feed an *and* gate, which produces the Boolean expression $(A + B) \cdot (B + C)$. Since $B \cdot B = B$, the expression can be restated as $A \cdot C + B$, and the redesigned circuitry results in the elimination of one *or* circuit. The logic conditions still prevail, since $B$ alone will produce an output for the second circuit just as it does for the first.

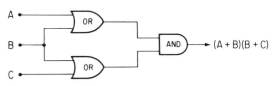

**Fig. 3-22.** Circuit simplification (Example No. 1).

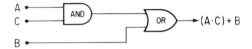

Another example is shown in Fig. 3-23, where a six-input system is shown with an output of $(A + B) \cdot (A + C) \cdot (A + D)$. This can be reduced to the simpler expression $A + B \cdot C \cdot D$ and thus can eliminate two *or* circuits. The same logic function is still performed after circuit simplification.

By observing the rules and laws detailed in this chapter, expressions similar to the examples illustrated can be simplified from

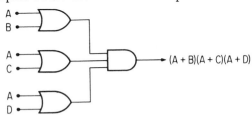

**Fig. 3-23.** Circuit simplification (Example No. 2).

their lengthier original structure. Assume, for instance, the original statement is $(A \cdot B) + (A \cdot \bar{B}) + (\bar{A} \cdot B)$. By simplifying the sum of the products we obtain $A \cdot (\bar{B} + B) + (\bar{A} \cdot B)$, since $A \cdot A = A$. Also, since $\bar{B} \cdot B = 0$, we can eliminate the first polynomial and obtain $A + (\bar{A} \cdot B)$, and, according to the rule expressed earlier, this is reduced to the final statement $A + B$ (a basic *or* circuit).

As mentioned earlier, a statement such as $\bar{A} + A$ is true, as is the expression $\bar{B} + B$, etc. Thus, when we state $\bar{A} + A$ and $A = 1$, then $\bar{A}$ is the complement of 1, or 0. Adding 1 and its complement, the sum will be 1: $1 + 0 = 1$. This simplifies the reduction of logic expressions, since such quantities can be replaced by their equivalent 1 values. This is exemplified by the expression

$$(\bar{A} \cdot C) \cdot (\bar{B} + B) + (\bar{A} + A) \cdot (B \cdot \bar{C})$$

If we assign 1 values to the $\bar{1} + 1$ expressions we obtain

$$(\bar{A} \cdot C \cdot 1) + (1 \cdot B \cdot \bar{C})$$
$$= (\bar{A} \cdot C) + (B \cdot \bar{C}) \qquad \text{(minimal form of original expression)}$$

## PROBLEMS

**1.** Briefly outline the growth of Boolean algebra to its present state.

**2.** A burglar-alarm system is so designed that opening a door closes a switch and sets an alarm. Another switch, in series, is used to make the system inoperative when the building is occupied. What type of logic circuit does this system represent?

**3.** Describe the characteristics of an *and* gate.

**4.** Prepare a truth table for a three-input *and* gate, using 1 and 0 designations for true and false.

**5.** What are the basic differences between the *inclusive or* and the *exclusive or*?

**6.** Prepare a truth table for a three-input *or* gate, using $A$, $B$, and $C$ for logic 1 expressions, and 0 for the logic 0 expression.

**7.** Explain what is meant by *two-level* diode logic circuitry.

**8.** Draw a circuit diagram for the DLC shown in symbol form in C of Fig. 3-7.

9. Draw a circuit diagram for the DLC shown in symbol form in C of Fig. 3-8.

10. Using logic symbols, draw a logic representation of the circuit shown in A of Fig. 3-9.

11. Describe the characteristics of a *not* circuit.

12. In Boolean algebra, of what significance are the De Morgan rules?

13. What are the advantages of transistorized logic circuits over the diode types?

14. Explain the characteristics of *nor* and *nand* gates.

15. Reproduce the circuits shown in Fig. 3-15, using NPN transistors. Show the polarity of input signals, and supply the Boolean expressions for these circuits.

16. Describe the characteristics of an *inhibitor* circuit.

17. Modify the circuit shown in B of Fig. 3-19 to perform the logic function $(A \cdot B) + (C \cdot D)$ using NPN transistors. Component values need not be given.

18. In Boolean algebra, what law is involved in the statement $(A + B) + C = A + B + C$?

19. In Boolean algebra, what law is involved in the statement $A + (B \cdot C) = (A + B) \cdot (A + C)$?

20. Simplify the expression $(A \cdot \bar{B}) + (\bar{A} \cdot B) + (A \cdot B)$.

21. Simplify the expression $(\bar{B} + B) \cdot (\bar{A} \cdot C) + (\bar{B} \cdot C) \cdot (A + \bar{A})$.

# FLIP-FLOPS, ACCUMULATORS, AND COUNTERS

**4**

**Introduction.** The Eccles-Jordan flip-flop circuit is one of the most important in digital computers. When a number of flip-flop units are connected in series they form what are termed *accumulators* or *registers*. As such, they perform the functions of accumulating counts (basic addition), scaling (a form of binary division), shifting numbers to left or right (useful in multiplication and division), storing numbers (a memory function), counting (producing the sum of a number of input pulses), switching (providing "on" and "off" conditions), and performing calculating functions as subsequently detailed. In order to do these things, a number of other components must be included in the basic flip-flop circuitry, plus the use of the logic gate systems discussed in Chapter 3. The manner in which this is done is discussed in this chapter after the basic principles of the flip-flop have been covered.

## The Saturated Flip-flop

A flip-flop circuit is a *bistable* device which produces no output signal unless a signal is applied to its input. The circuit contains two transistors (or tubes), one of which is in the conducting state and the other in the nonconducting state. Upon the application of an input signal, the transistor states reverse; the one which was conducting is cut off, and the nonconducting transistor is switched to the conducting state. The flip-flop can be considered as a *bistable multivibrator*, since it is essentially a two-stage amplifier with the output from one stage coupled to the input of the other. (As discussed in Chapter 1, the *astable multivibrator* is a free-running type which continuously produces an output signal, and the *monostable multivibrator* is the one-shot variety which is triggered by a signal but *reverts to its original* stage after a brief time interval. The flip-flop, on the other hand, is triggered into its *second state* upon the application of an input signal.)

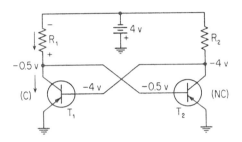

**Fig. 4-1.** Direct-coupled flip-flop.

A typical direct-coupled flip-flop circuit is shown in Fig. 4-1. Here, the collector of transistor $T_1$ is coupled directly to the base of transistor $T_2$. Similarly, the output at the collector of $T_2$ is coupled to the base input of $T_1$. Since these are PNP transistors, negative-polarity reverse bias is necessary for the collectors and this is supplied by the battery shown. With the negative terminal of the battery applied (through series resistors) to the collectors, the latter is made minus with respect to the emitters, which are at ground (plus) potential.

When power is first applied, any fractional differences between the transistors will cause one to conduct more quickly than the other. Assume that such a transistor is $T_1$ and current starts to rise through this unit initially. The electron flow is in the direction shown by the arrows, and a voltage drop occurs across resistor $R_1$. This lowers the collector potential of $T_1$ to a value near ground (positive). This lowered voltage is felt at the base of $T_2$ and reduces the forward bias potential (minus for the base and plus for the emitter in a PNP transistor). The reduction in forward bias for $T_2$ decreases current flow through this transistor, and the collector potential rises toward the negative supply value. This negative potential is applied to the base of $T_1$, which increases the forward bias for $T_1$ and increases the current flow. The process continues rapidly until $T_1$ is operating at maximum current flow (saturation) and $T_2$ is cut off. With $T_2$ nonconducting, there is no current flow through $R_2$, and hence the high negative potential at the collector of $T_2$ also holds $T_1$ at maximum current flow. Thus, the flip-flop remains in this stable state.

If the collector of the nonconducting $T_2$ transistor were shorted momentarily, the forward bias of the $T_1$ base-emitter would be removed and this transistor would be switched off. With no current through $R_1$, the $T_1$ collector voltage would rise to the full negative potential of the power source. This negative potential applied to the base of $T_2$ would permit the transistor to conduct. The resultant current flow through $R_2$ would then decrease the collector potential, which would bring it near the ground potential and thus reduce the forward bias for $T_1$. Thus, $T_1$ would remain in a nonconducting state, and $T_2$ would continue to conduct. The second stable state would now have been attained, and the circuit would remain in this state until again triggered by shorting out the collector of the nonconducting transistor. As will be shown later, the actual triggering is done by applying to the circuit a pulse signal having a polarity that negates the existing potential and flips (switches) the circuit to its other state.

Such a direct-coupled flip-flop utilizes a minimum of components, but, compared with the types discussed next, output-signal amplitudes

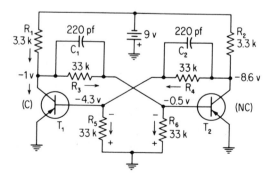

Fig. 4-2. R-C coupled flip-flop.

are low and require additional amplification. Also, because of direct coupling, $T_1$ collector voltage is limited to the base voltage value of the $T_2$ transistor, and the collector voltage of $T_2$ coincides with the base-voltage amplitude of $T_1$. The time interval for switching to the other state is rapid, however, and the circuit has been employed in a number of computers.

A conventional $RC$-coupled flip-flop circuit is shown in Fig. 4-2. Here, the voltage applied to the collectors can be increased above the base voltages both to develop a higher-amplitude signal outout than in the direct-coupled flip-flop and to increase circuit stability. Each transistor has a voltage-divider network across which the proper potentials will develop to hold one transistor in the "on" (conducting) state and keep the other in the "off" (nonconducting) state. Thus, transistor $T_1$ obtains the base bias from the junction of $R_4$ and $R_5$, while $T_2$ taps its bias at the junction of $R_3$ and $R_6$.

For Fig. 4-2, some typical values are given to help understand circuit function. If transistor $T_1$ is in the conducting state (at saturation), virtually the full power supply potential develops across $R_1$, reducing the $T_1$ collector potential to approximately $-1$ volt for a given type of resistor. If $R_3$ and $R_6$ have identical ohmic values, one-half this voltage appears at the junction and hence 0.5 volt is applied to the $T_2$ base. Because this is almost at ground potential, $T_2$ is cut off and hence nonconducting. Resistors $R_2$, $R_4$, and $R_5$ form a series string which shunts the supply potential. Hence, the voltage division across these resistors will be approximately 0.4 volt, 4.3 volts, and 4.3 volts, respectively, for a total of 9 volts (the supply potential). Thus, approximately $-8.6$ volts exists at the collector of $T_2$, which drops to $-4.3$ at the base of $T_1$.

The $-4.3$ volts at the base of $T_1$ provides the necessary forward bias for this transistor and keeps it in the conducting state. If the circuit is triggered to flip into its second state, the potentials reverse and those shown in Fig. 4-2 for the $T_1$ transistor will now prevail for $T_2$, and those at $T_2$ will exist at $T_1$.

Capacitors $C_1$ and $C_2$ are sometimes referred to as *commutating* capacitors and increase the switching speed. When short-duration trigger pulses are employed the circuit may not respond fast enough to change state before the pulse ends. Circuit-switching delay may be caused by minority-carrier storage time (discussed later) or by shunting effects of stray capacitance and the interelement capacitance of

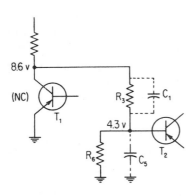

**Fig. 4-3. Effect of circuit capacitance.**

the transistors. How switching time is influenced by such shunt capacitance is illustrated in Fig. 4-3. Here, $C_s$ represents the lumped capacitance shunting the circuit. When transistor $T_1$ is switched into the nonconducting stage, the collector voltage rises from $-1$ volt (see Fig. 4-2) to 8.6 volts, as shown in Fig. 4-3. When this voltage appears at the base of $T_2$, it causes this transistor to conduct. The voltage at the base of $T_2$ does not rise immediately, however, because $C_s$ must reach a full charge. Because voltage rise in a capacitor lags current rise and because the charging path is in series with $R_3$, the time constant $RC$ is sufficiently long to delay the switching. By shunting $R_3$ with $C_1$, the shunting capacitance $C_s$ is permitted to charge more rapidly and thus reduce switching time.

## The Nonsaturated Flip-flop

In PNP transistors the *hole flow* is the primary carrier of current, while electron flow constitutes the minority carrier. For the NPN transistors, the electron flow becomes the primary carrier of current, and the hole flow, the secondary (minority) carrier. With a transistor conducting at saturation, the base region contains a large number of minority carriers which originate at the emitter and flow to the collector. When the transistor is triggered so it reverts to the nonconducting state, the minority carriers existing in the base area must flow through the base-collector junction before current flow can stop. Thus, a sufficient time interval elapses to produce a delay in the switching because of the equivalent *storage* of the minority carriers. The storage time (clearing the base of minority carriers) can be reduced by operating the transistor slightly below the saturation point. Flip-flop circuits, when so designed, are known as *nonsaturating* types.

One method for preventing transistor saturation in a flip-flop is by use of collector clamping diodes (also known as *limiting diodes*) as shown in A of Fig. 4-4. Here, diode $D_1$ connects from the $T_1$ collector to the $T_1$ base through resistor $R_5$. Diode $D_2$ connects from the collector of

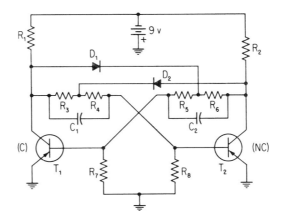

**Fig. 4-4. Nonsaturated flip-flop.**

$T_2$ to the $T_2$ base through $R_4$. The self-limiting function can best be understood by reference to Fig. 4-5 where the $T_1$ (conducting) section is illustrated with arrows showing the direction of electron flow.

Because of the conducting state of $T_1$ there is a voltage drop across $R_1$ and a reduced voltage at the $T_1$ collector. For $T_2$, however, the collector voltage is high because the transistor is nonconducting, and no voltage drop occurs across $R_2$. Resistors $R_2$, $R_6$, $R_5$, and $R_7$ form a shunting (voltage-divider) network across the power source, and for a specific value of $R_6$ the voltage at the right of the diode will be $-5$ volts as shown. Since the collector voltage for $T_1$ is $-3$, diode $D_1$ is forward biased and conducts. Thus, diode $D_1$ shunts, through the collector circuit of $T_1$, some of the current flow from the $-8.6$-volt source and reduces the current through the $R_5$ and $R_7$ branch. Consequently, the forward bias for the base-emitter circuit is reduced from the value

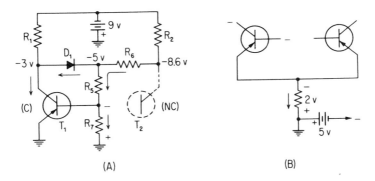

**Fig. 4-5. Nonsaturating circuit factors.**

which will prevail in the absence of $D_1$, and the transistor operation is brought to a point below saturation.

If transistor $T_1$ were in its nonconducting state, diode $D_1$ would not conduct, because it would have a reverse-bias potential across it. During nonconduction (for the values used in the illustration), the $T_1$ collector would be $-8.6$ volts and the $T_2$ collector, $-3$ volts, which would cause the left side of $D_1$ to be more negative than the right and prevent $D_1$ conduction.

The degenerative resistor shown in B of Fig. 4-5 is also useful for saturation reduction. Since this is in series with the emitter terminal, it will reduce the base-emitter potential (and hence the forward bias) by the amount of voltage drop which occurs across it. If electron flow through this resistor increases because of increased transistor conduction, the voltage drop across the resistor rises and thus reduces the forward bias by opposing the positive potential applied to the emitter. The reduction in forward bias, in turn, reduces the current through the emitter-collector portion of the circuit and minimizes the tendency toward reaching saturation. The emitter resistor shown in B is often included in the circuit shown in Fig. 4-4 to improve operation and circuit stability.

### *Flip-flop Triggering*

The flip-flop circuit is a binary device, that is, it has two stable states, one of which represents 1 and the other 0. Thus, in digital computer applications it is necessary to switch the flip-flop from one state to the other so it represents the desired 1 or 0. When successive stages of flip-flop circuits are connected together to form counters, it must be possible to apply a serial train of single-polarity pulses to the initial flip-flop for continuous triggering. Similarly, one flip-flop must be capable of triggering the next flip-flop and so on throughout the chain of circuits making up the counter.

Triggering is also necessary to *reset* (reverse the state of) the flip-flops containing 1's to *clear* the counter of its numerical representation when that is no longer needed. Similarly, at the start of operations, the various flip-flop circuitry must be triggered to represent zero counts.

The trigger-signal polarities as well as the output-signal polarities for a flip-flop using PNP transistors are shown in Fig. 4-6. For

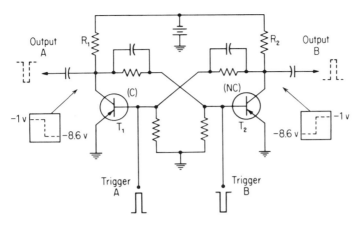

Fig. 4-6. Trigger and output signal polarities.

NPN transistors (and with the conducting and nonconducting states shown) the signal polarities indicated would be reversed.

Because $T_1$ is conducting, its base is negative with respect to the emitter, providing the necessary forward bias. Thus, if a positive-polarity pulse is applied (trigger $A$) as shown, the forward bias is overcome and $T_1$ stops conducting. If the voltage values prevail as shown earlier in Fig. 4-2, the $-1$ volt at the collector of $T_1$ will now change to almost the full supply-battery value, as shown in the graph at the left of $T_1$ in Fig. 4-6. This $-8.6$ value is felt at the base of $T_2$ and causes this transistor to go into conduction. Hence, the collector voltage for $T_2$ now changes from $-8.6$ to $-1$ volt, as shown in the graph to the right of $T_2$. This voltage is near the ground potential and hence, because of cross-coupling, holds $T_1$ at cutoff. Thus, the application of trigger pulse $A$ changed the flip-flop to its second state.

Note that, when the transistors were triggered, the collector voltages changed from one steady d-c value to another. With the flip-flop triggered to its second state, the collector voltages will again remain at a constant d-c level until the circuit is retriggered. However, during triggering, the *change* of voltage at each collector produces a rise and decline of signal amplitude at the output because of the coupling capacitors.

The circuit could also have been triggered into its second state by the application of trigger pulse $B$ to the base of transistor $T_2$. When this transistor is nonconducting, its base potential is near that of ground and hence the necessary forward bias to permit conduction is not present. The trigger pulse, having a negative polarity, supplies the proper forward bias potential and permits $T_2$ to conduct. The voltage drop across $R_2$ now decreases the negative collector potential from its original $-8.6$ volts to $-1$ volt, and this decrease is felt at the base of $T_1$, causing this transistor to cut off. Hence, trigger input $B$ also is capable of changing the flip-flop to its second state. The preferred method of triggering, however, is to cut off the conducting transistor. Reduced triggering speed may be encountered by triggering the non-conducting transistor because the cut-off bias potential has to be overcome and in some transistors the switching interval is longer than that for turning the transistor off.

When the flip-flop shown in Fig. 4-6 is in its second state (with $T_1$ nonconducting and $T_2$ conducting), the pulse polarity shown at trigger $A$ or trigger $B$ must be reversed to retrigger the flip-flop to its original state. If $T_1$ is now nonconducting, its base potential is near ground (positive) and the application of a positive pulse will drive the transistor more into the nonconducting region. Similarly, with $T_2$ conducting, the negative trigger pulse will increase forward bias rather than reduce it.

Note that when the flip-flop is triggered from one state to another, two output pulses are available, one with a positive polarity and one with a negative polarity. If the flip-flop is retriggered to its original state, the pulse polarity at output $A$ will be *positive* and that from output $B$, *negative*. This comes about because the $-8.6$ volts at the $T_1$ collector will revert back to the $-1$-volt value, which represents a change toward the positive direction. Similarly, the $-1$ volt at the collector of $T_2$ will change to $-8.6$ volts again, which represents a change in the negative direction.

### Steering Diodes

In the circuit shown in Fig. 4-6, the positive trigger pulse $A$ could have been applied to both base circuits at the same time and the circuit would still have been triggered. The positive pulse at $T_1$ base would have overcome the forward bias and triggered the flip-flop. The positive pulse at base $T_2$, however, would have been ineffectual because this transistor was already cut off (with the near positive potential). The use of a single pulse simplifies triggering, because the same polarity pulse will trigger the flip-flop to *either* state. With the flip-flop in the second state, for instance, a positive pulse at the base of $T_2$ (which is now conducting) will overcome the forward bias and stop conduction, which will change the flip-flop state.

Trigger inputs $A$ and $B$ of Fig. 4-6, however, cannot be tied together so that a single positive-polarity pulse can be entered, because this will obviously tie the bases together and make the circuit inoperative. Also, in practical circuitry, capacitive coupling between stages will change the pulse to one in which the d-c component is lost and both a negative and positive polarity exist in the signal (see Chapter 1, Clamping Circuit). With a dual-polarity trigger signal the positive portion will trigger, and the negative portion can retrigger, bringing the flip-flop back to its original state immediately, instead of to its second state. These disadvantages are eliminated by using *steering diodes*, as shown in Fig. 4-7. (These diodes must not be confused with the clamping diodes shown earlier in Fig. 4-4.)

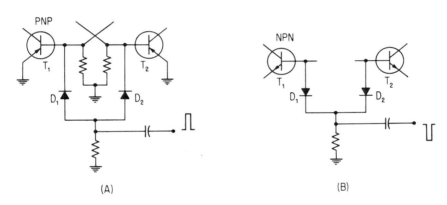

**Fig. 4-7. Base triggering.**

In A, a base-triggering steering circuit is shown, with the positive trigger pulse coupled by a series capacitor to two diodes $D_1$ and $D_2$. These diodes will only pass the positive-signal component to the bases of $T_1$ and $T_2$ and thus *steer* the proper polarity signal. With an NPN transistor flip-flop, the diodes are reversed as shown at $B$, and a negative trigger pulse is employed to cause the conducting transistor to be cut off. Thus, if $T_1$ in B of Fig. 4-7 is conducting, the forward bias is such that the base is *positive* with respect to the emitter. Hence, to stop conduction, a negative polarity signal must be applied to overcome the forward bias. If $T_2$ is nonconducting, its base will already be negative with respect to the emitter (reverse bias) and the negative pulse will increase the potentials so they will extend more into the cutoff region. Thus, the trigger pulse is again steered to the proper transistor.

The circuits shown in Figs. 4-6 and 4-7 use base triggering. The trigger amplitude must be sufficient to drive the conducting transistor into the nonconducting region, though little signal power is required. Collector triggering can also be employed, as shown in Fig. 4-8.

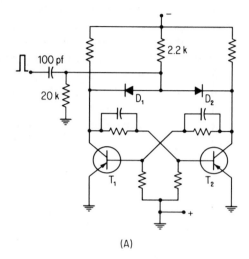

(A)

Fig. 4-8. Collector triggering and trigger amplifier.

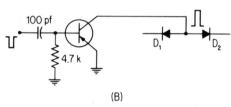

(B)

Since the trigger-signal amplitude is applied to the collector circuit, it is also felt at the base of the other transistor. Steering diodes are again used to direct the single-polarity signals to the respective collector circuits. Positive-polarity trigger pulses are again employed, as shown. If $T_1$ is conducting, its collector potential already has a low negative potential (near the ground positive polarity) and the application of a positive pulse has no effect. For $T_2$, however, the nonconduction places a high negative potential at the collector, which is reduced by the incoming trigger pulse. This reduction of the negative potential is felt at the base of $T_1$, which reduces the forward bias and triggers the flip-flop.

Collector triggering requires a pulse amplitude higher than that needed for base triggering. A trigger amplifier may be used to bring the trigger amplitude to the level required, as shown in B of Fig. 4-8. Because this transistor amplifier has phase-reversal characteristics (not circuit), the required signal polarity to the base of the amplifier transistor must be negative, as shown. With this system the 2.2 K resistor shown in A is not used, and the collector output from the trigger amplifier is coupled directly to the junction of the steering diodes.

A third possible method for triggering a transistorized flip-flop circuit is to apply the trigger signals to the transistor emitters. Such emitter triggering, however, requires high trigger current, and so the collector and base triggering methods are the most widely used.

## Trigger, Set, and Reset

To provide the flip-flop circuit with the versatility required to perform various computer functions, it is necessary to include additional terminals in the basic circuit. Earlier, in Fig. 4-6, individual base

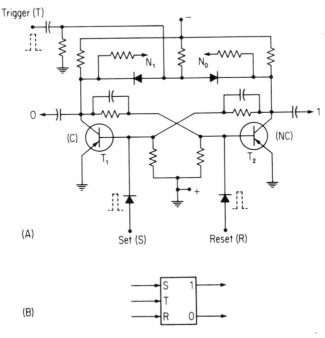

**Fig. 4-9. Terminal designations.**

trigger terminals were shown, and it was pointed out that either could be used to change the flip-flop state. In practice the trigger $B$ line can be used for resetting (clearing) the flip-flop stage after it has been set by either the trigger $A$ input or through the steering diodes shown in Fig. 4-8. The reset input, however, has the same polarity as the set-input signal, as shown in Fig. 4-9.

For the circuit shown in Fig. 4-9 the set input $S$ is only capable of changing the flip-flop to its second state when a positive signal is applied. A second positive signal applied here does not change the circuit to its original state because, while $T_1$ is nonconducting, the signal will only increase reverse bias and drive $T_1$ more into the non-conducting state. Similarly, the reset input $R$ can only "reset" the circuit to its original state. If the positive pulse is applied while $T_2$ is in the nonconducting state (its original state), the signal only increases the extent of the cutoff.

The initial state in Fig. 4-9, (when $T_1$ is conducting and $T_2$ non-conducting) represents 0, while its second state ($T_1$ cut off and $T_2$ conducting) represents 1. Thus we have the two representations need-ed for the binary system, the 0 and the 1. In the PNP flip-flop shown, positive pulse signals represent 1 and negative pulse signals represent 0. Thus, the injection of a positive pulse at either the trigger or set input flips the circuit to the second state for a 1 representation. As shown earlier in Fig. 4-6, a positive signal appears at the collector of $T_2$ (representing 1), and a negative signal appears at the collector of $T_1$ (representing 0). Thus, every time the flip-flop is triggered, there is a choice of either a negative or a positive output signal.

If the collector output from $T_1$ is used to couple to another flip-flop stage, a 1 representation signal will be applied to the second state only when the circuit is returned to the 0 state. Thus, when a number of flip-flops are connected to form a binary counter, it is important to remember that a flip-flop circuit will only trigger the next stage when changing from its 1 state to its 0 state.

Terminals $N_1$ and $N_0$ in Fig. 4-9 may be applied to indicator-light circuits to provide a visual indication of either the 1 or 0 state of the flip-flop. Thus, when the circuit is in the 0 state, collector voltage at $T_1$ is low and the $N_1$ indicator light is out. At the same time the col-lector voltage for $T_2$ is high and $N_0$ is on. When the stage is in the 1 state, the cut off $T_2$ transistor has a high collector voltage, which turns on light $N_1$ to indicate the 1 state of the flip-flop. At this time $N_0$ is out, indicating the circuit is *not* in the zero state. A block diagram repre-sentation of the binary flip-flop is shown in B of Fig. 4-9.

If NPN transistors are employed for the flip-flop shown in Fig. 4-9, negative-polarity signal pulses are used for the trigger, set, and reset inputs. Thus, a negative pulse would represent 1 and a positive pulse (or the absence of a pulse) would represent zero. As in the PNP flip-flop, however, either a positive or a negative signal polarity is available from the output terminals, as required in specific applications. Also, the circuit shown in Fig. 4-9 with PNP transistors could be considered in the 0 stage when $T_2$ is conducting and $T_1$ cut off. Since the flip-flop is a symmetrical circuit, operation would be the same, except that the set signal would be applied to $T_2$ and the reset signal to $T_1$.

## The Binary Counter

A two-stage binary counter is shown in Fig. 4-10, and an analysis of these circuits will indicate the method of operation. The circuit sequence is from *right to left* in contrast to the nomal left-to-right circuit sequence used in electronic schematics. The right-left sequence is used so that the count representation will coincide with that of our arithmetic place system and thus aid our understanding of the operation. In some publications the left-to-right circuit sequence will be encountered, but the right-to-left will be used throughout this text.

Initially, assume both stages are in the zero state, with the $T_2$ and $T_4$ transistors conducting as shown. Thus, these two stages represent a count of 00. When one pulse is entered at the $T$ input of the first

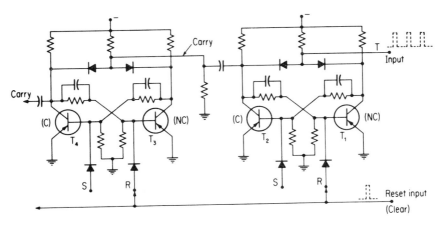

**Fig. 4-10. Two-stage binary counter.**

(right-hand) stage, it will trigger this circuit to its second state representing the count of 1. When this first stage is triggered, a negative-polarity pulse is developed in the collector circuit of $T_2$ and appears at the steering diodes of the second stage at the left. The negative pulse, however, is ineffectual at the diode junction of the second stage because it is the reverse of the polarity which permits diode conduction. Thus, the two stages now represent the count of 01.

Upon the application of a second pulse at the $T$ input at the right, this flip-flop stage is triggered to its original 0 state. At this time, however, a *positive* pulse is produced at the $T_2$ collector output, and this has the proper polarity for diode conduction when it appears at the junction of the steering diodes of the second stage at the left. Now this stage is triggered to its 1 state, and the count representation is now 10, which is the binary 2.

The third pulse entered into the counter will trigger the first stage to 1 again, giving a representation of 11, the binary 3. If no more pulses are now entered, the counter will retain this 11 binary number for so long as power is applied to the circuit. Hence, the counter has storage capabilities. In practice, however, the flip-flops of the computer are used only for temporary internal storage as required during calculation processes. For permanent storage, the devices detailed in Chapter 7 are utilized. When the numbers are no longer needed in

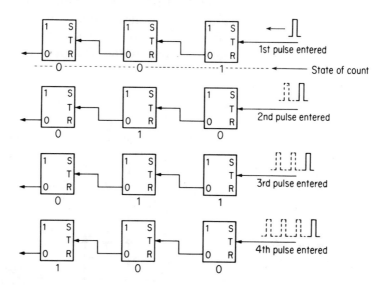

**Fig. 4-11.** Count sequence.

the counter, a positive signal pulse is applied to the reset line. This appears at all the $R$ terminals of the flip-flop stages and thus resets (clears) the flip-flops of their stored numbers and returns them to zero.

The count sequence and the state of each flip-flop are shown in Fig. 4-11 for a count up to four. Here a three-stage counter is shown with a maximum count capability of 111 (7). For higher counts, additional flip-flop stages are added until the maximum count for which the computer is designed is reached. In analyzing the count sequence in Fig. 4-11, it must be remembered that two pulses (digits) must be entered into a flip-flop before the next stage is triggered. This follows the binary addition rule of $1 + 1 = 0$, carry 1. Hence, if two digits are entered into a flip-flop stage, it will trigger twice $(1 + 1)$ to zero, and transfer a trigger (carry) pulse to the next stage for a binary 10 count.

Flip-flop stages are often represented on the console of a computer by indicator lights. When the flip-flop is in the 1 state, the indicator bulb will light up. A four-stage counter is shown in Fig. 4-12 with accompanying indicator lights showing a stored count of 1011. Some computers have also used indicator lights in the other half of the flip-flop to show the 0 state, or the complement representation, as discussed for Fig. 4-9.

For the counter in Fig. 4-12, assume that initially seven digits (pulses) are applied to the $T$ input of the first stage at the right. These seven digits would create a binary count of 0111 for the stages shown. If, at a somewhat later time, four additional digits were entered, the final count in the circuits would be the binary number 1011, as shown. Thus, a number of flip-flop circuits, when strung

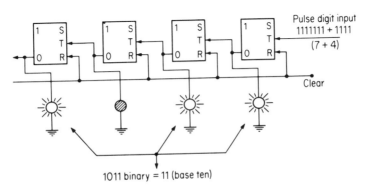

**Fig. 4-12. Four-stage binary counter.**

together, will convert a train of pulses, representing individual digits, into their binary equivalent sum, as well as store them; and the counter will "accumulate" the binary numbers as well as add up groups of sequential digits applied to the input. In the four stages shown in Fig. 4-12, the 11 digits which had been applied result in the three bulbs' being lit, as illustrated, representing a 1011 binary number which had been converted from the decimal equivalent 11. Four stages such as shown in Fig. 4-12 will count up to 15 (with all the bulbs lit and indicating the binary number 1111). For a higher count, additional stages must be added.

When a number of stages of flip-flops are connected together to form a counter, the indicator lights bear a similarity to the wheel registry of the mechanical binary counter, as will be seen by reference to the table given in Chapter 2, page 40. Thus, the numeral in the binary column would indicate a lighted bulb (or bulbs) for the decimal figures shown in the right-hand column. For example, when six pulses have been inserted into the counter, the second and third indicators would be lit, with the first and fourth being out. On the other hand, at the count of nine, the first and fourth bulbs would be lit, with the second and third out.

If consideration is given to the number of times an indicator bulb lights up for the number of pulses entered into a particular flip-flop, it would be found that a flip-flop circuit performs a function known as *scaling*, since it will scale down, or divide, an input by a base 2 relationship. If, for instance, two pulses are injected into the first stage, the bulb will light only once, indicating that this stage divides by 2. The addition of a second stage will cause the device to divide by 4, because, for every four pulses inserted into the first stage input, only one pulse appears at the output of the second stage. The output from the third stage would consist of only one triggering pulse for every eight triggering pulses entered into the input of the first stage, etc. Hence, the system actually is a divider as well as a binary counter. The output from the fourth stage is one pulse for every sixteen entered into the first stage.

The binary counter of Fig. 4-12 counts in ascending order; that is, the count stored in the stages increases as additonal input pulses are applied. The binary counter can also be used to count in *descending* order by employing the other output from each flip-flop stage, as shown in Fig. 4-13. Here, each stage is in the 1 state, providing a count of 7 and a binary representation of 111, as shown in A. If a

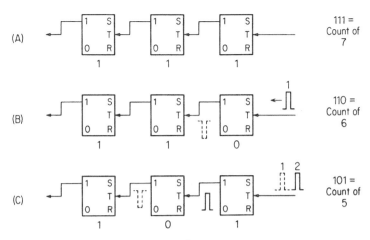

**Fig. 4-13. Binary count reduction.**

pulse is now applied to the trigger input at the right, it will trip this stage to zero as shown in B. Because the upper output is used, however, the triggering of the first stage to zero results in the production of a negative output signal which is not passed by the steering diodes of the second stage, and hence the second stage remains at the 1 count. Now the counter contains a reduced binary number, 110, representative of the number 6.

When another pulse is applied to the input, as in C of the figure the first stage at the right is triggered to the 1 state and a positive output pulse is procured from the upper output terminal. Now the second stage is triggered to 0, resulting in an additional count reduction to 101, representing 5. Thus, for each input pulse the total count is reduced by 1.

## Decade Counter

There are a number of computer applications (including data processing) for which it would be convenient to have a counter operating in a *decade* fashion instead of in pure binary. Thus, instead of four stages counting to 15 (1111), four stages would count to 9 (1001) and trigger to 0 at the count of 10. At this time, the four stages would send a triggering pulse to the input of the succeeding four-stage counter in order to trip it. In such a system the decade counter oper-

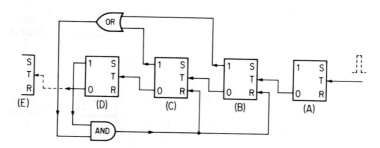

**Fig. 4-14.** Decade counter.

ates in a base-10 system while still using the binary system for each stage.

There are several methods for adding circuitry to the basic binary counter to form a decade counter. One such system is shown in Fig. 4-14, and it utilizes an *or* circuit as well as an *and* circuit, as shown. Note that the second outputs from the flip-flop stages *C* and *B* feed an *or* circuit, which in turn supplies one of the terminals of an *and* circuit.

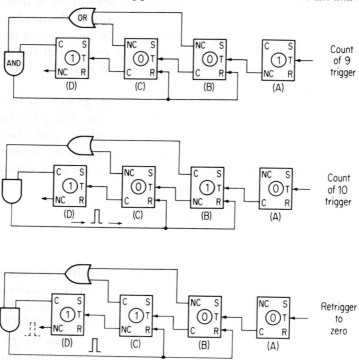

**Fig. 4-15.** Decade trigger operation.

The other input to the *and* circuit is from the upper output terminal of stage *D* as shown. The *and* circuit, in turn, is applied to the reset inputs of both the *B* and the *C* stages. Thus, whenever coincidence occurs for the *and* circuit, an output pulse will be applied to stages *B* and *C* which will reset (clear) these stages if they are in the 1 state.

The method of operation can best be understood by reference to Fig. 4-15. As shown, each stage of the decade counter has one output terminal designated as *C* to represent *conduction* and another *NC* to indicate *nonconduction*. For the purpose of explanation, we shall assume that positive pulses are the significant ones; hence each positive pulse represents a 1 count. At the upper four stages shown, a count of 9 has been reached; hence the first and last stages are in the 1 state as shown. Note that at this time there is no coincidence of the inputs to the *and* gate since the output terminals from stages *C* and *B* do not coincide with the output terminal from stage *D*.

When the tenth pulse is entered into the trigger input of the four stages, the first stage is triggered to 0 and a positive output pulse is produced, which, in turn, triggers the second stage *B* to the 1 state as shown in the center illustration. When this occurs, however, there will be coincidence at the *and* circuit, since the upper output from stage *B* coincides with that of stage *D*, and the result is the application of a positive pulse to the reset inputs of both the *B* and the *C* stages. Since the *C* stage is already in its 0 state, however, a reset pulse is ineffectual here. The *B* stage, however, is triggered by the reset pulse to 0, and momentarily the four stages show 1100, as in the lower drawing. Now, however, coincidence again occurs at the upper outputs of the *C* and *D* stages, and another reset pulse is applied to the *B* and *C* stages. Now, the reset pulse clears the *C* stage, producing a positive output pulse which triggers the *D* stage to 0. When the *D* stage is triggered to 0, it also produces a positive output pulse which triggers the fifth stage. Thus, at the count of 10, the four stages of the decade counter all become zero, and the fifth stage is triggered into the 1 state. (The fifth stage would be the *first* stage of the next decade counter.)

Interconnected decade counters are shown in Fig. 4-16. Here each flip-flop of a particular counter is drawn in a vertical plane, and it is assumed that the interconnections are as previously shown in Fig. 4-14. Thus, the first stage is at the upper right and the binary count value is as shown in Fig. 4-16. The fourth flip-flop stage of the first decade counter is connected to the first flip-flop stage of the second decade counter, as shown. Thus, the output from each decade counter

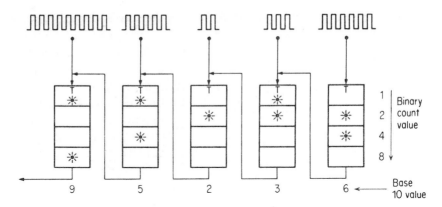

Fig. 4-16. Interconnected decade counters.

is coupled to the input of each successive decade counter to form a continuous decade-circuit train.

If six pulses are entered into the first decade counter at the right, the respective lights which indicate this count would be lit as shown, representing the binary number 0110, which is equal to the base-10 value of 6. When three pulses are applied to the second decade counter, the binary representation will be 11, indicating the base-10 value of 3. Similarly, assume that successive stages contain the count of 2, 5, and 9, as shown. In consequence, these interconnected decade counters now indicate a base-10 value count of 95,236 as shown. The decade system shown in Fig. 4-6 will also accumulate counts since, if four more pulses are entered into the first stage at the right, because of the decade-counter circuit this stage will then trigger to 0 and a pulse will be sent to the second decade counter, changing the 3 count to a 4 count, for a total of 95,240. Similarly, an additional pulse could be entered into the fourth decade counter to increase the total count by an additional thousand.

To represent the numbers contained in the decade counters indicated in Fig. 4-16, it is necessary to code each decimal number in terms of its binary equivalent, and hence this system is known as *binary-coded decimal*. This is necessary to indicate the true count. For instance, if 23 were expressed in pure binary notation, it would be 10111. To express this number as contained in a decade-counter system, we should have the following notation:

0010  0011

Four binary bits (0's or 1's) are used for each decimal digit to make them uniform with the four bits required for 8 (1000) and 9 (1001). Thus, when expressing a number such as 984, we have the same number of bits for each binary-coded decimal number:

1001   1000   0100

For the number shown in the decade-counter system of Fig. 4-16, the following binary-coded decimal representation applies:

1001   0101   0010   0011   0110

In coding binary numbers in groups to provide decimal representation in this fashion, the first nine digits would, of course, be in pure binary form. After the ninth number, however, the binary-coded notation consists of separate four-bit number groups as shown below:

| Decimal Number | Binary-Coded | | |
|---|---|---|---|
| 01 | | | 0001 |
| 02 | | | 0010 |
| 03 | | | 0011 |
| 04 | | | 0100 |
| 05 | | | 0101 |
| etc. | | | |
| 09 | | | 1001 |
| 10 | | 0001 | 0000 |
| 11 | | 0001 | 0001 |
| 12 | | 0001 | 0010 |
| 13 | | 0001 | 0011 |
| etc. | | | |
| 20 | | 0010 | 0000 |
| 21 | | 0010 | 0001 |
| 22 | | 0010 | 0010 |
| 23 | | 0010 | 0011 |
| etc. | | | |
| 364 | 0011 | 0110 | 0100 |
| 365 | 0011 | 0110 | 0101 |
| etc. | | | |

From the foregoing it is evident that the binary-coded decimal system provides a convenient notation method for expressing the large numbers which may be handled by interconnected decade counters. It is particularly useful in certain data-processing computer systems and is also utilized with other code groups, as explained more fully in the next chapter.

## Parallel and Serial Operation

As mentioned in Chapter 1 under Digital Signals, binary numbers can be handled in either serial or parallel form in digital computers. Thus, when reading out from a series of flip-flop stages (registers) or when reading in, provisions must be made to accommodate the mode of operation used. Previously we entered a series of pulses into the first stage of a group of flip-flop circuits, with one pulse representing 1, two pulses, 2, etc. Similarly, in the decade counters, we entered five pulses to represent 5, eight pulses to represent 8, etc. Often, however, it is necessary to read in and read out groups of pulses or signals representative of the *binary number*, such as 101 for 5, 110 for 6, etc.

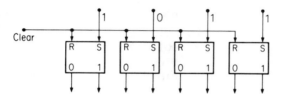

Fig. 4-17. Parallel read-in and read-out methods.

The circuit arrangement shown in Fig. 4-17 provides for parallel binary number read-in and read-out procedures. Here, the binary number 1011 is entered in parallel form into the *S*-input lines, as shown. This number can then be read out in parallel form from the lower output lines, as shown, to provide for either the pure binary or the complement number, as more fully described in Chapter 6.

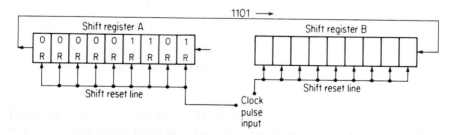

Fig. 4-18. Serial read-in and read-out.

Serial read-in and read-out methods for binary numbers are shown in Fig. 4-18. Here, special flip-flop registers are used so that the binary numbers can be shifted progressively to the left by the application of reset pulses to the clearing input. Such shift registers are described in Chapter 6. If the number 1101 is stored in register $A$ as shown, it can be transferred to register $B$ by shifting the number 9 times. This would run the number out at the left of the $A$ register and into the first flip-flop of the $B$ register in progression, as shown. The number of clock pulses which must be entered is determined by the number of stages contained in the flip-flop registers. If each register had 20 flip-flop circuits, it would require 20 reset pulses to perform a complete serial transfer of any number from the $A$ register into the $B$ register. The process clears the $A$ register of the number it contained. This method can, of course, also be used to read the number from the $A$ register into a permanent storage device or to route it to any destination which will accept a serial-form binary representation.

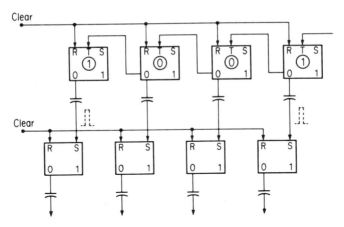

Fig. 4-19. Number transfer by clearing input.

The *steady-state* voltages at the 0 and 1 output lines of flip-flop stages can be applied to other circuits to represent 0 and 1 signals. When, however, capacity coupling exists between two stages, a binary signal can only be transferred by either triggering or clearing the stage, since the steady-state of the flip-flop will not produce the desired signal coupling through a capacitor. This is exemplified in Fig. 4-19, where a counter has the binary number 1001 stored in it. In order to transfer this binary representation to a storage register through ca-

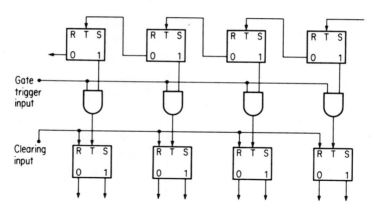

Fig. 4-20. Number transfer by *and* gates.

pacitor coupling, a clearing pulse is inserted in the counter to clear all the stages. Since only the first and fourth stage will be reset, an output pulse is produced which then enters the lower storage register, as shown. Thus, the upper counter register is now clear, and the binary 1001 is stored in the lower register.

If a steady-state representation of a number is to be transferred from one unit to another, *and* gates can be used as shown in Fig. 4-20. Here the 1-output terminals are utilized, since these will provide the proper steady-state polarity when the circuit is in the 1 state. Thus, if the upper counter again contains 1001, the first and fourth *and* circuits will have the proper polarity applied to the left-hand terminals for coincidence when a gate trigger-input pulse is applied. Consequently the number stored in the upper counter can be transferred to the lower register by the application of a gate trigger-input signal having a polarity that coincides with the output steady-state voltages existing at the first and fourth flip-flop stages. If the second and third stages contain a zero representation, the polarity at the output terminal would be opposite to that of the gate trigger input, and hence the second and third *and* circuit will not transfer a number to the lower flip-flop stages. By a method shown in Fig. 4-20, a number contained in the upper counter is transferred to the lower flip-flop stages without clearing the number from the upper counter. Hence, the number is still retained by the upper counter and can be utilized for other calculation purposes by the computer if the operational routines require this. If the number in the upper counter is to be erased, reset pulses must be applied in conventional form.

## Overflow

Regardless of how many flip-flop stages are used in counters and registers, there is a limit to the magnitude of the number they can handle. When a register obtains a number which has a value in excess of that it can handle, the condition is termed *overflow*. When overflow occurs, an overflow light is illuminated and in most instances the computer stops. Often the final flip-flop of a given register is used to sense the overflow condition, turn on the light, and initiate other functions deemed necessary by the design engineers. Separate overflow indicators may be used for the various registers.

The sensing of overflow is also useful in some computing procedures such as the division process, as detailed in Chapter 6.

## PROBLEMS

1. List some of the functions which can be performed by a series of flip-flop stages.

2. Explain the essential differences between the bistable multivibrator and the astable type.

3. Summarize the circuit operation of a direct-coupled transistor flip-flop.

4. For what purpose are *commutating* capacitors used in a flip-flop circuit?

5. What factors influence the switching speed of a flip-flop circuit?

6. Why is it desirable to operate a flip-flop below the saturation region?

7. What is the purpose of the degenerative resistor shown in B of Fig. 4-5?

8. Briefly explain the purpose of using *steering* diodes.

9. Draw a circuit schematic of a collector-triggered flip-flop stage using NPN transistors, preceded by a trigger amplifier feeding steering diodes.

10. What circuit interconnecting changes are made to convert a binary counter which counts in ascending order into one which counts in descending order?

11. Briefly explain how the basic binary counter is converted to a decade counter.

12. Reproduce the block diagrams of Fig. 4-15, but show the conducting and nonconducting stages for the counts of 6, 7, and 8.

**13.** Reproduce the drawing shown in Fig. 4-16, but show a count of 46,781.

**14.** Express the number 34 in pure binary and also in binary-coded decimal form.

**15.** Reproduce the drawing shown in Fig. 4-18, showing 15 stages for each register, and explain how a number such as 11011 can be transferred from the $A$ register to the $B$ register.

**16.** How may numbers be read out of a register in parallel form while their representation is still retained in the register?

# SPECIAL CODES
# AND NOTATION

**5**

**Introduction.** In addition to the pure binary code described in Chapter 2 (and the binary-coded decimal system explained in Chapter 4), other codes and notations are employed in various digital computers. Some of these special codes are employed to minimize errors, others are utilized to reduce the number of 1 digits in a binary group, and still others are employed for special purposes as the occasion demands. All, however, are based on the pure binary notation described in Chapter 2; hence the information contained in that earlier chapter should be thoroughly assimilated before undertaking a study of the special codes described in this chapter.

The pure binary code described in Chapter 2 is also known as a *weighted code*, because each bit has a value (weight) such as 8, 4, 2, 1. By adding the weights of the digits represented, the base-10 value of the group is ascertained: 1111 = 15, 1001 = 9, etc. An *unweighted* code is one in which the sum of the digit values (weights) is not equal to the number represented by the group of bits. Unweighted codes are special purpose types, such as the excess-three code described in this chapter.

The binary-coded decimal system described earlier, and the octal system described initially in this chapter are basically variations on the method of notation of the pure binary code and should not be considered as special codes. The excess-three, the Gray, and similar codes

**115**

are special codes which have differences other than notation variations. The specific application of such special codes and notations are given for each one described in this chapter.

### Octal Notation

Octal notation simplifies the conversion of large binary numbers to their decimal equivalent and vice-versa. From the standpoint of convenience, it can be likened to the binary-coded decimal notation described in Chapter 4. The binary-coded decimal system, however, applies specifically to decade-counter circuitry, whereas the octal notation relates to the pure binary counting devices. Octal notation is of particular advantage when large binary numbers must be notated for certain programming phases, or when it is necessary to write or record binary numbers. It is highly useful when it is necessary to place information directly into computer circuitry piecemeal for the evaluation of the performance of certain computer sections or for the testing of specific parts of a program.

In octal notation a binary number of any length is broken up into sets of three bits each. Thus, a binary number such as 1011011 is expressed as 001 011 011. Because only three digits are contained in each group, decimal equivalents range only from 0 to 7 (eight digits including zero). Thus, the octal system has a radix (base) of eight. Each three-bit binary group (from right to left in conventional place system) increases by a power of eight and is thus related to the increase by a power of two of each digit in the pure binary notation. It is this relationship which simplifies the conversion of a binary number to its decimal equivalent or the change of a decimal number to its binary equivalent.

Since octal notation is based on the powers of eight, each power of eight which a triad place (group of three binary bits) represents can be set down in similar fashion to the binary-system powers of two shown earlier on page 41:

|       |       |       |       |       |       | *Triad Group* |
|-------|-------|-------|-------|-------|-------|----------------|
| 000   | 000   | 000   | 000   | 000   | 000   | ←*Place*      |
| $8^5$ | $8^4$ | $8^3$ | $8^2$ | $8^1$ | $8^0$ | ←*Power*      |
| 32,768| 4096  | 512   | 64    | 8     | 1     | ←*Value*      |

etc.

Thus, from the foregoing, it is evident that a first-place group of three bits has unit power values just as in pure binary notation. Hence, $001 = 1$, $010 = 2$, $011 = 3$, etc., up to a value of 7 (111). A second-place group of three digits increases in a power-of-8 value related to the *binary number represented by the group*, $001\ 000 = 8$ (as is obvious if we express this as $001000$); $010\ 000 = 16$ (since the second-place group has a binary number representation of $010 = 2$ and $2 \times 8 = 16$). Similarly, if the number is $011\ 000$, it represents $3 \times 8 = 24$, which is the true value of the binary number if the bits are bunched together as $011000$, which has a value of $16 + 8 = 24$. The second-group value increases to the limit of the number of digits in the group, $111\ 000 = 7 \times 8 = 56$. If 1 digits are also present in the first-place group, their value is added to that obtained for the second-place group, as, $111\ 001 = (7 \times 8) + 1 = 57$. Similarly, $101\ 101 = (5 \times 8) + 5 = 45$, as is evident if we group these to produce the binary number $101101$, which equals $32 + 8 + 4 + 1 = 45$.

For the third-place group, the powers of $8^2$ increase in relation to the binary number value represented by the three bits. If the number is $010\ 000\ 000$, the third-place group has a binary value of 2 and a power value of $8^2$; hence $2 \times 8^2 = 2 \times 64 = 128$. If the value of the binary number $011011011$ is to be found, the grouping by three bits produces $011\ 011\ 011$. These groups yield

|  | 011 | 011 | 011 |  |
|---|---|---|---|---|
|  | $3 \times 64 = 192$ | $3 \times 8 = 24$ | $3 \times 1 = 3$ |  |
| $=$ | 192 $+$ | 24 $+$ | 3 | $= 219$ |

For the number $1011101$ (93), extra zeros are added to the last place to represent the three bits:

|  | 001 | 011 | 101 | $=$ | *octal* 135 |
|---|---|---|---|---|---|
| $=$ | $1 \times 64$ | $3 \times 8$ | $5 \times 1$ |  |  |
| $=$ | 64 $+$ | 24 $+$ | 5 | $=$ | 93 |

These principles form the basis of the octal system of notation, and the numerical binary value of the group of three bits is the *octal* value. Thus, the *octal* value of $101\ 111\ 001\ 011 = 5713$. The following table shows decimal, octal, and binary values up to a count of 25:

| Decimal | Octal | Binary |
|---|---|---|
| 0 | 00 | 000 000 |
| 1 | 01 | 000 001 |
| 2 | 02 | 000 010 |
| 3 | 03 | 000 011 |
| 4 | 04 | 000 100 |
| 5 | 05 | 000 101 |
| 6 | 06 | 000 110 |
| 7 | 07 | 000 111 |
| 8 | 10 | 001 000 |
| 9 | 11 | 001 001 |
| 10 | 12 | 001 010 |
| 11 | 13 | 001 011 |
| 12 | 14 | 001 100 |
| 13 | 15 | 001 101 |
| 14 | 16 | 001 110 |
| 15 | 17 | 001 111 |
| 16 | 20 | 010 000 |
| 17 | 21 | 010 001 |
| 18 | 22 | 010 010 |
| 19 | 23 | 010 011 |
| 20 | 24 | 010 100 |
| 21 | 25 | 010 101 |
| 22 | 26 | 010 110 |
| 23 | 27 | 010 111 |
| 24 | 30 | 011 000 |
| 25 | 31 | 011 001 |

The octal system is also convenient for finding the binary equivalent of a given decimal number, since the octal equivalent of a base-10 number can be found by dividing successively by 8 and writing down each remainder. The sequence of remainders forms the octal number. (A similar method was shown for pure binary in Chapter 2, where successive divisions by 2 were made.) Once the octal number is obtained, the binary equivalent is set down.

As an example, assume we wish to find the binary equivalent of 382. We divide by 8 as shown below:

| | | Quotient | Remainder |
|---|---|---|---|
| $\frac{382}{8}$ | = | 47 | 6 |
| $\frac{47}{8}$ | = | 5 | 7 |
| $\frac{5}{8}$ | = | 0 | 5 |

Reading the remainder upward produces 576, the octal equivalent of 382. The equivalent binary values are then set down:

$$101\ 111\ 110 = 101111110 = 382$$

Similarly, if the binary equivalent of 349 were to be found, the division process is

*Remainder*

| $\frac{349}{8}$ | = | 43 | 5 |
| $\frac{43}{8}$ | = | 5 | 3 |
| $\frac{5}{8}$ | = | 0 | 5 |

Thus, the octal number is 535, producing 101 011 101, which, when bunched together, forms the binary number 101011101, which has a decimal value of 349. This simplifies considerably the ease with which a long binary number can be written for a given decimal value. This is clearly exemplified by the following additional example where the binary number for 7562 is to be written:

*Remainder*

| 7562 | ÷ | 8 | = | 945 | 2 |
| 945 | ÷ | 8 | = | 118 | 1 |
| 118 | ÷ | 8 | = | 14 | 6 |
| 14 | ÷ | 8 | = | 1 | 6 |
| 1 | ÷ | 8 | = | 0 | 1 |

By this division method we find the decimal number 7562 produces the octal number 16612, and this is converted to the octal notation:

$$001\ 110\ 110\ 001\ 010 = 001110110001010 = 7562$$

## Gray Code

In industrial and military electronics there are numerous occasions when a shaft rotation, a lever movement, or other physical change must be converted to an equivalent numerical expression such as a binary number. This conversion of a physical variation to a binary-

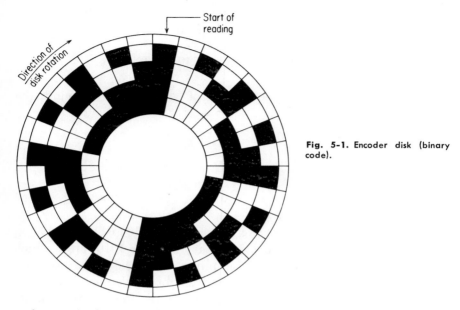

**Fig. 5-1.** Encoder disk (binary code).

value equivalent, permits a digital computer to process the information thus received for purposes of computation, control, or both. Hence this process finds important usage in guidance and tracking systems in military applications and in industrial control of lathes, machine tools, and other equipment.

A convenient method of converting a physical change (such as a shaft rotation) into a binary representation uses an encoder disk such as shown in Fig. 5-1. Such a shaft encoder disk consists of alternate segments of holes (the light areas in the illustration) through which the binary number can be sensed by using a pick up device such as photocells or electric feeler brushes as shown in Fig. 5-2. For photocell usage,

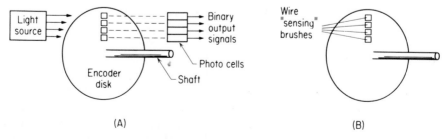

**Fig. 5-2.** Encoder disk signal sampling.

the disk is sometimes constructed of alternate transparent and non-transparent sections (using a plastic disk). Disks in which the segments are of the printed-circuit type are also employed.

The encoder disk shown in Fig. 5-1 produces a pure binary output. In the starting position shown, all segments are black and the output which is read is 0000. When the disk moves by one outer-ring segment in a clockwise rotation, the number 0001 is sensed (reading from the inside of the circle outward). Upon another one-segment rotation, the number 0010 is sensed. Continued rotation senses an ascending numerical value of binary numbers up to a maximum count of 15 at the 180° rotational point. Additional rotation starts the count over again.

Such encoder disks can be constructed with additional rings to provide higher-number read-outs if smaller segments of the circumference are to be sensed. When very slight rotational changes are to be converted to a numerical representation, however, the danger of error is increased, particularly when the read-out consists of pure binary. To facilitate the coding of a small variable into a number expressed in a given code, it is desirable to change only one digit at a time when going from one number to the next highest number. In pure binary notation there are instances when several digits change during the numerical progress. For instance, in binary, when changing from the number 3 (0011) to 4 (0100), three digits must change since the two digits in 0011 must revert to 0's and the third-place 0 must be changed to a 1. Similarly, going from 7 (0111) to 8 (1000) involves a change of four digits. From 15 (1111) to 16 (10000) involves a change of five digits. Operational errors are reduced considerably if only one digit at a time changes as the numerical value increases. An ideal code for this purpose is the *Gray code* named after its inventor, Dr. Frank Gray. The Gray code is sometimes called the *cyclic code*, or *minimum-error code*. Another term applied to this code is the *reflected binary*. The following table shows the Gray code equivalent of decimal numbers up to 12.

| Decimal Number | Pure Binary | Gray Code |
|---|---|---|
| 0 | 0000 | 0000 |
| 1 | 0001 | 0001 |
| 2 | 0010 | 0011 |
| 3 | 0011 | 0010 |

| Decimal Number | Pure Binary | Gray Code |
|:---:|:---:|:---:|
| 4 | 0100 | 0110 |
| 5 | 0101 | 0111 |
| 6 | 0110 | 0101 |
| 7 | 0111 | 0100 |
| 8 | 1000 | 1100 |
| 9 | 1001 | 1101 |
| 10 | 1010 | 1111 |
| 11 | 1011 | 1110 |
| 12 | 1100 | 1010 |

An inspection of the foregoing table will indicate the technique used to obtain the Gray code. To convert a binary number to its Gray code equivalent, the binary number is added to itself without carrying, but the added number *is indexed (moved over) to the right by one place, dropping the digit which would extend beyond the original number.* Thus, to express the binary number 2 (10) in Gray code, the process is

$$
\begin{array}{ll}
\phantom{+}10 & \text{(binary 2)} \\
\underline{+1} & \text{(binary 2 indexed to right by one number)} \\
\phantom{+}11 &
\end{array}
$$

When a carry function is indicated, it is ignored. The following indicates this process, where the number 6 (110) is converted to the Gray code:

$$
\begin{array}{ll}
\phantom{+}110 & \text{(6)} \\
\underline{+11} & \text{(6 indexed)} \\
\phantom{+}101 & \text{Gray code 6}
\end{array}
$$

Note in the foregoing that in second place the addition of 1 plus 1 equals 0 with 1 to carry. In converting to the Gray code, however, the carry function is not performed. This holds true even though a number of digits would be involved, as the following indicates:

$$
\begin{array}{ll}
\phantom{+}1111 & \text{(15)} \\
\underline{+111} & \text{(15 indexed)} \\
\phantom{+}1000 & \text{Gray code 15}
\end{array}
$$

To convert from the Gray code back to the binary, the operation is set down as shown below. The numbers have been given alphabetical designations to facilitate explanation.

$$\begin{array}{c}
A \;\; B \;\; C \;\; D \;\; E \\
1 \;\; 1 \;\; 1 \;\; 0 \;\; 0 \quad \text{Gray code} \\
+\overline{1 \;\; 0 \;\; 1 \;\; 1 \;\; 1} \quad \text{binary equivalent} \\
F \;\; G \;\; H \;\; I \;\; \mathcal{J}
\end{array}$$

Initially, the Gray code number 11100 is written as shown above, and the first digit to the left, $A$, is brought down and forms the extreme left number of the binary equivalent $F$. This $F$ number is now added to the upper $B$ number *without carry*, which results in zero, number $G$. Now $G$ is added to $C$, and $0 + 1 = 1$, the $H$ number. In turn this $H$ number is added to $D$, producing the $I$ number 1, and this is added to $E$, producing another 1, the $\mathcal{J}$ number. This process yields the binary equivalent of the Gray code. For any numbers thus handled, it must be remembered to *add without carry*. The circuit equivalent for Gray-to-binary conversion is shown later.

An encoder disk which produces a five-place Gray-code binary number is shown in Fig. 5-3. As in the starting position of the pure binary disk shown earlier, the reading is zero, the number 00000, being sensed, since the black areas indicate solid sections which permit no light entry (or no wire brush contact sensing through them). If the disc rotates for one of the outer-ring segments (1/64 of its diame-

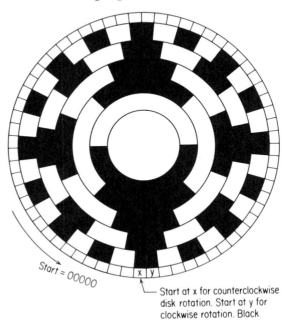

**Fig. 5-3.** Encoder disk (Gray code).

Start at x for counterclockwise disk rotation. Start at y for clockwise rotation. Black squares are solid

# 124     Special Codes and Notation     Chap. 5

ter), the number 00001 will be sensed, starting from the innermost
segment and reading outward toward the rim. In this encoder, after
the disk has turned 180°, the output Gray binary numbers repeat
themselves. Thus, a rotation to 190° produces the same output number as at the 170° position.

Sensing methods for this disk are the same as for the earlier disk
shown in Fig. 5-2. The read-out system would be modified to accommodate five binary numbers. Using photocells, the light passing
through the transparent slot sections is intercepted by the photocells
to produce a five-bit binary representation. When one of the photocells receives no light, a binary zero is represented. After producing
the binary digits, the information is channeled to flip-flop stages or
other computer circuits for evaluation of the information for calculating or controlling purposes.

A typical parallel-input Gray-to-binary conversion system is
shown in Fig. 5-4. Here, so-called *half adders* are used, which perform
the logic *exclusive-or* function described earlier in Chapter 3. Such a
half adder will perform the addition of 1 + 1 *without* carry, and the
circuitry is shown in Chapter 6. The truth table for the half adder
(exclusive or) is

$$0 + 0 = 0$$
$$1 + 0 = 1$$
$$0 + 1 = 1$$
$$1 + 1 = 0$$

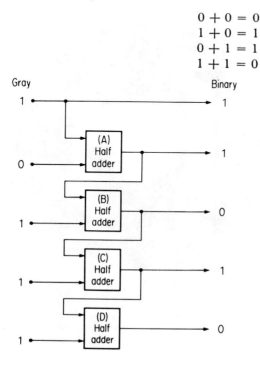

Fig. 5-4. Gray to binary conversion.

With the logic expressed by this truth table, assume the Gray code number 10111 is entered into the converter system. In such an instance, the half adder marked *A* receives 0 and 1 and produces a 1 output in conjunction with the upper 1 output. The *A* half-adder *output* is also fed to one of the inputs of the *B* half adder. Since the *B* half adder receives 1 + 1, it adds *without carry* and produces a 0 output as shown. This is fed to one of the inputs of the *C* half adder to produce a 1 output. The latter is fed to the lower *D* adder, and the output without carry is zero.

Thus, a binary output of 11010 is produced for the Gray code number 10111 entered. If the magnitude of the input number exceeds five bits, as many half adders would have to be included as required for the additional number length.

## Excess-three Code

A special-purpose variation of the binary-coded decimal notation described in Chapter 4 is the one known as the *excess-three code*. In this system, each decimal digit is coded in binary form, except that a value of three (011) is added to the number formed by the binary coding. For numbers above 9, binary-coded decimal grouping is employed. The following table indicates this method of notation:

| Decimal Number | Excess-Three Code | |
|:---:|:---:|:---:|
| 00 | 0011 | |
| 01 | 0100 | |
| 02 | 0101 | |
| 03 | 0110 | |
| 04 | 0111 | |
| 05 | 1000 | |
| 06 | 1001 | |
| 07 | 1010 | |
| 08 | 1011 | |
| 09 | 1100 | |
| 10 | 0100 | 0011 |
| 11 | 0100 | 0100 |
| 12 | 0100 | 0101 |

The excess-three code is useful in simplifying subtraction processes in digital computers employing binary-coded decimal notation, because of the characteristic complement of *nine* for each pair of related digits. You will note from the foregoing table that the 0 and the 9 are symbolic opposites—that is, 0011 and 1100. In the decimal number 0, the excess-three code has the 0 where the 1's are in the excess-three code equivalent of the decimal number 9. In this case, the 0 replaces the 1 and vice versa. This factor also holds for the numbers 3 and 6, wherein the 3 is expressed as 0110 and the 6 is expressed as 1001. The decimal numbers 2 and 7 also are symbolic opposites, indicated as 0101 and 1010. Numbers 4 and 5 also have directly opposite characteristics because the 4 is expressed as 0111 and the 5 is expressed as 1000. This complementing feature means that any number subtracted from 9 indicates the remainder by simply interchanging the 0's and 1's in the number to be subtracted. For instance, if 2 is to be subtracted from 9, the excess-three code for 2 is 0101. Replacing the 0's with 1's and the 1's with 0's in the latter number gives us 1010, which equals 7 in the excess-three code. Thus, by interchanging 0's and 1's in the number which was to be subtracted, we immediately arrive at the remainder. The following is an additional example to help illustrate this process:

| Decimal Number | | Excess-Three |
|---|---|---|
| 9 | = | 1100 |
| −4 | = | 0111 |
| 5 | = | 1000 |

Because a value of 3 was added to each excess-three code group of four bits, such a value must obviously be subtracted to convert to pure binary. This applies to each four-bit group, as shown below:

```
1100   1000   1001   excess-three number 956
−11    −11    −11
────   ────   ────
1001   0101   0110   binary number 956
```

The nines complement feature with end-around carry (discussed in Chapter 2) applied to the excess-three code, yields a pure binary answer. Assume, for instance, we wish to subtract 2 from 8. In excess-three form these numbers are

```
 1011   (8 in excess-three code)
−0101   (2 in excess-three code)
```

If we now change the excess-three subtrahend to its complement excess-three equivalent, we can thus add and perform the end-around carry:

$$
\begin{array}{ll}
\phantom{+}1011 & \text{(8 in excess-three)} \\
+\ 1010 & \text{(complement of 2 in excess-three)} \\
\hline
1\ 0101 & \\
+\quad 1 & \text{(end-around carry)} \\
\hline
\phantom{1}0110 = 6 & \text{(in pure binary)}
\end{array}
$$

Similarly, assume we wish to subtract 4 from 9:

$$
\begin{array}{ll}
\phantom{+}1100 & \text{(9 in excess-three)} \\
+\ 1000 & \text{(complement of 4 in excess-three)} \\
\hline
1\ 0100 & \\
+\quad 1 & \text{(end-around carry)} \\
\hline
\phantom{1}0101 = 5 & \text{(in pure binary)}
\end{array}
$$

As a final example of this procedure, the following show the subtraction of 38 from 79, expressing both in excess-three code and in binary-coded decimal notation:

$$
\begin{array}{lll}
\phantom{+}1010 & \phantom{+}1100 & \text{(79 in excess-three code)} \\
+\ 1001 & +\ 0100 & \text{(complement of 38 in excess-three)} \\
\hline
1\ 0011 & 1\ 0000 & \\
+\quad 1 & +\quad 1 & \text{(end-around carry)} \\
\hline
\phantom{1}100 & \phantom{1}1 = 41 & \text{(in binary-coded decimal)}
\end{array}
$$

## Biquinary Code

The biquinary code was used in earlier digital computers as a decimal-coded binary type to reduce the number of counter circuits. It is still employed, however, in visual-display tube circuitry, as discussed and illustrated in Chapter 8. In the biquinary code, dual groups of bits are used, one containing two bits (*bi-*) and the other containing five bits (*quinary*). The quinary part uses only a single 1 digit and progressively moves this digit to the left, as 00001, 00010, 00100, etc. Since only five bits are employed, the maximum quinary number is reached after a count of 5, and the sequence is repeated. The two-bit bi- part identifies the number of times the five steps occur in the quinary part. Thus, 01 identifies the first five sequential steps of the quinary part, and 10 the remaining five steps. The following table illustrates the biquinary code:

| Decimal | Biquinary |
|:---:|:---:|
| 0 | 01 00001 |
| 1 | 01 00010 |
| 2 | 01 00100 |
| 3 | 01 01000 |
| 4 | 01 10000 |
| 5 | 10 00001 |
| 6 | 10 00010 |
| 7 | 10 00100 |
| 8 | 10 01000 |
| 9 | 10 10000 |

The biquinary system was actually in existance for many years, since it is the basis for the number system used in the abacus mentioned in Chapter 1. The two-bead section of an abacus corresponds to the bi- part of the biquinary system, and the five-bead section, to the quinary part. Thus, the various number representations are set up as shown in Fig. 5-5:

```
o o o o o o o o o o o
o o o o o             o
          o o o o o
─────────────────────────
  o o o o   o o o o
    o o o     o o o
o       o o o       o o o
o o       o o o       o o
o o o       o o o       o
o o o o   o o o o   o
o o o o o o o o o o o
0 1 2 3 4 5 6 7 8 9 0
```

**Fig. 5-5. The abacus.**

## 7, 4, 2, 1 Code

A code which had been found useful in older vacuum-tube computers is the 7, 4, 2, 1 code, which conserved electric energy. This code was devised to minimize the number of 1's in the code group. In this system, simplification occurs because the number of 1's in any code group is limited to two. In the pure binary system, the value of the first-place digit is 1, the second-place, 2; the third-place 4; and the fourth-place, 8. Hence, the binary system is sometimes referred to as the 8, 4, 2, 1, system (or 1, 2, 4, 8). In the 7, 4, 2, 1, system, the fourth-place digit has a value of 7, as shown in the column below. In the older vacuum-tube computers this code was of value because it reduced electric energy consumption because of the reduction in the number of pulses which must be applied for a particular number or numbers. This code, and the equivalent decimal values, are given below.

| *Decimal Number* | *7, 4, 2, 1 Code* |
|:---:|:---:|
| 0 | 0000 |
| 1 | 0001 |
| 2 | 0010 |
| 3 | 0011 |
| 4 | 0100 |
| 5 | 0101 |
| 6 | 0110 |
| 7 | 1000 |
| 8 | 1001 |
| 9 | 1010 |

## Error-detecting Codes

In digital computers there are several special codes that have been specifically designed for detecting any errors which might occur. Such codes are particularly useful where punched cards or perforated tape is employed for feeding information into the computer. One method for establishing a particular error-detecting code is to use only two 1 digits plus three 0's for numbers from 0 to 9. By keeping the number of bits which represent 1's to a minimum, there is less chance for error. If the coding is such that only two 1's are employed in conjunction with three 0's, any number with only two 0's or four 0's is incorrect. The following is an example of such a code:

$$
\begin{array}{rcl}
0 & = & 00011 \\
1 & = & 00110 \\
2 & = & 01100 \\
3 & = & 11000 \\
4 & = & 10001 \\
5 & = & 10010 \\
6 & = & 10100 \\
7 & = & 01010 \\
8 & = & 00101 \\
9 & = & 01001 \\
\end{array}
$$

There are various combinations of three 0's and two 1's which can be employed for coding a series of numbers from 0 to 9, and the particular one employed in a computer may be different from the one shown above. If desired, the designer can employ 11000 to represent the number 1, 10001 for 2, 10010 for 3, etc. This type of code is sometimes called the *two-out-of-five* code because only two of the five symbols are 1's and need be represented by pulses.

Another method for error detecting is that known as *parity check*. Parity refers to the quality of being equal and hence a parity check is actually an equality checking code. The coding consists of the use of an additional digit in conjunction with a given binary number. The additional digit is known as a *parity digit* and may be either a 0 or a 1. The parity digit is chosen to make the number of all digits in the binary group either even or odd. If the system is chosen where the digits in the binary number, plus the parity digit, are even, it is known as *even parity*. If not, the system is referred to as *odd parity*. The following indicates the addition of a parity digit to representative binary numbers:

| Decimal Number | Parity Digit | Binary Number |
|:---:|:---:|:---:|
| 1 | 1 | 0001 |
| 2 | 1 | 0010 |
| 3 | 0 | 0011 |
| 4 | 1 | 0100 |
| 5 | 0 | 0101 |

In the foregoing, it will be noted that the even parity system was employed, since the number of all the digits in the binary group (plus the parity digit) are even. For odd parity, the following would be used:

| Decimal Number | Parity Digit | Binary Number |
|---|---|---|
| 1 | 0 | 0001 |
| 2 | 0 | 0010 |
| 3 | 1 | 0011 |
| 4 | 0 | 0100 |
| 5 | 1 | 0101 |

In either of the foregoing cases, an error is immediately detected because the occurrence of an error changes the parity of the number. In even parity, an error is indicated by the presence of an odd parity number.

# PROBLEMS

**1.** What are the advantages of octal notation?

**2** (a) How should 10110101 be grouped to represent an octal number?
(b) What is the base-10 equivalent of the octal expression for 10110101?
(c) What is the true base-10 value of 10110101?

**3.** What are the octal and binary number equivalents of the decimal value 499?

**4** (a) What is the purpose of using the Gray code?
(b) What are some of the other terms applied to the Gray code?

**5.** Convert the decimal value 16 to the Gray code.

**6.** Convert the Gray-code number 11011 to its binary equivalent.

**7.** Describe the purpose of using a disk encoder and the principle of operation.

**8** (a) Reproduce Fig. 5-4, and increase the number of half adders to process the conversion of a Gray-code number 110101 to binary.
(b) Apply the Gray-code number 110101 to the circuit drawn, and show output. Explain the circuit operation.

**9.** Express the excess-three number 0100 0100 in binary-coded decimal form.

**10.** Express 392 in excess-three code.

**11.** Subtract 241 from 988, using excess-three code in the nines-complement *addition* process.

**12.** Explain how the biquinary code is formed.

**13.** Rearrange the five-bit error-detecting code given in this chapter to form a new code of this type starting with 0 = 11000 and ending with 9 = 10001.

**14.** Write an odd-parity code from 1 to 9.

**15.** Write an even-parity code from 1 to 9.

# CALCULATION
# CIRCUITS

**6**

**Introduction.** For a computer to perform the basic operations of addition, subtraction, multiplication, and division, a number of logic circuits (see Chapter 3) are combined to form individual adders, subtractors, multipliers, and dividers. To provide operational versatility, some of these perform their function by accepting binary numbers in serial form and others by accepting the numbers in parallel form. Once the four basic arithmetic operation systems have been designed for the computer, other calculation processes can be performed by proper programming, as discussed later. Where certain arithmetical processes are to be performed often, a sequential program of instructions is compiled and permanently stored by the computer for usage as required. These are called *subroutines* and are discussed more fully in later chapters.

The basic units making up the fundamental calculation circuitry are discussed in this chapter. The representation for the circuits are in standard block symbol form to conform to conventional diagrams. In following the logic which applies to the arithmetic circuitry, the reader should have full knowledge of the logic-gate characteristics which were covered in Chapter 3, as well as the counter principles covered in Chapter 4; otherwise the discussions of the modes of operation of these devices will be difficult to follow.

**133**

## Adders

The flip-flop counters discussed in Chapter 4 can be employed for parallel addition because they have the ability to accumulate counts. If, for instance, four stages of flip-flop circuits contained the binary number 1001, the entry of the binary number 0110 in parallel form would place the second and third flip-flop stages in the 1 state and the resultant number contained in the four stages would be 1111. Here, no *carry* function was required. But, if the number 0011 were to be added to the original 1001 contained in the flip-flop stages, the triggering of the first stage by the first-place 1 in 0011 would cause the first stage to send a triggering pulse to the second stage at the same time that the second-place 1 in 0011 arrives; this double application of a trigger pulse would not permit the proper carry function to be performed and a false sum would result.

For proper carry function, circuits must be designed to prevent the arrival of two significant bits at any one time. One method of doing this is to utilize delay lines between the stages, so that interstage triggering pulses are delayed while such stages are triggered by parallel entry. This then permits repeated additions in parallel form with proper carry functions.

The use of interstage delay lines is shown in Fig. 6-1. Here, two separate flip-flop register accumulators are shown, each having four stages. The lower accumulator stages, $B$, already have stored in them the binary number 0011. The upper register $A$ contains the binary

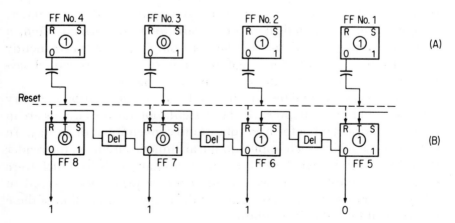

**Fig. 6-1.** Parallel addition.

number 1011 which is to be added to the number 0011 stored in the lower $B$ stages. When the upper stages of $A$ are cleared, the number 1011 is entered in parallel form to the lower flip-flop stages of $B$.

When the triggering pulse from *FF* no. 1 enters *FF* no. 5, the later trips to 0 and produces an output triggering pulse which enters the delay line. At the same time, *FF* no. 2 also triggers *FF* no. 6 to 0, and this stage also sends a triggering pulse into its output delay line. When *FF* no. 4 triggers *FF* no. 8, the latter trips to the 1 state and no output triggering pulse is developed in *FF* no. 8. Thus, for a very brief time interval the $B$ flip-flops only contain the number 1000. When the pulses in the delay lines reach the triggering inputs of *FF* no. 6 and *FF* no. 7, these stages are tripped to the 1 state, producing the sum of the two original numbers, 1110. Thus the delay lines between the stages of the flip-flops perform the proper carry function and will permit the register to accumulate counts up to the limit of the stages used.

The exclusive-*or* circuits which form half adders have already been mentioned in Chapter 3 and Chapter 5, with an application illustrated in Fig. 5-4. Such half adders have no recirculating carry function and hence cannot perform complete addition. By combining two half adders, however, a full adder is formed which accepts serial-train binary numbers of any length. Half adders are formed by using the logic circuits described in Chapter 3, consisting of *or*, *and*, and *inhibitor* circuits. A half adder will provide a true sum if no carry function is involved, as shown in A of Fig. 6-2, where the Boolean algebra notation is shown. The *or* circuit provides an output for either the $X$ or $Y$ or for both inputs. The *and* circuit provides an output only if both $X$ and $Y$ inputs are present. When the *and* circuit provides an output signal, it will inhibit any signal appearing at the upper input to the *inhibitor* circuit. Thus, for the $X$ and $Y$ inputs, the *sum* output produces $(X + Y)(\overline{XY})$, and the carry output is $XY$.

In A of Fig. 6-2, the binary number 101 is to be added to 010, and these numbers are applied to the inputs, as shown, and appear at the *or*-circuit input terminals as well as the *and*-circuit input terminals.

Since an *or* circuit will produce an output when a signal of proper polarity appears at either input, the *or* circuit in A has an output of 111, which is applied to the *inhibitor* circuit. Because there is no pulse coincidence at the *and* circuit, it provides no signal to inhibit the output of 111 from the *inhibitor* circuit. Hence, the true sum is produced.

In B of Fig. 6-2, a false sum results because the carry function was not applied to the output number. Here, the binary number 101

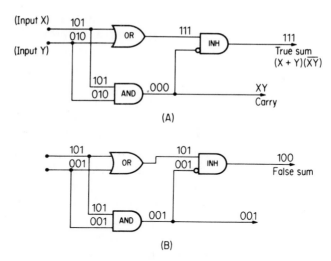

**Fig. 6-2.** Half adder.

is to be added to 001. In this instance, the first-place digits $1 + 1$ should add to 0 with one digit carried to the second place. The *or* circuit produces an output of 101, since it will have an output for either or both of the input signals. The *and* circuit, however, produces 001, since only the two first-place digits produce coincidence. At the *inhibitor*, the first-place digits produce an inhibiting function and an output of 100 is produced instead of the true sum 110.

By combining two half adders and including a delay line, as shown in Fig. 6-3, the carry digits are recirculated and delayed by one place to form a full adder capable of producing true sums in serial form. Assume, for instance, that the binary number 111 is to be added to 011. These are applied in serial form to the two inputs and hence appear at both the *or* circuit and the *and* circuit, as shown in Fig. 6-3.

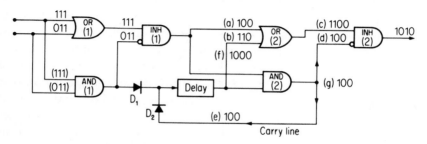

**Fig. 6-3.** Carry function of full adder.

The addition of these two numbers necessitates that the circuit add the two first-place digits to produce 0 with one digit to carry. In the second-place digits, the carry digit plus the two digits in the input numbers would equal 1 with 1 to carry to the third place. The third-place addition of the two digits would result in 0 with another digit to carry to the fourth place, producing the true sum of 1010. Here, it can be seen that it is necessary to carry a number from the first place to the fourth place successively. The manner in which this is done can be seen from the illustration.

When the binary numbers 111 and 011 are applied to the *or* circuit, the output will be 111, since the *or* circuit will produce an output for either or both of the input signals. When, however, the two binary numbers are applied to the *and* circuit, only the two first-place numbers appear, since the third-place digit input to the *and* circuit has no corresponding input to produce an output pulse. Thus, the output from the *and* circuit consisting of 011 and the output from the *or* circuit consisting of 111 are applied to the inhibiting circuit no. 1. The output from the *and* circuit produces two inhibitory pulses and hence limits the output from the *inhibitor* circuit to the binary number marked *A*, consisting of 100. However, the output of 011 from the first *and* circuit is also applied to a delay circuit, and at the output of the delay circuit this number is 110 (marked *B* in the drawing). The *A* and *B* signals are applied to the *or* circuit no. 2, and the output from the latter is designated as *C* and consists of the number 1110. The inputs to the second *or* circuit are also applied to the second *and* circuit, and, since only third-place digits occur simultaneously, the output from the second *and* circuit consists of the binary number 100 and is designated as *D* in the drawing. The latter is recirculated to the delay circuit and appears at the output of the delay circuit as the *F* binary number of 1000. Since this fourth-place digit will go through the *or* circuit, it contributes the fourth-place digit to the *C* output of the *or* circuit. Because the fourth-place digit in the *F* number cannot enter the second *and* circuit (since there is no corresponding digit occurring at that time), there is no further output from the second *and* circuit. Hence, the input binary numbers to the second *inhibitor* circuit consist of the *C* number 1110 and the *D* number 100. Since this *D* number has only a third-place digit, the latter acts as an inhibitory pulse for the third-place digit of the *C* number and cancels this third-place digit from the output of the second *inhibitor* circuit. Thus, the output of the *inhibitor* circuit consists of 1010, which is the true sum of the two binary numbers applied to the input of the full adder. Diode $D_1$ serves to prevent the carry pulses from entering the first inhibiting circuit. Diode $D_2$ prevents signals from the first *and* circuit from entering the carry line and reaching the second *inhibitor* circuit.

The full adder will take any two numbers and add them together, regardless of the number of digits in either of the input numbers applied to the full adder. Because of the recirculation of the carry signal in the delay line, it can perform the carry function for an infinite number of places from the first place on up.

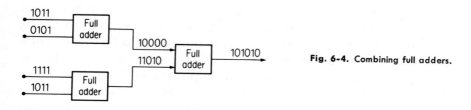

Fig. 6-4. Combining full adders.

Multiple addition can be performed by combining adders as required, as shown in Fig. 6-4, where four binary numbers are added simultaneously by applying each serial train to the respective input at the same time. The output sums from the first two adders are then added by a third adder, as shown.

Full adders can be designed with a third input to enable them to accept carry numbers from registers or half adders if required. The circuit arrangement for a three-input adder with a sum and carry output is shown in A of Fig. 6-5, using an additional *or* circuit for the carry output. The carry output can be recirculated through a delay line to form a full adder with a carry input as shown in B. The two numbers to be added are applied in serial form to the upper two terminals, and the true sum is obtained from the output, as was the case for the adder shown in Fig. 6-3. The logic-circuit operation follows the same pattern as detailed for the one shown in Fig. 6-3.

## Subtracters

As described in Chapter 2, it is possible to perform the subtraction process by *addition*, using the ones-complementing method with end-around carry. The process simplifies subtraction in a computer and

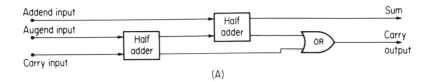

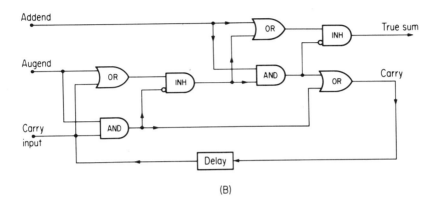

Fig. 6-5. Three-input serial adder.

handles the binary numbers in parallel form. Assume, for instance, that the following subtraction is to be performed:

$$
\begin{array}{rl}
1011 & \text{minuend} \\
-101 & \text{subtrahend} \\
\hline
110 & \text{remainder}
\end{array}
$$

Using the ones-complementing method with end-around carry as detailed in Chapter 2 yields

$$
\begin{array}{rl}
1011 & \text{minuend} \\
+\,1010 & \text{complement} \\
\hline
1\,0101 & \\
+\quad 1 & \text{end-around carry of last-place digit} \\
\hline
110 &
\end{array}
$$

There are various ways of handling this subtraction-by-addition process in a computer, and one method is illustrated in Fig. 6-6. Since the minuend in the foregoing problem involves only four bits, this sets the maximum bit content of the complement. Thus, only four flip-flop stages of a particular group forming a register are used. As shown in Fig. 6-6, the subtrahend (0101) is placed in one set of flip-flop stages as shown, using four flip-flop circuits as the significant group. This number is now read out in complement form to four places, that is, the binary complement number 1010. The complement number is read into the second flip-flop register, as shown. Since the latter already contained the minuend 1011, the addition of the complement number 1010 produces the sum 10101, with the last-place digit contained in the fifth flip-flop stage. Because the complement number is always a 1, this is held in storage in the lower flip-flop register as shown. Now, the sum (of the complement and minuend) in the second string of flip-flop stages is read into the lower register from the four significant stages only, the number contained in the fifth stage not being read out. Thus, only 0101 is read into the lower flip-flop stages, and this, added to the 1 already in the latter, produces the true remainder of 0110.

The complement selection circuitry, shown in Fig. 6-7, uses *and* circuits for switching either the true binary number or the complement to the lower output terminals. Note that the steady-state values of the

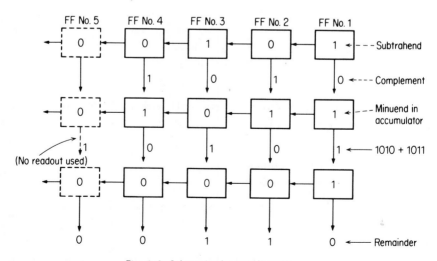

**Fig. 6-6.** Subtraction by complementing.

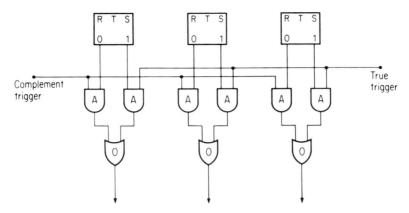

**Fig. 6-7. Complement selection.**

0 and 1 output lines from the flip-flops are employed to apply a potential to the *and* gates. Thus, if a flip-flop is in the *zero* state, the voltage from the 0 lines coincides in polarity with that of the complement trigger pulse and the *and* circuit thus produces an output pulse representing logic *one*, (the complement of 0). If a flip-flop is in the *one* state, no polarity coincidence prevails for the complement pulse, and a *zero* output is produced (the complement of 1).

Similarly, if a flip-flop is in the *zero* state, the voltage from the 1 lines is opposite in polarity to the true trigger pulse and no coincidence prevails; hence a *zero* output is obtained upon the application of such a pulse to the true trigger line. If the flip-flop is in the *one* state, the 1 line has a polarity coinciding with that of the true trigger pulse. When the latter is applied, the *and* circuit passes the pulse and produces a *one* output from the lower terminal.

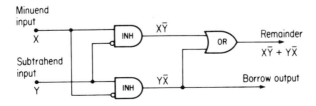

**Fig. 6-8. Half subtracter.**

Like the serial adders, subtracters can be formed from logic circuits to perform subtraction of serial numbers. A typical half subtracter is shown in Fig. 6-8. Here, two *inhibitor* circuits are used as well as an *or* circuit, as shown. This circuit does not have the ability to borrow a number from the next place, and, as with the adders, a recirculation procedure is necessary to form a full subtracter. If a three-input subtracter is required, the two half subtracters are connected as shown in A of Fig. 6-9, using an *or* circuit for the borrow-output line. The recirculation with delay line is shown in B.

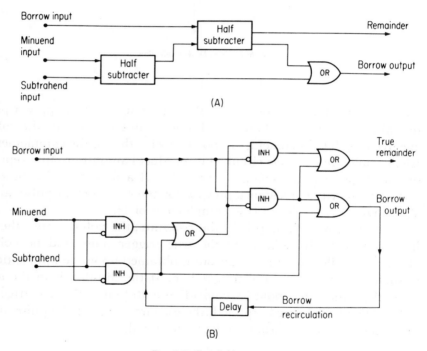

**Fig. 6-9.** Serial subtracters.

The operation of the serial subtracter is illustrated in Fig. 6-10. Here the $Y$ number 0001 is to be subtracted from the $X$ number 1100, and these binary numbers in serial form are applied to the lower two inputs as shown, with the borrow-input $B_1$ line not used. Note that the $X$ and $Y$ numbers are reversed for the lower *inhibitor* circuit. Thus, the upper input *inhibitor* 1 produces an output of 1100, since no inhibiting pulse is present for the two binary digits in third and fourth place. The lower input *inhibitor* 2, however, only produces an output of 0001, since the inhibiting number does not appear at the output. In consequence the *or* circuit receives the numbers 1100 and 0001 and produces an output of 1101 which is applied to the second pair of *inhibitors*. Note that the binary number 0001, which is applied to the first *or* circuit, is also applied to the third *or* circuit feeding the borrow-output $B_o$ line.

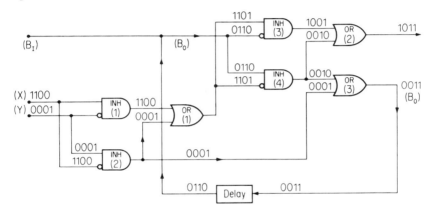

**Fig. 6-10.** Serial subtracter operation.

The first-place 1 applied to the third *or* circuit recirculates and passes through the delay line, where it is shifted to the left one place to form 10. When this appears at the fourth *inhibitor*, an output is produced and places a second-place 1 at the input of the third *or* circuit. This also recirculates, and hence the borrow-output number appearing at the third and fourth *inhibitor* circuits is the number 0110. At the third *inhibitor* this produces an output (in conjunction with the 1101 input) of 1001. At the fourth *inhibitor*, the numbers 0110 and 1101 produce only a 0010 output, which is applied to the second *or* circuit as well as to the third *or* circuit. The output from the second *or* circuit is 1011, representing the true remainder of the subtraction process.

As with the serial adder, the serial subtracter will handle binary numbers of any length in serial form. Multiple subtracters or combined adders and subtracters can be used when it is desirable to perform calculations involving several numbers or processes. For instance, two subtracters can be used simultaneously for handling four binary numbers as shown in A of Fig. 6-11. Here, the subtrahend binary 0011 is to be subtracted from the minuend 1101 while at the same time a second subtrahend 01 is to be subtracted from 1001. By employing two subtracters as shown, each subtracter performs its individual function; the first subtracter produces a remainder of 1010 and the second subtracter produces a remainder of 1000. If these two sums are now to be added together, a full adder can be used as shown; or, if the number from the second subtracter is to be subtracted from the number from the first subtracter, then a third subtracter can be employed.

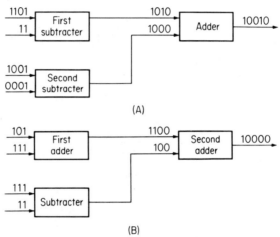

Fig. 6-11. Combined adders and subtracters.

Simultaneous additon and subtraction can also be performed by combining adders and subtracters as shown in B of Fig. 6-11. Here, the binary number 11 is to be subtracted from 111 and the remainder then added to the sum of 101 plus 111. Hence, the latter two numbers are applied to an adder which produces the sum of 1100, and the subtraction process of 11 from 111 produces the binary number 100. The latter number can be subtracted from the binary number 1100 by use of another subtracter, or it can be added by using an adder as shown in the illustration.

Other combinations can be employed, though often particular sums or products are rerouted through the computer as required to produce the final sum. The allocation of the various numbers of a particular problem to the individual circuits of the computer must be established by the program of instructions which are set up beforehand for the particular problem involved.

## Multipliers

One method of doing a multiplication problem is to add the multiplicand to itself by the number of times indicated by the multiplier. Thus, if 438 is to be multiplied by 65, the multiplicand of 438 can be added together 65 times to obtain the product. This is a simple method of performing the multiplication in digital computers without the necessity for complex circuitry, the only drawback being that it takes longer for the calculation to be performed compared with the speed of the addition and subtraction methods previously detailed. While the repetitive addition of the multiplicand is employed in some digital computers others employ circuitry which will solve the multiplication in the same manner that it is done in the arithmetic formula for procuring partial products and adding them together. There are several circuit combinations which can be employed for performing the multiplication process in this manner. As for adders and subtracters, special circuit combinations are necessary to perform the functions of offsetting the multiplicand by the number of places required during the initial adding process. After this has been done, adders must be utilized to procure the sum of the offset multiplicand numbers. The multipliers must be designed to handle binary numbers, where the multiplicand and multipler are inserted simultaneously into the multiplier or at different time intervals.

The requirements of a multiplier can be better understood by examining a typical problem.

$$
\begin{array}{r}
111 \quad (7) \\
\times 11 \quad (3) \\
\hline
111 \\
111 \\
\hline
10101 \quad (21)
\end{array}
$$

In the foregoing example, the multiplicand 111 (7) is to be muliplied by 11 (3). This means that the multiplicand must be set down twice, with the second multiplicand moved to the left by one place as in regular multiplication. When these two figures are added together, the result is 10101 (21). Hence, it is obvious that a multiplier must use the multiplicand for addition purposes in the manner indicated by the number of binary digits in the multiplier. In the example just given, the multiplier indicated that the multiplcand had to be added to another number equal to the multiplicand but moved over one place. After the multiplier does this, it is also necessary to feed the original multiplicand, plus the delayed multiplicand, into an adder so that the sum can be procured. Actually, the adder would receive at one input the binary number 111 representing the initial multiplicand and then the binary number 1110 which represents the displaced or the delayed multiplicand.

The foregoing was a simple example of multiplication, but the multiplier must also be capable of displacing the multiplicand initially when the multiplier ends in a 0. This type of multiplication is represented by the following:

$$\begin{array}{r} 111 \quad (7) \\ \times 10 \quad (2) \\ \hline 000 \\ 111 \\ \hline 1110 \quad (14) \end{array}$$

Here, the multiplicand again consists of 111 (7), but now the multiplier is 10 (2). Hence, the multiplier must delay the multiplicand by a one-place interval and then add the delayed mutiplicand so that the answer is 1110 (14).

Another instance where a combination of the two foregoing conditions occur is the following:

$$\begin{array}{r} 1101 \quad (13) \\ \times 101 \quad (5) \\ \hline 1101 \\ 11010 \\ \hline 1000001 \quad (65) \end{array}$$

In the foregoing, the binary number 101 representing the multiplier now has 0 between the first- and third-place digits. Thus, the multiplicand must be set down once, then delayed by a two-place interval, and set down again. These two figures must then be added to produce the answer shown. From the foregoing it is evident that the multiplier must be such that any combination of binary digits or 0's, in either the multiplier or the multiplicand, will be taken care of automatically.

The formation of partial products by displacing the multiplicand to the left can be accomplished by using only delay circuits (discussed in Chapter 1) or *shift registers* which may contain delay circuits. Shift registers are formed from a series of flip-flop stages which have been modified so that a clearing pulse applied to the reset line causes a binary number to be shifted through the stages instead of being cleared. A shift register of this type is shown in Fig. 6-12, where four flip-flop circuits are indicated for purposes of analysis. Many more stages can, of course, be used to handle larger numbers and to permit a more extensive shifting of arithmetical places.

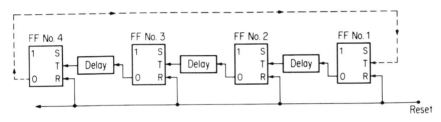

**Fig. 6-12.** Left-shift register (and ring counter).

A shift register is capable of shifting a single binary digit 1 or a larger binary number such as 101, 1101, 1111, etc. Initially, for Fig. 6-12, assume that the first flip-flop stage had been triggered to represent the 1 state, and all other stages are in the 0 state. Now, when a clearing pulse is applied to the reset line, it will not affect those stages which are in the 0 state but will clear the first flip-flop stage which registers 1. When this stage is cleared, it produces an output pulse which enters the delay circuit. After the clearing pulse duration is terminated, the pulse signal leaves the delay circuit and enters the trigger input of the second stage, tripping this stage to represent 1. If another clearing pulse is entered on the reset line, the second stage is cleared and sends a signal into the second delay circuit, which, in turn, trips the third stage to its 1 state after the clearing pulse duration has terminated.

Successive clearing pulses progressively shift the binary number to the left through as many flip-flop stages as are contained in the register. With delay circuits between the flip-flop stages, the clearing pulses

entered on the reset line are incapable of clearing the shift register and
their only effect is to produce a shift. If the stages are to be cleared, a
conventional coupling must be re-established between stages, with the
delay circuits not in effect. Repeated entry of clearing pulses would, of
course, shift the number to and through the last flip-flop of the register
and thus clear the flip-flop chain.

In some applications the output from the last flip-flop is routed
back to the first flip-flop stage, as shown by the dashed line in Fig.
6-12. When this is done, repeated entry of clearing pulses results in the
numbers being returned to the first stages, and hence the number can
be continuously circulated through the shift register in ring fashion.
Hence, such a shift register is also known as a *ring counter*. Specific
applications for the ring counters are given later in this chapter.

By shifting a number to the left, the shift register *permits multiplication by the base 2*. If, for instance, the binary number 11 (3) were
stored in the shift register and a reset pulse was entered, the binary
number would shift one place to the left and become 110 (6), or 11
$\times$ 10 = 110. Similarly, if the number were shifted again by the entry
of another reset pulse, another place shift would occur and the number
would become 1100 (12), again undergoing a multiplication by a
factor of 2. If the number 111 (7) were originally in the register, a
single shift would produce 1110 (14), or 111 $\times$ 10.

When the shift register is used for the multiplication process, a fair

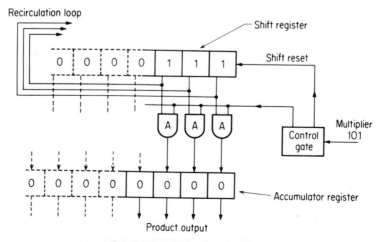

**Fig. 6-13. Multiplication by shifting.**

degree of routing and rerouting of numbers between registers becomes necessary. While binary number routing in a computer can become complex, the basic operations for a multiplier function are shown in Fig. 6-13. Additional signal routing principles are covered later in this chapter and in subsequent chapters. Assume the operation is to consist of multiplying the binary number 111 by 101. The multiplicand 111 can be stored in the shift register as shown, and the multiplier placed in a temporary storage register where it can be sampled by a control gate system. (In arithmetic operations the numbers involved are originally in storage and are read into registers according to the program sequence, as detailed in Chapters 9 and 10.)

The first-place bit of the multiplier is sampled by the control gate, and, since in our example this is the numeral 1, the control gate sends a pulse to the *and* circuits. When there is polarity coincidence with the 1 states of the flip-flop, the multiplicand is transferred to the accumulator register as the original number 0111. (Had the multiplicand been 101, the second *and* circuit would not have transferred any pulse digit to the second flip-flop of the accumulator register.) If only the steady-state signals of the shift register were used for the *and* circuits, the multiplicand would still be present in the shift register. If the shift register were actually cleared for read-out purposes, the number would have to be rerouted by a recirculation loop circuit and placed back into the shift register.

After the number in the shift register has been read into the accumulator, the control gate sends a shift (reset) pulse to the shift register and the multiplicand now becomes the partial product 1110. Because the next (second-place) bit of the multiplier is 0, the appearance of this at the *and* circuit inputs prevents the partial product 1110 in the shift register from appearing at the output of the *and* circuit. Now the control gate sends another reset pulse to the shift register and the partial product becomes 11100. The third-place digit of the multiplier now opens the *and* circuits and the number 11100 is added to the number 00111 already in the accumulator, forming the product 100011. Since this is the final result of the multiplication process, the routing and gating stop. Since the product of two three-bit numbers contains six bits, the accumulator-register product will occupy twice the number of stages than either the multiplicand shift register or multiplier register. The control gate can be designed to sense the magnitude (number of bits) of the multiplier and stop op-

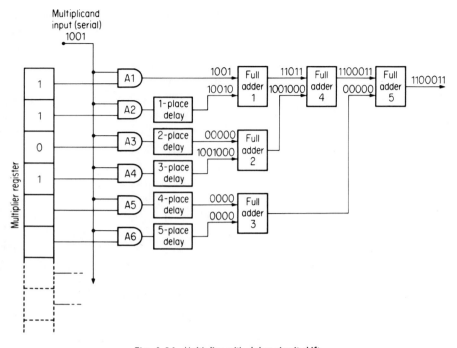

**Fig. 6-14. Multiplier with delay circuit shift.**

eration when the last bit has been processed. The magnitude of the number in the accumulator can also be sampled to indicate the conclusion of the multiplication.

A multiplier using delay circuits for producing the necessary shifts for forming partial products is shown in Fig. 6-14. Here, the multiplier is fed into a storage register which applies signals of proper polarity to open *and* gates when a flip-flop stage is in the 1 state. The multiplicand is fed in serial form into the input line feeding the upper terminals of the *and* circuits as shown. The magnitude of the multiplier that can be used is limited by the number of *and* circuits and delay lines employed. Each succeeding delay circuit will shift a binary number by an additional place. Full adders are then used to accumulate the sum of the partial products formed.

If the number 1001 is to be multiplied by 1011, for instance, the latter is stored in the multiplier register as shown, and the 1001 applied in serial form to the multiplicand input. Thus, each succeeding bit of the multiplicand is applied simultaneously to all the upper input terminals of the *and* circuits. Since the first-place 1 of the multiplicand appears first, it produces coincidence in *and* circuit no. 1 because of the similarity to the potential applied by the first flip-flop stage of the multiplier register. Hence, this number is applied to the upper input of the first full adder. The first-place bit of the multiplicand also enters the second *and* circuit and enters the one-place delay line, appearing at the second input of the first full adder as 01. The same first-place multiplicand number does not enter the third *and* circuit since the third flip-flop of the multiplier register does not apply a coinciding polarity, and the third *and* circuit remains closed. Entry is established at the fourth *and* circuit, however, and the delay line produces a three-place delay and an output number 1000. Successive bits of the multiplicand encounter the same open or closed gate conditions, and the final product is procured in serial form from the last adder circuit as shown.

### Dividers

When the sequence of the flip-flop stages for the left-shift register shown in Fig. 6-12 is reversed, a right-shift register is formed, as shown in Fig. 6-15. As discussed for the left-shift of Fig. 6-12, when a number is shifted to the left, multiplication by base 2 is performed. When, however, a number is shifted to the right, division by base 2 is the result. Thus, if the number 1100 (12) were entered into the shift register of Fig. 6-15 and a reset pulse applied, the number would become 0110 (6), indicating a division by 2. An additional shift would produce 0011 (3), again a division by 2. Thus, just as the left-shift register can be employed for multiplication, so can the right-shift register be used for division purposes.

The division process can be performed either by repeated subtraction or by the conventional long-division process. In repeated subtraction we must determine by how many times the divisor can be subtracted from the dividend before a positive remainder no longer

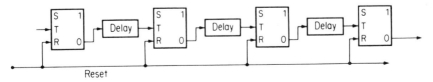

**Fig. 6-15. Right-shift register.**

results. The number of times this can be done provides us with the quotient (the final answer). While this method can be employed in computers, it is a time-consuming affair because the repeated subtraction may involve a number of steps. If, for instance, 105(1101001) is to be divided by 7 (111), it will require 15 sequential subtractions to procure the quotient of 1111:

$$
\begin{array}{ll}
1101001 & \\
- \quad 111 & \text{(1st subtraction)} \\
\hline
1100010 & \\
- \quad 111 & \text{(2nd subtraction)} \\
\hline
1011011 & \\
- \quad 111 & \text{(3rd subtraction)} \\
\hline
1010100 & \\
- \quad 111 & \text{(4th subtraction)} \\
\hline
111001 & \\
\end{array}
$$

etc., for a total of 15 steps

In the long-division method, however, the process is less complex and fewer steps are involved:

$$
\begin{array}{r}
1111 \quad (15) \\
(7) \quad 111 \, ) \, \overline{1101001} \quad (105) \\
111 \quad\quad\quad \\
\hline
1100 \quad\quad \\
111 \quad\quad \\
\hline
1010 \quad\quad \\
111 \quad\quad \\
\hline
111 \quad\quad \\
111 \quad\quad \\
\hline
00 \quad\quad \\
\end{array}
$$

Division in a digital computer is a much more complex operation than those for the other arithmetical processes. In parallel mode, the subtraction of the divisor from the dividend is by the addition process using ones complementing and end-around carry (see Fig. 6-6 and related discussions). In the example above, when the divisor is placed in a register, it occupies a six-bit position, since the first three arithmetical places are zeros. Hence, as the divisor is shifted to the right, it occupies one less place each time:

```
                    1111
          111 ) 1101001
                111000    (divisor)
                110001
                011100    (1 right shift)
                010101
                001110    (2 right shifts)
                000111
                000111    (3 right shifts)
                000000
```

The process, for the same example, would be as follows for the ones complement method which the computer undertakes:

```
                 1111
       111 ) 1101001
         + 1000111    (divisor complement)
         1 0110000
         +      1    (end-around carry)
           110001    (remainder)
         + 100011    (complement shifted to right 1 place)
         1 010100
         +     1
           010101    (remainder)
         + 010001    (complement shifted to right)
         1 00110
         +   1
           00111
         + 1000      (complement shifted to right)
         1 111
         +   1
           000
```

In the last operation, the remainder 111 plus 1 would yield 1000, but since the remainder 111 occupies only three flip-flop stages (with the complement in the fourth) the read-out is from only three stages, producing 000.

The division process using ones-complement subtraction of the shifted divisor appears straightforward, but problems in design arise because the computer must ascertain whether or not the divisor complement is in correct position with respect to the dividend. The correct position was, of course, employed in the foregoing examples, since we knew the divisor had to be displaced to the right initially because the divisor 111 could not be subtracted from 110:

$$111 \overline{)\ 1101001} \qquad 111 \overline{)\ 1101001}$$
$$\underline{111000} \qquad\qquad \underline{1000111} \quad \text{(complement)}$$

Had the dividend been 1111001, however, the divisor 111 would have had no initial shift:

$$111 \overline{)\ 1111001} \qquad 111 \overline{)\ 1111001}$$
$$\underline{1110000} \qquad\qquad \underline{0001111} \quad \text{(complement)}$$

Thus, the computer cannot be designed to provide an automatic shift initially, because during various division processes there are occasions when *no* shift should be made initially. Hence, the computer must be able to *sense* whether or not the position of the divisor is correct in its relation to the dividend. Thus, a decision type of operation must be performed by the computer to ascertain if the position is correct and, if not, to make such a correction automatically. On occasion, a decision on shifting is also necessary somewhere along the division process, as the following example indicates, where 100011 (35) is to be divided by 111 (7) producing a quotient of 5:

```
                      101
          111 ) 100011
                11100
              ──────
                  111  (remainder)
(shifted divisor)  1110  (remainder smaller than divisor,
              ──────       requiring an additional shift)
                  111
                  111
              ──────
                  000
```

The computer can be designed to sense when an additional shift of the divisor is necessary by taking advantage of two conditions inherent in the ones-complement end-around-carry principle.

1. When the subtrahend is smaller than the minuend, *an* end-around-carry digit is produced.
2. When the subtrahend is larger than the minuend, *no* end-around-carry digit is produced.

These conditions are illustrated in the following examples:

| Conventional Binary Subtraction | Complement Subtraction Process | | Incorrect Digit Alignment | | |
|---|---|---|---|---|---|
| 1010 | 1010 | | (1010) | = | 1010 |
| −110 | + 1001 | | −(1100) | = | +0011 (complement) |
| 100 | 1 0011 | | | | 1101 (no carry) |
| | 1 | (carry) | | | |
| | 100 | | | | |

Hence, the division process is formulated so the computer undertakes the following steps:

1. The complement divisor is aligned with the dividend and added (subtraction process).
2. If no carry digit is produced, a *zero* is added to the quotient, the dividend is restored to its original value, and the divisor shifted one place to the right. Now the complement divisor is again added to the dividend (subtraction process).
3. If a carry digit is produced, a *one* is added to the quotient. The complement divisor is again shifted one place to the right and added to the remainder (complement subtraction process).
4. The process continues until the full quotient has been achieved.

As an alternative, the complement divisor could retain its place position and the dividend and remainders could be shifted to the left. In either case, each time the subtraction process produces an end-around-carry digit, a 1 is added to the quotient, and, when the subtraction produces no carry digit, a 0 is added to the quotient, the subtraction process for that particular step is cancelled, and the one-place shift is made before the subtraction process is repeated.

The previous example, where 100011 (35) is divided by 111 (7), would produce the following steps (the binary subtraction is shown for simplicity):

$$111 \overline{)\,10011}$$
$$\phantom{111)\,}11100$$

$$111 \overline{)\,100011}$$
$$\phantom{111)\,}111000 \quad \text{no subtraction—place 0 in quotient register, shift divisor, and subtract again}$$

$$111 \overline{)\ 100011}$$
$$11100$$
$$\overline{\ \ 111}$$

subtraction—place 1 in quotient register and continue (shift divisor and subtract)

$$111 \overline{)\ 100011}$$
$$11100$$
$$\overline{\ \ 111}$$
$$1110$$

no subtraction—place 0 in quotient register, shift divisor, and subtract again

$$111 \overline{)\ 100011}$$
$$11100$$
$$\overline{\ \ 111}$$
$$111$$
$$\overline{000}$$

subtraction—place 1 in quotient register and stop operation when there is no positive remainder

Thus, the quotient register contains 0101, the correct answer to the division problem. The basic system in block diagram form is shown in Fig. 6-16. Here, the divisor is placed in the top register, complemented, and added to the dividend (subtraction) by the parallel adder, as shown. The complement-sense section ascertains whether or not the end-around carry 1 is present and will add 1 to the quotient register if the carry digit is sensed.

Because the dividend was recirculated by the rewrite register, the control system clears the dividend register and places the remainder in

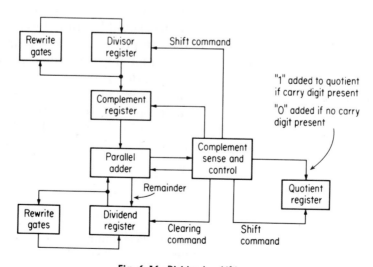

**Fig. 6-16. Division by shifting.**

it. The divisor was also recirculated back into its register by the re-write gate system and is shifted by the control section. Again, the shifted divisor in complement form is added to the remainder in the dividend register (subtraction) by the parallel adder. If no end-around-carry digit is sensed by the control unit, a 0 is added to the quotient register and the remainder in the parallel adder is cancelled by clearing. The divisor is shifted and its complemented form again added in the parallel adder to the recirculated dividend (the re-mainder from the previous operation). Thus, if the subtraction pro-cess (by the complementing-adding method) does not yield a carry digit, the number in the dividend register is not cleared but instead is retained for a repeated arithmetical process once the divisor has been shifted to the right.

The complement-sense unit is sometimes referred to as an *overflow* circuit, because it senses the carry digit which overflows the number of places involved in the complement-addition procedure. The quotient register is under shift control by the overflow section, and the entry of each new binary bit is preceded by a shift to the left of the digits al-ready contained therein. Thus, if the first sensing places a 1 in the quotient register and this is followed by a 0, the 1 is shifted to the left and thus the proper place relationships of the quotient are main-tained, 10. If the next digit is a 1, the 10 is shifted to the left and the new 1 entered to form a quotient of 101.

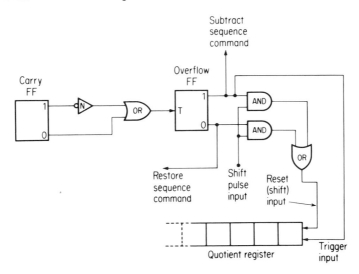

**Fig. 6-17.** Quotient register control system.

Complex routing is necessary for the divider, as indicated by Fig. 6-17, which shows the general circuitry involved in the quotient register. The flip-flop holding the end-around-carry bit, when present, has both outputs applied to an *or* circuit, so that either of its states will trigger the overflow-control flip-flop. A *not* circuit inverts the signal polarity from one output so that the proper polarity signal is applied to the overflow flip-flop and the latter trips for each change of state of the carry flip-flop. When a carry bit is sensed, the 1 output of the over-flow flip-flop applies a trigger pulse to the quotient register, which enters 1 into this register. A quotient-register shift is also initiated, and a subtract-sequence-control command signal is issued. If the carry flip-flop has no carry bit, the overflow flip-flop is triggered to its second state and the 0 output issues a restore-sequence command; no trigger pulse enters the quotient register, but the latter is shifted to produce a new binary value of 10. The process continues until the full quotient is reached.

An alternative method of division can be employed when the absence of a carry bit indicates incorrect positioning of the divisor. The false remainder can be added to the divisor to restore the dividend, instead of the dividend recirculation process being used as shown in Fig. 6-17. The remainder which is produced when the divisor is incorrectly positioned (divisor larger than the dividend) represents a *negative number*. Thus, to restore the dividend, the negative number is added to the divisor by using the end-around-carry process (see Chapter 2, Negative Numbers). The following illustrates the principles involved.

*Correctly positioned:*

```
  1001   (dividend)            1001   (dividend)
 - 101   (binary divisor)    +1010   (complement divisor)
 ------                      ------
   100   (remainder)         1 0011
                                +1   (end-around carry)
                             ------
                               100   (remainder)
```

*Incorrectly positioned:*

```
  1001   (dividend)            1001   (dividend)
 -1010   (binary divisor)    +0101   (complement divisor)
 ------                      ------
                              1110   (negative remainder,
                                      no end-around carry)
```

*Restoration of dividend:*

$$
\begin{array}{ll}
\phantom{+}1010 & \text{(binary divisor)} \\
+1110 & \text{(negative remainder)} \\
\hline
1\,1000 & \\
\phantom{1\,10}+1 & \text{(end-around carry)} \\
\hline
\phantom{1}1001 & \text{(restored dividend)}
\end{array}
$$

Serial mode of operation can also be employed for the division process. Essentially the sequence of operations remains the same except for serial read-in and read-out and serial addition. When the subtraction procedure (addition of dividend and complemented divisor) does not produce a negative answer, a 1 is placed in the lowest significant position of the quotient register. If the subtraction is not successful and a negative remainder results, 0 is placed in the quotient register. The divisor is shifted to the right one place after each subtraction process (or the remainder could be shifted to the left instead, producing the same results). As new bits are added to the quotient register, its contents are shifted to the left so that the latest entry is positioned in the first-place flip-flop.

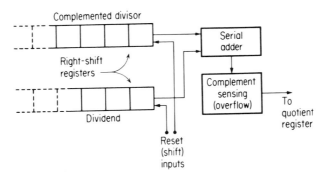

**Fig. 6-18. Serial division.**

The contents of the divisor and dividend registers are read into the serial adder by shifting the binary numbers to the right. By this process the numbers are emitted sequentially (in serial form) and enter the serial adder input sections, as shown in Fig. 6-18. This right-shifting for read-out purposes must not be confused with an arithmetical place shift. In the latter a binary number takes on a new value, whereas in the unloading process of a serial register the number value remains intact. If, however, the divisor precedes the dividend by one place in the unloading procedure, the divisor will undergo a right *place* shift (arithmetical) with respect to the dividend.

Circuit rearrangement or system modification will be encountered in digital computers. The general principles given herein, however, indicate the logic design and basic modes of operation of arithmetical processes. Reference should also be made to Chapter 4, The Binary Counter, for a review of scaling and count-down procedures in flip-flop registers. Related data will be found in Chapters 9 and 10 covering the programming aspects of problem solving.

## Timing Control

In the serial division process shown in Fig. 6-18, it is essential that the start of the unloading of both the divisor register and the dividend register begin at precisely the same time; otherwise serial addition will be inaccurate. Similarly, in other serial-mode operations involving

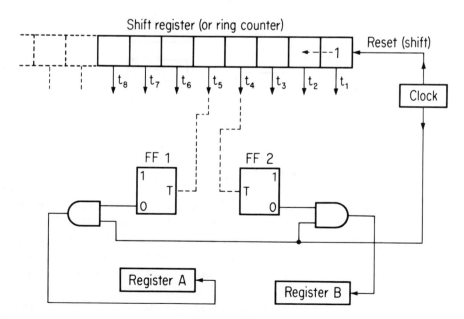

**Fig. 6-19.** Timing control.

read-in and read-out processes, precision timing must be maintained. For this purpose, ring counters and shift registers are employed in conjunction with the pulse train obtained from the clock pulse generator. An illustrative system is shown in Fig. 6-19, where two registers are pulsed in a one-place time sequence.

As shown, if the first flip-flop at the extreme right of the shift register is in the 1 state, the application of a train of clock pulses will progressively shift this 1 state to the left. As the 1 state shifts to the left, a pulse output is obtained from the successive flip-flop stages, corresponding to time 1 ($t_1$), time 2 ($t_2$), etc., of the initial state. In the shift register the pulse will eventually be lost as it is gated through all the stages comprising the register. If the 1 state is to be retained, the output from the last stage is fed to the first, to form a ring counter.

If the output terminal representing the fourth place $t_4$ is connected to a flip-flop stage as shown, and terminal $t_5$ to another flip-flop, sequential tripping, gating, resetting, or other functions can be obtained. This comes about because both flip-flop stages have the output connected to an *and* circuit which is also fed a continuous train of clock pulses. Initially, the steady-state polarity of the flip-flop stages is set so it does not coincide with that of the clock pulses; hence the clock pulses do not enter registers $A$ and $B$. (Here, register $B$ could contain the divisor in serial division which is to be shifted to the right in relation to the dividend contained in register $A$.)

When the 1 state in the upper shift register reaches $t_4$, the second flip-flop is triggered and its output terminal provides a steady-state polarity which coincides with that of the clock pulses. Thus, the clock pulses are gated into the $B$-register reset line, and the register contents will be read out in serial form. Flip-flop no. 1, however, receives its triggering pulse one time interval (one place) later to initiate the serial read-out process. If the contents of both the $A$ and $B$ registers are fed to an adder, the $B$-register binary number will assume a 1-place left-shift position in relation to the binary contents obtained from register $A$. In ring-counter operation, the recirculation of the 1 state will cause both flip-flop stages to retrigger to the original state when the 1 state of the upper shift register again passes through the fourth and fifth stages and produces a pulse at $t_4$ and then at $t_5$. If only one pulse is to leave the *and* circuits for purposes other than serial read-out, the $t$ terminals of the upper shift register can be connected directly to the *and* circuits or through a monostable one-shot type of multivibrator described in Chapter 1.

## PROBLEMS

1. What is the purpose of the interstage delay lines in Fig. 6-1?

2 (a) Reproduce the half adder shown in Fig. 6-2, and show the addition of the binary numbers 10101 and 1001.
   (b) Is the output a true or a false sum?

3. Reproduce the three-input adder shown in Fig. 6-5B, and show the addition of the binary numbers 0011 and 0101. Indicate the binary numbers present at each circuit input, as well as the output binary number (sum).

4. Briefly explain how a computer subtracts by ones-complement addition.

5. In what manner can flip-flop stages be triggered to produce a complement output?

6. Reproduce the serial subtracter shown in Fig. 6-9B, and show the subtraction of the binary number 0111 from 1110. Indicate the binary numbers present at each circuit input, as well as the output binary number (remainder).

7. Show in block diagram form (as in Fig. 6-11) how two subtracters may be used to handle four binary numbers, and a third subtracter employed to subtract one remainder from the other. Place the numbers 1101 and 0101 in the first subtracter, and the numbers 1111 and 1011 in the second subtracter.

8. If the binary number 101 is placed in a *left-shift* register and three reset pulses applied, what is the arithmetical value of the shifted number?

9. If the binary number 11000 is placed in a *right-shift* register and three reset pulses applied, what is the arithmetical value of the shifted number?

10. In what type of multiplier is the multiplicand entered in serial form?

11. Complete the following division, retaining six places for each step:

$$\frac{1}{110 \overline{)\,101010}}$$
$$\overline{011000}$$

12. In the "division by shifting" system shown in Fig. 6-16, how does the computer sense when an additional shift of the divisor is necessary?

13. In Fig. 6-16, under what circumstances is a zero added to the quotient register?

**14.** In serial division, how is a binary number read out of the dividend register?

**15.** In the division process, the computer incorrectly subtracted the binary divisor 111 from the dividend 1101. It placed the complement divisor under the dividend as

$$
\begin{array}{ll}
\phantom{+}1101 & \text{(dividend)} \\
+\ 0001 & \text{(complement divisor)} \\
\hline
\phantom{+}1110 &
\end{array}
$$

How may the negative remainder of 1110 be used for restoration of the original dividend?

**16.** How is precise unloading in serial form from a register accomplished in computers?

**17.** What changes must be made in the system shown in Fig. 6-19 if only one pulse is to be emitted from the *and*-gate circuits?

# STORAGE SYSTEMS
# AND COMPONENT
# LOGIC

**7**

**Introduction.** As discussed in Chapter 1 (and illustrated in Fig. 1-1), a digital computer must have provisions for storing information which it can call on as required during computing processes. Because the information handled by a digital computer is in binary form, a storage device need only be capable of registering either a 0 or a 1 state. Thus, as detailed earlier in Chapter 4, the flip-flop registers constitute one method of storage of digital information. Such flip-flop registers, however, have limited storage capabilities, and, if electric power is removed, the stored contents are lost. Thus, computer versatility requires other storage systems capable of holding a considerable amount of information for as long as required. Adaptable to the 0- and 1-state conditions are many other types of storage devices, most of them based on magnetic principles. Included in this category are magnetic drums, tapes, disks, and ferrite cores. The drums, tapes, and disks have ferromagnetic coatings which permit sectors to be magnetized to represent binary digits. Ferrite cores can be energized so they retain residual magnetism to indicate a binary bit. These and other devices are covered in detail in this chapter.

Punched cards and paper tape may also be considered as storage devices since the information can be read out at any time desired.

However, because these are related to input and output systems, they are discussed in detail in the next chapter.

The term *memory* is also used to refer to computer storage, since the retention of information by the computer simulates the memory function of living creatures. The storage facilities of a computer are only limited by cost and space factors, since external storage units can be added as required to increase memory capabilities.

## Storage Terminology

Flip-flop registers can be considered as short-term storage devices as compared with drums, tapes, and other systems. The flip-flop storage registers are used during calculation processes for short periods of time. Thus, for a simple addition process, for instance, both the addend and the augend would be in a permanent type of store location. The addend would then be placed in a flip-flop register and the computer instructed to add to this the augend located in a specific permanent storage location. The sum may then be left in the register awaiting the next instructional command.

The stored information to which the computer has immediate *access* (*rapid read-out* and *read-in*) is often referred to as the *internal storage*, since it has operational characteristics which relate to internal computer circuitry. The term internal storage does not necessarily imply that the storage unit is contained within a particular computer console but only to its usage for the computer operation. Devices designed to store information which is to be retained over long periods of time (and which may have slow access) are referred to as *external* storage.

Drum and ferrite storage, as well as flip-flop registers, are of the internal-storage type, while magnetic tape is of the external type. In arithmetic operations the external storage may contain sequential steps for finding square roots or for performing other often-needed calculations (called *subroutines*). In data processing, external storage is the primary reservoir of business data and is comparable to the business filing system. Thus it holds in readiness for processing such information as statistical data, inventories, names and addresses if required, and other pertinent information.

*Buffer storage* is the term often applied to an auxiliary storage system which augments the storage capabilities of the *primary storage* unit.

Thus, a ferrite-core storage system could be backed up by a slower-speed type of storage. Sometimes the latter is used to hold information temporarily before being read out of the computer.

*Permanence* is a word used to describe the information retention capabilities of a storage system. Two other terms related to permanence are *destructive* and *nondestructive*. Punched cards or punched paper tape are a nondestructive type of storage, since the information can be read from them and still retained. Ferrite cores (as explained more fully later) are of the destructive type, since the reading of information from them destroys the retained information. The terms *erasable* and *nonerasable* are also employed on occasion.

*Rewrite* is the process of recirculating information back into storage in cases of destructive memory systems. Thus, even though the information is temporarily lost during read-out, it is immediately read in again if it must be retained for use again at a later time.

*Word* is a term applied to any group of digits which is handled as a single group and not as individual 0- and 1-bit units. (A *bit* is a binary 0 or 1.) A particular digital computer may be designed to accommodate 10 bits to a word in its storage units, while others may have a 30-bit word, or a 56-bit word, etc. Stored words are preceded by a polarity sign, as covered in greater detail later.

*Address*, as the term implies, is a binary number which indicates the particular location of a word or group of words in storage. Address applications are discussed in Chapter 10 as they are related to computer programming.

*Access time* relates to the time interval required to retrieve data from storage. Thus, the access time refers to the elapsed time between the initiation of the read command and obtaining the information. Access time for a punched card may be 0.08 second, while that for a ferrite magnetic core may be less than 5 microseconds.

*Mode of access* refers to the manner in which stored information is read out. *Sequential* access is the procurement of stored information in serial form, one bit at a time. A typical example is magnetic tape, where continuous tape progression occurs, and read-out in serial form occurs when the proper storage address is reached. *Parallel* access occurs when the bits comprising a word are read out simultaneously. A magnetic drum storage device may utilize both serial and parallel access processes by reading out the individual bits of a word in parallel form and reading the series of words in sequence (serial access). *Random access* is the term used to indicate the ability of the computer to retrieve information from storage at random, without having to search out the required storage address by relating it to a previous address. Thus, the information stored in a particular address is available with an access time identical to that of other storage locations. (Ferrite-core storage is of the random-access type.)

*Storage capacity* is the sum total of bits (or words) which a digital computer can store, or which a particular memory system can hold. Some magnetic drums have a storage capacity of over a million bits, while some ferrite-core frames can hold 5000 bits. By increasing the number of drums or core frames, the total capacity can be enlarged as required.

## Magnetic-Tape Storage

Magnetic-tape storage is used as an auxiliary external memory in digital computers. It is a permanent type of storage (nondestructive during read-out) with a longer access time than the primary internal-storage devices. Magnetic tape provides a convenient method for feeding information into a computer, and in such an application it has a much faster read-in speed than the punched cards or paper tape described in the next chapter.

The principle involved in recording digital data on magnetic tape is similar to that used in home tape recorders. Where, however, home recorders use tape reels up to 7 inches in diameter, the computer types use a standard $10\frac{1}{2}$-inch diameter size, containing approximately 2400 feet of tape.

In home tape recorders, $\frac{1}{4}$-inch-wide tape is employed, and, during recording or playback, tape speeds of $1\frac{7}{8}$ to $7\frac{1}{2}$ inches per second may be used, depending on the quality of reproduction desired. Computer tape speeds, on the other hand, range from 30 inches per second to as high as 150 inches per second for some units, with tape widths available from $\frac{1}{2}$ to 3 inches. Common widths are $\frac{1}{2}$ and 1 inch.

The plastic tapes for both home recorders and computer storage have one side coated with a magnetic material combining a red oxide with a binder. The oxide, like iron or steel, can be magnetized by subjecting it to a magnetic field. Once magnetized, the tape coating retains its magnetism for an indefinite period, and can thus store information imparted to it in the form of varying magnetic densities.

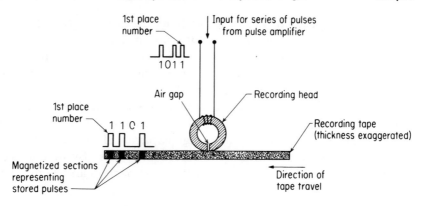

**Fig. 7-1. Tape recording principle.**

During the storage process, the side coated with the oxide is passed over a recording head in a manner such as shown in Fig. 7-1. The recording head consists of a laminated core and a coil, and, when pulses or other types of signals are applied to the input leads of the coil, a magnetic field is generated across the very small air gap. As the tape passes over this air gap, the alternating magnetic field will change the molecular structure of the oxide material and magnetize sections of it in accordance with the intensity and polarity of the fields generated across the air gap of the recording head. When it is necessary to procure the stored information from the tape, it is again run over a recording head (now called a playback head), and the varying degrees of magnetism along the tape will now induce a voltage in the pickup coil. The output leads from the coil will then contain the pulses or other signal information which were originally placed on the tape when the tape was run through initially. Some recorders utilize one head both as a recording head and a playback head, while others have separate heads for recording and playback.

For tape recorders used for voice and music, recording and playback with good fidelity requires that a supersonic bias signal (usually above 50,000 cycles) be applied to the tape prior to the actual recording. Such supersonic bias permits operation of the recording on a more linear portion of the hysteresis loop of the magnetic recording curve and provides a minimum of distortion and a maximum approach to high fidelity. (The magnetic hysteresis curve is discussed with the ferrite-core storage systems in this chapter.) For computer magnetic-tape storage, however, the linearity of recording is not a factor, since stored signal information is in the form of pulses and no supersonic type of bias is required. Fixed-voltage bias, however, is used in some recording methods. In one method the recording head has a current circulating through it of such a polarity that it records a negative magnetic flux on the tape during the time no digit pulse is being recorded. When a 1 digit is to be written, the circulating-current polarity changes to positive. Because of the negative-polarity magnetism of the tape between the recording of digits, no erasure of the tape is required during the recording of data over that already present on the tape (and no longer required). This method is sometimes called *non-return-to zero*. In the *return-to-zero* method, no current flows through the recording-head winding except when either a 1 or a 0 is to be written. Each bit has a signal polarity opposite to the other. Thus, the logic 1 may be represented by a positive pulse and the logic 0 with a negative pulse. Since logic 0 has an opposite-polarity pulse representation, the current through the write head returns to 0 after a bit has been recorded.

Computer storage tapes have many more tracks (channels) than found in the two- or four-track home recorder tapes. Each track, however, records the information in serial form as shown in Fig. 7-1. If, for instance, a pulse sequence of 1011 is being recorded, the first-place digit signal is applied to the recording head and a magnetized area is placed on the tape. The second bit signal enters the recording head after the tape area which stored the initial digit has moved away. Thus, the second bit is stored. The tape then moves past the head for a longer interval without any signal pulse being applied to the head, representing the zero bit of the binary serial train. The fourth-place digit will then enter the recording head and magnetize a section of the tape. Thus, the left-hand section of the tape will have stored the first-place digit and the right-hand section of the magnetized area contains the fourth-place digit. If this is then run through a similar head for playback, the direction of the tape past the head will be in the same direction initially used. Hence, the output from the tape will produce 1011. Read and write heads have similar designs, and a single head can be used for both reading and writing as is often done in home recorders and computer applications. On special occasions, however, separate read and write heads are employed.

A typical multichannel magnetic computer tape recording method is shown in A of Fig. 7-2. Here, 14 tracks are used, with two read-write heads positioned to activate alternate tracks and thus interlace the recorded data. In this way, one head is capable of recording seven

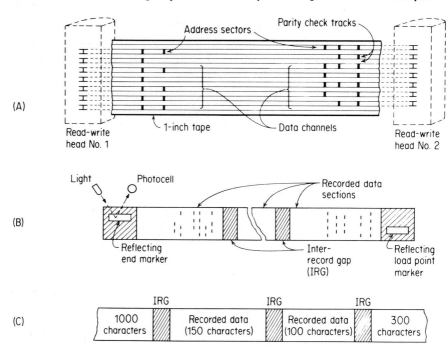

**Fig. 7-2.** Tape storage characteristics.

characters across the tape simultaneously, including the bits making up the address channel and the parity check. The bits recorded in the address channel permit the selection of the desired information contained in a predetermined segment of the tape. The parity channel contains the necessary digits to make the total digit count in a word even, for even parity, or odd, for odd parity. Thus an error check can be maintained on the written information and the data read-out. (See Chapter 5, Error-detecting Codes.)

For each word read from the tape storage, the number of 1 digits is compared with the odd (or even) parity requirement. If coincidence occurs, normal operation is continued. If the number of 1 digits in the read-out word does not match the required parity, an error is sensed and machine operation is suspended while the operator makes the necessary check and correction. The recorded bits shown in A of Fig. 7-2 form even-parity words.

As indicated in Fig. 7-2, each track contains, in serial form, one bit of a word. The word itself can be in pure binary or in binary-coded decimal form as required (see Chapter 4, Decade Counter).

Each word can be read out or written simultaneously, in parallel form. Words, however, are placed on the tape in serial form.

One or more computer words are recorded in a section (sometimes called a record) containing a specific address code for identification. Random record lengths may be used, or fixed lengths can also be employed containing a specific maximum number of bits. As shown in B of Fig. 7-2, interrecord gaps (IRG) are left between records. These gaps occupy approximately $\frac{3}{4}$ inch of tape and are necessary to permit the tape to decelerate to a stop after a record is read out, or to provide sufficient time for the tape to come up to proper speed before data are rewritten on the tape. Exact IRG length is related to the speed with which the start-stop mechanism of the unit operates. After the tape has come to a stop, the read-write head is positioned at the approximate center of the interrecord gap. In C is shown a segment of tape with record lengths differing from each other. Generally, however, the record segments on tape are of identical length for a particular system.

Various methods are employed for sensing tape direction, the beginning of recorded data, end of tape, etc. When the computer, upon an instructional command from the program, is to seek out a specific block of information on tape, the given identifying address is held in a computer register while a tape search is undertaken. If the address sensing indicates a widening numerical difference between the required address and those being sensed while the tape is moving, the computer recognizes that the tape is moving in the wrong direction. The tape movement is then stopped and reversed, and the search for the correct identifying address continues. Once found, information is read out and the tape movement comes to a halt, placing the read-write head at the center or the IRG.

In loading the tape, it is necessary to locate the starting point of the information which is recorded or which is to be recorded. One method is to attach a reflecting foil to the tape (called the *load-point marker*). A light directed at the place where the reflecting foil is positioned produces a reflected light which is sensed by a photocell, as shown in Fig. 7-2. Thus, if an operator pushes a button to rewind the tape, the tape will move in the proper direction toward the load point, and, when the photocell senses the marker, the control unit stops the tape movement and the read-write heads are positioned at the beginning of the usable portion of the tape. Read or write procedures can now be undertaken.

At the tape end another reflector marker is used (usually on the opposite side of the tape so it can be distinguished from the loading marker). Writing of information is continued on the tape until the photocell senses the end of the usable tape length. A signal is then sent to the contol unit which halts tape movement. In some tape systems the load point and end markers are composed of silver-coated conductive leaders spliced on each end of the tape. The tape runs through sensor posts which indicate the beginning-of-tape (BOT) and the end-of-tape (EOT) points. Perforated tape ends may also be used to stop or reverse tape movement by tripping switches when the perforations are sensed by feeler wires.

### Tape Control

The rapid starting and stopping of tape movement during the reading or writing process necessitates careful design of the tape transport mechanisms. One method that has been widely used is illustrated in Fig. 7-3. Here, the feed reel is shown at the upper left, and the take-up reel at the right. Tape-guide rollers direct the tape toward the bottom of the console to form two loops as shown. Tape-

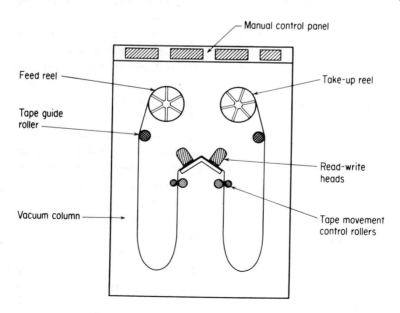

**Fig. 7-3. Tape system console.**

movement-control rollers grip the tape between them and permit quick start and stop operations. Since tape movement must be initiated (and stopped) more rapidly than permitted by the inertia of the tape reels, the slack tape in the loops is taken up as required and reel movement is permitted to follow a short time later to restore the slack making up the loops.

The tape loops are suspended in vacuum columns and a slight air pressure is applied to the top of the tape to provide some tension. This permits even tape winding on the reels and prevents the tape's whipping during rapid movement. Photocell sensing of loop lengths is used to control the motors driving the reel rotation. Thus, the formation of too long (or too short) a loop is prevented.

Tape reels may be positioned one over the other as shown in Fig. 7-4 for a narrower housing. The tape unit shown is the Model 234 of the Philco-Ford Corporation. Some of these units are capable of handling 90,000 characters per second and others up to 240,000 per second, depending on design factors.

The storage capacity of a reel of magnetic tape used in computers depends on the lengths used for the information segments and the lengths of the IRG. Also factors are the tape speed and the width of each magnetized area (recorded digit). A 2400-inch length of tape is, however, generally capable of storing in excess of 2,500,000 characters. Total external storage capacity can be increased for a given computer by adding more tape storage units as required.

**Fig. 7-4.** Model 234 tape unit. Courtesy, Philco Corp.

## Magnetic-Drum Storage

Because of the rapid access time, magnetic-drum storage units may be employed as internal (primary) storage devices in digital com-

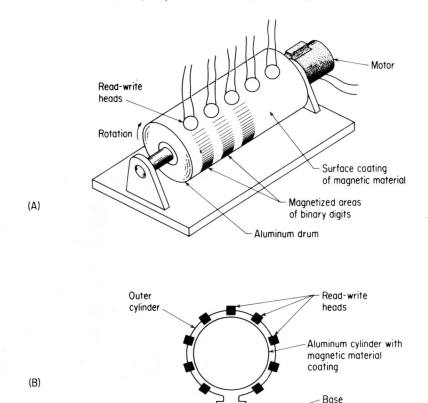

(A)

(B)

**Fig. 7-5.** Magnetic storage drum detail.

puters. The basic principle of operation is the same as for magnetic tape; a magnetic material coating is energized to represent a binary digit. Read-write heads function in the same manner as described for the magnetic tape.

Magnetic-drum storage units utilize a large cylindrical drum (usually aluminum) which has its surface coated with the magnetic material, as shown in Fig. 7-5. The drum is rotated at a high speed and information is stored in narrow tracks along the circumference. A series of recording heads is placed so that it spans the width of the drum, and succeeding rows span the circumference as shown on a typical drum in Fig. 7-6. An outer cylinder holds the read-write heads.

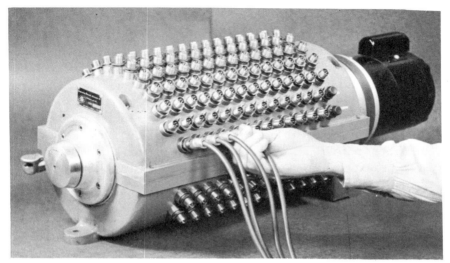

Fig. 7-6. Typical drum storage unit. Courtesy, UNIVAC Division, Sperry-Rand Corp.

Total storage capacity is related to the drum-surface size, the rotation speed, and the number of heads used.

On the commercial unit shown in Fig. 7-6 (Remington Rand Univac), 224 tracks are employed, with each track accommodating approximately 2100 binary digits (bits). Thus, the drum has a capacity to store 470,400 bits (224 × 2100). The drum has a diameter of 8.5 inches and a usable length of 14.5 inches. Approximately 80 binary digits can be stored in one circumferential inch, with a maximum access time of 17 milliseconds. The nominal revolutions per minute are 3510, and the motor develops $\frac{1}{3}$ horsepower at this speed. The approximate weight of the unit is 125 pounds.

Other such units vary in size, capacity, cylinder rpm, and weight. Some drums have a diameter of less than 5 inches, and others have a diameter which exceeds 20 inches. Larger drums use $1\frac{1}{2}$-horsepower motors and weigh well over 500 pounds. Some have cylinder revolutions that are in excess of 15,000 rpm and storage capacities of over a million bits.

As in magnetic-tape storage, the information recorded on a drum is of the nondestructive type, and, when read out, the stored data are retained. Read-out requires precise timing and control because of the high-speed rovolution of the drum cylinder. Thus, at the start of the read-out the binary bit or word recorded first must be read-out first.

Otherwise, at the start of the read-out the drum may be in such a position that the read-out starts at the middle or toward the end of the group of binary bits which are stored. The methods for accomplishing accurate read-out generally depend on whether serial or parallel modes of recording prevail. As on the tape, individual bits making up a word can be recorded in parallel and the sequence of whole words in serial mode. In this method, one circumferential track is reserved for each bit of the word and the entire word is written in a one-bit time factor (parallel). Thus, the recording technic shown for tape in Fig. 7-2 resembles a one-word track around the drum circumference.

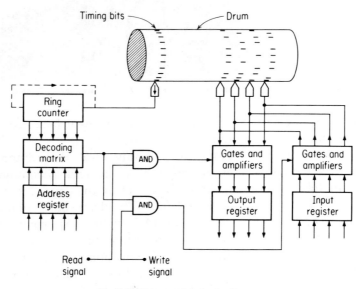

**Fig. 7-7.** Drum read-write circuitry.

One read-write method is shown in Fig. 7-7, where timing pulses are recorded for permanent storage around one track of the drum. These 1 bits of magnetized areas are picked up by a read head and applied to a ring counter having as many stages as there are bit positions on the circumference. The first timing bit position coincides with the initial value of a number stored in the ring counter. As the drum rotates, successive timing pulses progressively shift the ring counter. Thus, each successive timing pulse is identified by a specific ring-counter number, and thus each information area is coded automatically. After a complete cylinder revolution, the ring counter is returned to its original position.

As shown in Fig. 7-7, for either read-in or read-out procedures, a signal is applied to the appropriate *and* circuit during the time the address for the required stored data is applied to the address register. When coincidence occurs between the address and the ring counter, the decoder matrix produces an output signal which is applied to the read-out gate circuits. If a write signal has been applied to the lower *and* circuit, the number applied to the input register will be recorded on the drum when coincidence prevails between the address location desired and the proper positioning of this area under the recording heads.

A decoding network can be formed by using *and* and *or* circuits as shown in Fig. 7-8. Here, the binary number in the address register (steady-state voltages) is applied to the left terminals of the *and* gates

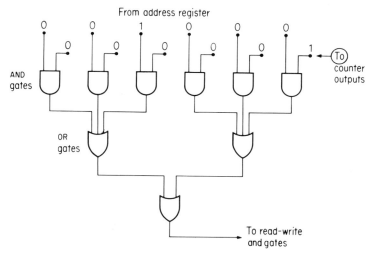

**Fig. 7-8.** Decoding (coincidence) matrix.

as shown. In the starting position of the drum, the ring counter represents a 1 count. For each timing pulse applied to the ring counter, a left shift occurs, progressively producing 000001, 000010, 000100, etc. When the ring counter represents 001000, coincidence occurs for the fourth *and* circuit from the right and a pulse is sent throught the *or* gates to the read-write *and* circuit, with a routing as shown in Fig. 7-7.

The input gating system detail is shown in Fig. 7-9. The same system would be used for the read-out section. When the write *and* circuit produces an output signal, it will permit the number stored in the input register to be applied to the amplifier circuits and the write heads. Because the write *and* circuit only produces a signal when the address register number coincides with the drum's circumferential possition number in the ring counter, the information writing is applied to the drum at the precise time required for that particular address.

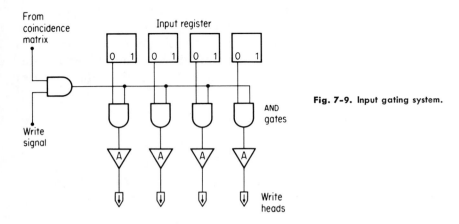

Fig. 7-9. Input gating system.

Instead of a sequential digit single-track timing channel, several channels can be used to store the address for the information applied to the drum. Thus, the address for each data sector is written in channels around the drum circumference instead of the drum's rotational position being sensed by timing pulses and a ring counter. Each bit of the address is then sensed by read heads and applied to a decoding matrix for comparison with the address in question.

As in magnetic tape storage, one track for each word sector is reserved for a parity-check pulse for error-detection purposes.

### Magnetic-Disk Storage

Magnetic-disk storage devices provide extensive external storage capacity. Such units consist of iron-oxide-coated disks resembling phonograph records. The disks are stacked and rotated by a common shaft at 1000 rpm or more. Spacing is provided between each stacked disk for insertion of a read-write head. The tracks are in the form of concentric circles around the disk, and each track is read serially. With multiple recording units, the bits comprising the word can be written in parallel form, using a group of tracks as in tape and drum recordings. Successive words are written serially.

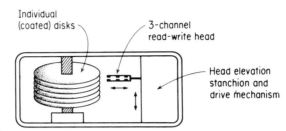

**Fig. 7-10.** Disk storage assembly.

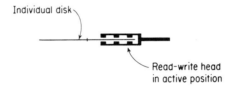

In some units a single read-write head mechanism has been used, as shown in Fig. 7-10. Here, a hydraulic positioning stanchion is used for elevating the head mechanism as well as for positioning it horizontally over the disk. Other units employ multiple heads for each disk, and, as these require no elevation movement but need only move into position over the disks, the access time is reduced. In modern units the head positioning over the desired tracks takes less than 100 milliseconds.

Storage capacity depends on the rpm rate, the disk diameter, and the magnetic density used for each bit. With a 40-inch disk coated on both sides, a storage capacity in excess of 10 million bits can be realized. Thus, when 10 or 20 such disks are stacked, total storage capacity reaches extensive proportions.

Disk tracks are grouped into zones, each zone accommodating a number of tracks. The zones for a particular system may be two per disk side, while another system may use as many as six or more zones. Since the magnetized areas representing bits are bunched closer together as the inner track circles have progressively reduced circumferences, the innermost track of each zone has magnetized bit areas of

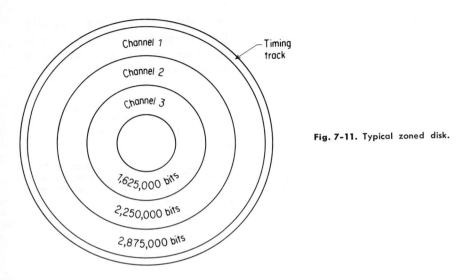

**Fig. 7-11.** Typical zoned disk.

highest permissable intensity. A typical three-zone disk is shown in Fig. 7-11. As in magnetic-drum storage, a timing track is provided which contains a permanently-recorded series of bits for rotational positioning sensing for the address function. Several tracks can also be used for multiple-bit code addresses. With a single timing track, an additional index track containing a single bit is used to identify the starting (zero) position of the disk during rotation.

In Fig. 7-11, assume each channel is allocated one read-write head which can be positioned over 100 segments of a single channel. If this particular disk permits the storage of 250 bits of information per inch of track, an average channel circumference of 115 inches would provide $250 \times 115 = 28{,}750$ bis per track. With 100 tracks per channel, the first channel could accommodate 2,875,000 bits. If the second channel has an average circumference of 90 inches per track, each track in this second channel could store $90 \times 250 = 22{,}500$ bits. With 100 tracks, the total capacity for the second channel is 2,250,000. The innermost track, with an average circumference of 65 inches, has a total channel capacity of 1,625,000 bits. Thus, the total capacity for a single disk side would be approximately 6,750,000 bits.

### Ferrite-Core Storage

Ferrite cores have been widely used as an internal storage system in computers because of their short access time. Ferrite is a hard, brittle material composed of spinel crystals consisting of a mixture of such metals as nickel, manganese, and zinc. Ferrite has found extensive usage as the cores of built-in antennas in radios and as the cores for special-purpose transformers, because of the extremely high $Q$ obtained with resultant high permeability.

For computer storage applications, the ferrite material is formed into tiny rings sometimes referred to as *ferrite toroids* or *ferrite memory cores*. Core sizes vary, with some smaller ones having an outside diameter of only 0.02 inch and an inside diameter of 0.015 inch. In a single computer system as many as 20 million ferrite cores may be used.

Thin wire is strung through the ferrite ring center for energizing purposes. When a short-duration signal current of sufficient amplitude is made to flow through the wire, magnetic fields are created which cause the ferrite cores to become magnetized with a polarity coinciding with that of the energizing current. The polarity of the magnetic field thus created in the ferrite ring is retained for an indefinite period. If current of opposite polarity is applied to the wire, the ring magnetism reverses and the ring retains the reversed-polarity magnetism. Thus, the ferrite ring has the ability to store either a 0 or a 1 representation.

When it is necessary to store information, a particular pulse of energy will magnetize the core along a nearly rectangular hysteresis loop. Figure 7-12 illustrates the hysteresis loop of ferrite represented by the solid lines compared with ordinary magnetic material shown by the dashed lines. Note that the ferrite hysteresis loop almost represents a rectangle in comparison with the curved type of loop for the ordinary magnetic material.

The vertical axis represents flux density $B$, and the horizontal axis represents the magnetizing force $H$. Such a graph is called a *B-H curve* of magnetic characteristics. The unit of flux density, or magnetism is known as *gauss*, while the unit for the magnetizing force is *oersted*. The relationship between the two is that a magnetizing force of 1 oersted produces a flux density of 1 gauss. (One gauss represents one magnetic line per square centimeter of cross-sectional area in air.)

The *B-H* curve is procured by increasing the magnetizing force on the magnetic material and noting the increase in flux density. Magnetizing force to soft iron can be applied by forming a loop of wire around the iron and running current through the wire. The wire itself forms a field composed of magnetic lines of force which act to energize the soft iron. If the current is increased, the magnetism in the iron will also become stronger until the leveling off portion as shown in the graph. The rise in flux density for ordinary material curves upward from the center zero line and tapers off to the right as shown by the dotted lines. In reducing the magnetizing force, the curve fails to retrace the curve back on the forward trace line to the zero point, but curves back down at the left as shown by the arrows in the dotted section. Thus, when the magnetizing force is zero, the flux density is still quite high (known as *residual* magnetism or a remnant magnetism). Thus, the flux density $B$ lags behind the magnetizing force $H$. This lag phenomenon is known as *hysteresis*, hence the graph of the curve is called a *hysteresis loop*. With reversing polarity, the curve drops down to the left below the zero line as shown. Decreasing the magnetizing force causes the right-hand trace upward, again failing to intercept the zero line. The entire magnetic material would have to be thoroughly demagnetized to be able to start at zero again and trace upward.

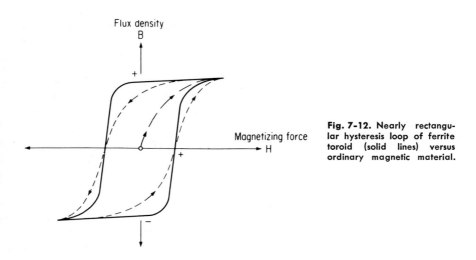

**Fig. 7-12.** Nearly rectangular hysteresis loop of ferrite toroid (solid lines) versus ordinary magnetic material.

Because the ferrite magnetic cores have a rectangular hysteresis loop, the ferrite core is inherently a bistable element. An inspection of Fig. 7-12, which shows the rectangular loop, will indicate that the magnetic induction of the core can be equivalent to a charge in the plus direction or a charge in the minus direction, depending on the polarity of the magnetizing field current. For computer usage, when the magnetic field is in the positive direction it is assigned either 0 or 1, with the negative direction being assigned the opposite designation. For instance, when in the plus direction it can represent 0, and when in the minus direction it can represent the binary digit 1. Hence, when the core is magnetized in the negative direction it would store the digit 1 and this direction would be the *write* direction. When the core is now magnetized in the positive direction, the information can be

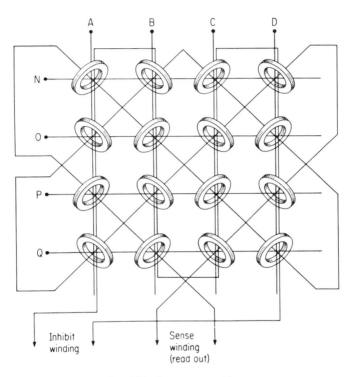

**Fig. 7-13. Core storage wiring.**

read out; hence the positive direction can be considered the *read* direction. If the core is magnetized in the so-called negative direction, it can be switched to the positive direction by the application of a read pulse which has full amplitude. During the change from the negative condition to the read-out condition, a voltage is induced in the sense wire (described later) which runs through the center of the core. On the other hand, if the core is in the zero state (positive), the application of a read pulse will produce very little voltage in the sense (output) winding. Hence, the ferrite core, because of its rectangular hysteresis loop, has the ability to select or discriminate between two conditions or states. For this reason it is particularly adaptable for binary arithmetic, where only 0 and 1 are utilized.

For digital-computer storage use, the cores are assembled on a flat panel and connected together by cross-wiring to form what is known as a *matrix*, in similar fashion to the enlarged section of a typical unit illustrated in Fig. 7-13. Independent and insulated wires are run through the cores as shown, with the vertical series marked *A*, *B*, etc., intercepting at the core a series of horizontal wires marked *N*, *O*, etc., in the illustration. Thus, each individual ferrite core has one pair of coded wires at intersection. Voltage applied to any coded horizontal or vertical line will cause current to flow in that wire and hence create a magnetic field around the wire.

In practice, however, the current amplitude is held at only half that which would produce a change of magnetic state in the core. Such a current is sometimes termed *half-select current* because it creates a magnetic field in one wire which is only one-half the amplitude required to shift the magnetic field of the core. When the other intersecting wire of that core is energized, however, the coinciding fields of the two wires are sufficiently high to change the magnetic state of the core. Thus, if current is made to flow through the wire designated as *B*, a field will be set up all along this wire, but it will be of insufficient amplitude to reverse the magnetic state of the cores in the vertical row. If a coinciding half-select current flow is now produced in the horizontal line marked *N*, the two magnetic fields established at the intersection of *N* and *B* will be greater than the coercive force of the core and hence of sufficient magnitude to reverse the state of that

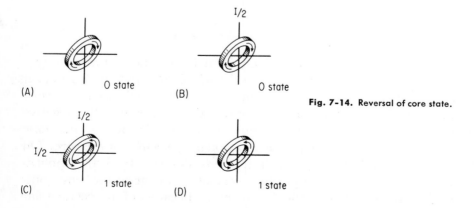

(A)     0 state     (B)     0 state

(C)     1 state     (D)     1 state

**Fig. 7-14.** Reversal of core state.

particular core. If the core was in the 0 state it will now be magnetized to represent the 1 state and will resist any change in polarity of the magnetism it acquired. Since the two half-select currents must be in coincidence to change the core state, the term *coincident-current core storage* is often applied to this memory system.

The reversal of the core state is more clearly indicated in Fig. 7-14. In A the 0 (zero) state is shown, with the arrows representing the direction of the magnetism. In B one-half the necessary current for tripping the core flows through the vertical winding and hence a 0 state still exists. In C half-select currents are made to flow through both the vertical and horizontal wires and hence the core state of magnetism changes as indicated by the arrows. After the energizing currents leave, the core remains the reversed magnetic field representative of the 1 state, as shown in D.

When half-select currents of opposite polarity to read-in currents are caused to flow through a vertical and a horizontal wire, the core again undergoes a change in its magnetized state and is switched to 0. This shift in its magnetic state creates a changing magnetic-flux field which induces a voltage on the wire intersecting the core at an angle. As shown in Fig. 7-13, this is a continuous winding, the ends of which terminate at the bottom and are designated as the *sense* winding, or read-out wire. The voltage induced in the read-out wire thus represents the stored bit of binary information which had been retained by a particular ferrite core. This output signal voltage, ranging in amplitude from 20 to 50 millivolts, is amplified to the required degree and channeled to the necessary circuits of the computer to be processed as required.

The half-select currents applied to the vertical and horizontal wires during read-out is a noise source. Because half-select currents are circulating through all the cores threaded by the vertical and horizontal wires, such cores, even though not reversed, tend to induce additive noises in the sense wire. To minimize this, the sense wire is wound in opposite directions through the various diagonal core groups. The result is that noise voltages induced in the sense wire by one diagonal core group have polarities opposite to those of the noise voltages induced by the other diagonal group. Hence, noise cancellation occurs. With such noise-cancellation sense-wire threading, the output signal produced from a particular core will have a polarity opposite to that for a signal produced from a core in another group. Thus, the sensing of an output signal of either positive or negative

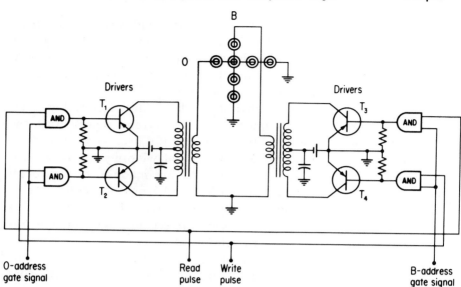

**Fig. 7-15.** Read-write core driver system.

polarity constitutes a 1-value read-out. If a core is already in the 0 state, no output voltage is obtained from the sense wire, because the core is already magnetized in the direction produced by the two half-select read-out currents.

A typical read-write system is shown in Fig. 7-15. Here, transistor driver circuits are used which, in the absence of a base signal, are in a nonconducting state. The circuits shown are actuated only when the address registers of the computer indicate that the $O$-$B$ core is to be energized to either the 1 or 0 state, and a read or write pulse is applied. If a read pulse is applied, coincidence occurs with the $O$-address signal at the upper-left *and* circuit and an output pulse from the *and* circuit applies the necessary forward bias to transistor $T_1$ for conduction. Thus, a half-select current flows in the transformer secondary winding, and all the cores in the horizontal $O$ line are half energized. At the same time the $B$-address gate signal and the read pulse open the upper right *and* circuit, and thus transistor $T_3$ conducts and causes a half-select current to flow in the vertical $B$ cores. Consequently, the core at which the lines addressed $O$ and $B$ intersect is switched to the 1 state. For a write pulse, the lower *and* circuits are actuated and permit transistors $T_2$ and $T_4$ to conduct, which produces a half-select current in both the $O$ and $B$ lines, but now of opposite polarity. The core is now switched to the 0 (zero) state, and an output signal is produced from the sense wire.

On read-out the stored information is lost because the core must be switched to the 0 state to pulse the sense wire. Thus, this storage system is of the destructive type, and, to retain the information upon read-out, it must be recirculated and reapplied to the core to regenerate it again. Thus, for every read-out, a write pulse is applied to restore the information. If, however, a particular core was initially in the 0 state, a restoring write-pulse switching must be nullified so that a 0 state is not changed to an erroneous 1 state. When a core is to be switched is in the 0 state, an inhibiting pulse is applied to the inhibit winding shown in Fig. 7-13, which prevents the writing of a 1. The appropriate circuitry for accomplishing this is shown in Fig. 7-16. If

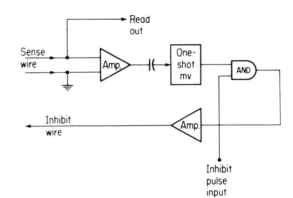

**Fig. 7-16.** Inhibit-sense circuits.

a signal is obtained from the sense wire, it is amplified and applied to the monostable (one-shot) multivibrator (see Chapter 1). The multivibrator thus applies to the *and* circuit a pulse of opposite polarity to the inhibit pulse. In consequence, the *and* gate remains closed, and no inhibit pulse is applied to the inhibit wire. After the sense-wire signal leaves, the one-shot circuit reverts back to its original state, producing signal coincidence at the *and* circuit. When no sense signal is obtained during read-out, the *and* circuit passes the inhibit pulse to the inhibit winding, preventing a write function.

For illustration simplification, the core matrix shown in Fig. 7-13 consists of only 16 ferrite cores. In commercial units, a single frame may contain thousands of cores. The core frame shown in Fig. 7-17, for instance, contains 64 cores in both the vertical and horizontal rows,

for a total of 4096 cores contained in an area of 4 square inches (2 $\times$ 2 inches).

Generally, switching time ranges from 1 to approximately 5 microseconds, depending on the type and quality of the ferrite cores used. Driving currents range from 400 to 800 milliamperes.

For parallel modes of operation, ferrite-core frames are stacked with the particular core of one frame having identical identifying codes with the other cores in the same frame position. Thus, an $A$-$N$ address (as given in the example in Fig. 7-13) would apply to each first core of each frame stacked above the other. The code identification would apply to a complete computer *word* instead of only one bit. This is shown in Fig. 7-18, which shows the stacking of six planes to provide six bits to a word. Since there are 64 cores per frame, this particular stack holds a maximum of 64 six-bit words. The cores which are energized to store the binary number 101100 are shown in Fig. 7-18. Thus, as in other storage systems described, words can be written or read

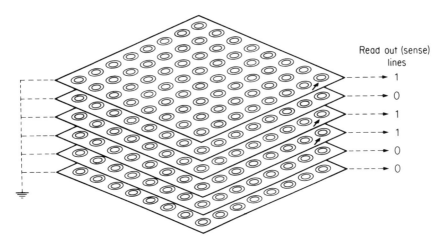

Read out (sense) lines

1
0
1
1
0
0

**Fig. 7-18.** Stacked planes.

**Fig. 7-19.** Core memory stack.
Courtesy, Fabri-Tek, Inc.

in bit parallel, and sequential words in serial mode operation. With a frame having a 4096-bit capacity, 9 can be stacked to provide 4096 words, each containing 9 bits. Thus, total bit capacity for such a unit would be 36,864. In some commercial stacks such a capacity would be contained in a 5- by 5- by 3-inch unit. A typical core-memory stack with output jacks for vertical, horizontal, sense, and inhibit wires is shown in Fig. 7-19.

### Transfluxer-Core Storage

When, during manufacture, two or more apertures are introduced in a ferrite core, several separate legs and flux paths are formed when the core is magnetized. This permits such a multiaperture device (abbreviated MAD) to be used as a nondestructive storage system. The magnetic flux can be transferred from leg to leg in controlled fashion, and so the term *transfluxer* has been used for such cores. The two-aperture core is shown in A of Fig. 7-20. Here, the unequal diameter holes are used for separate write and read purposes, as opposed

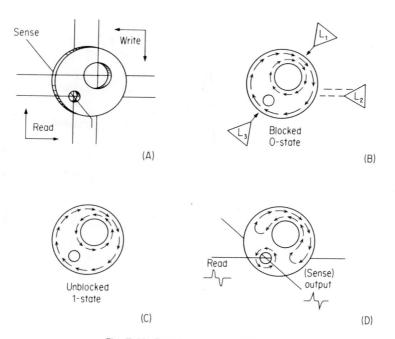

**Fig. 7-20. Transfluxer characteristics.**

to the single read-write design of the ferrite-core storage previously discussed.

Two write wires are threaded through the larger aperture, and the smaller aperture contains the read and sense wires. Initially, to represent the 0 state, the write wires have a voltage applied to them so that half-select currents are produced for the proper core selection, as was the case with the ferrite-core system discussed previously. The write current magnetizes the ferrite transfluxer core to produce the flux-flow direction shown in B of the figure. Now, three flux legs or areas are produced: one narrow area between the large aperture and rim, $L_1$; another between the large aperture and the small aperture, $L_2$; and a third leg $L_3$ between the small aperture and rim. The narrow $L_2$ and $L_3$ areas become magnetically saturated and because of the rectangular hysteresis loop will remain virtually so after the write signal is gone.

If a voltage which creates a clockwise flux flow is now applied to the read winding, the magnetic field thus created in the small aperture would normally have the effect of increasing $L_3$ flux and decreasing $L_2$ flux. However, $L_3$ is already at saturation and the flux cannot be increased, while the saturated $L_2$ flux field is in such a direction as to oppose the read-winding flux. Hence no change occurs, and no output read signal is sensed. An identical condition prevails if the read current is such as to produce a counterclockwise flux field. This would tend to increase $L_2$ flux, but the latter is already at saturation, and the $L_3$ flux field opposes the read-winding flux. Again no change occurs, and no read signal is produced. Thus, no output signal is generated, regardless of whether the read signal is positive, negative, or a-c in character. Since the production of an output signal is blocked, the core represents the 0 state.

When the core is switched to the 1 state, the current polarity is such that a counterclockwise magnetic force is produced. The write current is limited to that amount which reverses the flux direction around the rim area of the larger aperture only, without affecting the $L_3$ area, as shown in C. Now the core is in an unblocked state and capable of producing an output signal in the sense wire when a read signal is applied to the read wires.

If a signal is applied to the read winding, having a polarity to produce a counterclockwise field, the flux around the small aperture will reverse, as shown in D of Fig. 7-20. With a flux reversal, an output signal is induced in the sense winding. The field reversal around

the small aperture does not affect the 1-state (unblocked) characteristic of the core. If a current of opposite polarity is now caused to
flow again in the read winding, a clockwise field is produced and the
flux is reversed again and remains so after the reading current ter-
minates. Thus, an a-c signal can be applied to produce a read-out,
with the first alternation of the signal causing a flux reversal around the
small aperture and the second alternation of the a-c signal restoring
the original flux-field direction. Because of this, repeated read-out
without information loss is possible (nondestructive storage). To
change the 1 state to a 0 state, the proper polarity signals must be
applied to the write windings to cause the core to be switched to the
blocked 0 state, with flux directions as shown in B.

The wiring shown in A of Fig. 7-20 is repeated in matrix fashion to
form a core storage frame similar to those illustrated in Figs. 7-13 and
7-17. Stacked planes permit parallel word storage as illustrated for
the ferrite-core storage in Fig. 7-18. Because the core is not switched
during read-out, no current coincidence is required in the read
aperture. The read wire through a horizontal row of cores can be
energized to an amplitude producing flux reversal in the small aperture, and the vertical read wire running through the core can be used
as the sense (read-out) line.

### Core Logic

Both the basic ferrite cores and the MADs (multiaperture devices)
can also be employed to form logic-function circuits. Each has ferromagnetic properties with residual-magnetism characteristics, and so
logic gates, flip-flops, and shift registers can be designed. Typical of
such applications are the ferrite-core circuits shown in Fig. 7-21.

In A is shown a core with a primary and secondary winding forming a toroidal type of transformer. Like the transformer *not* circuit
described in Chapter 3, this performs an inverting function as shown
in B, where the schematic representation is given plus dot notation.
As shown, a positive-polarity input pulse produces a negative-polarity output pulse. Similarly, a negative input produces a positive
output.

An *or* type of circuit can also be formed, as shown in C. Here, a
two-input *or* gate is illustrated, though additional inputs can be employed as required. An input at either *A* or *B* (or both) will cause core

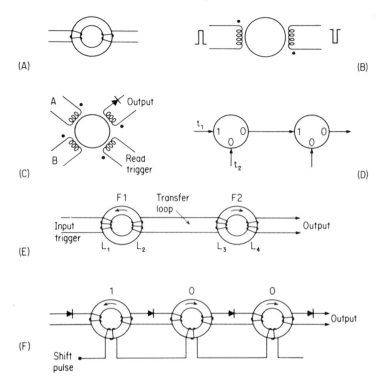

**Fig. 7-21. Core logic circuitry.**

saturation, and, when a read-out pulse is applied to the trigger input, a unipolar output signal is procured. The diode prevents an output during the time the core is energized. When the read trigger pulse reverses the core state, the changing magnetic fields induce a voltage across the output winding. If the polarity of the $B$ signal is reversed, it will prevent the $A$ signal from causing core saturation, and thus forms an *inhibitor* circuit.

When the circuit shown in B is coupled to a similar section, the secondary of the first core is coupled to the primary of the second core to form a transfer loop. Flip-flop and shift-register circuits can thus be formed. When two or more cores are coupled in this manner, the symbol representation shown in D is sometimes used. The two wires to the input primary are represented by a single arrow, with a digit representing the core state obtained with an input signal. The 0 at the start of the output line indicates the core state necessary to produce this numerical output. Thus, when a pulse is applied at the input

$t_1$, the left core is set at the 1 state. If a pulse is now applied at $t_2$, the core state is reversed to 0 and the next core is set at its 1 state.

The mode of operation described for D can be used to form a bistable flip-flop circuit. This is shown in E, where the full schematic representation of the basic circuit is given for ease of analysis. Here, assume core $F_1$ is magnetized in a counterclockwise state to represent a state comparable to the "on" state of a transistor flip-flop. At the same time the second core $F_2$ is magnetized in the clockwise direction, or "off" state. Thus, the core circuit now resembles a transistor flip-flop where one transistor conducts and the other is cut off.

If a pulse of proper polarity is now applied to the input, current circulates in winding $L_1$ and a field is produced which will energize the first core (at the left) in a clockwise flux condition, which reverses its state. The changing field of $F_1$ will now induct a voltage across $L_2$, causing a current circulation through the transfer loop and thus through $L_3$. Current through $L_3$ produces a magnetic field which changes the "off" state of $F_2$ to the "on" state. Thus, the second state of the bistable circuit has been reached. Winding $L_3$ has fewer turns on it than $L_2$ to prevent the reflipping of $F_1$ as $F_2$ reverses its state.

In F of Fig. 7-21 is shown a shift register with third core winding for shifting purposes. Here, the left core is in the 1 state with counterclockwise flux circulation. The other two cores are in the 0 state with clockwise flux rotation as shown. When a shift pulse is applied, fields are produced which would cause the cores to assume a clockwise flux position. Since cores 2 and 3 are already in this position, however, the shift pulse has no effect. In the first core at the left, however, the shift pulse causes field reversal. In consequence, the left core reverts to the 0 state, and an output voltage is produced which flips the second core to the 1 state (counterclockwise flux). When the second core is energized in a counterclockwise flux rotation, it also develops an output signal. Such a signal, however, is of a polarity opposite to that produced from the first core; hence its output will consist of a magnetic force in the same direction which already exists in the right-hand core. This signal is blocked by the series diode. The use of series isolating diodes also blocks any reverse currents which might occur.

The transfluxer and other MADs can also perform logic functions. A three-aperture MAD, for instance, can be used as a dual-input sequential gate, as shown in Fig. 7-22. The inputs (designated as $M$ and $N$) are threaded through the two separate apertures as shown in A. The third aperture near the rim is used to obtain the output when

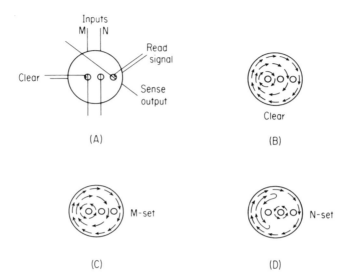

Fig. 7-22. Pulse sequential gate characteristics.

a read signal is applied, in a fashion similar to that described for the two-aperture transfluxer. A clearing line is used to obliterate the input pulses after the gate function has been terminated. This is necessary because of the storage characteristics of such ferrite-core materials.

In the cleared state, the magnetic-flux directions are as shown in B, and no signal can be obtained from the rim aperture because of the parallel direction of the flux lines, as was the case with the two-aperture transfluxer. If a pulse is now applied to the $M$ input, the flux lines around the $M$-line aperture will reverse as shown in C. At the rim aperture, however, flux lines are still parallel, and no output signal can be obtained.

If the application of an $M$ input is followed by an $N$ input, the flux lines become as shown in D, and now the output is unblocked since the flux lines at the rim aperture are in opposite directions. A read pulse will now produce an ouput from the sense winding. With a bipolar read signal, the read-out aperture is reset for continuous subsequent readings. When the MAD is cleared, the device is blocked and no output is obtained from the sense wire when a read pulse is applied. Note that the input signals must be in an $M$-$N$ sequence to obtain an unblocked core status. If an $N$ input is applied initially, it will be ineffectual since the center aperture in the clear state also has parallel flux lines.

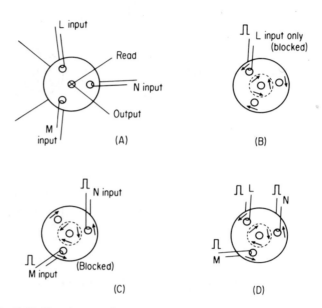

**Fig. 7-23.** Three-input *and* gate with four-aperture transfluxer.

Multiaperture core devices can form logic circuits without the need for additional resistors or capacitors, as shown in Fig. 7-23. Here, a four-aperture transfluxer is shown, having characteristics which permit its operation as a three-input *and* circuit. The three inputs ($L$, $M$, and $N$) surround the center aperture as shown. The output flux direction around the three legs of the center aperture can be blocked by any *one* or *two* of the legs by applying an input. When, however, three inputs are applied simultaneously, an unblocked condition occurs and an output reading from the sense wire can be obtained.

If, for instance, only an $L$ input signal is applied as shown in B, the center legs do not have unipolar flux lines and hence no output can be obtained. For only an $N$ and $M$ input as in C, the center legs again have no unipolar flux lines. For three simultaneous inputs as in D, the center legs have the required unipolar flux lines to produce an output when the read signal is applied. Thus, this three-input device functions as an *and* circuit requiring coincidence in three input signals to obtain an unblocked status for readout. With a five-aperture MAD having four rim apertures and one center aperture, a four-input *and* circuit can be obtained, with operation similar to that of the three-input described.

## *Thin-film Storage*

Thin-film storage is one phase of *microminiaturization*, the fabrication and assembly of components and circuits into microscopic dimensions. By such processes, the hardware bulk of all electronic circuitry, including computers, has been reduced to an extraordinary degree so that units which formerly took up considerable room, are now miniaturized to the point where they occupy less space than a small coin. Several circuits complete with components can be combined (integrated circuit) in a silicon wafer *chip*, or so-called *monolithic block*, of microminiature proportions. Such formation of semiconductor chips into usable circuit elements is performed by a variety of processes, including electroplating, electrodepositing of material on glass or ceramic substrates, photoengraving and etching procedures, and vacuum deposition. In the last, the active material is placed in a vacuum chamber with the substrate and heated for vaporization deposit of a thin film of the material on the substrate.

High voltage, currents, and electric power are not necessary to perform electronic amplification, signal modification, logic circuit functions, etc. Hence, microminiaturization does not hamper such functions if noise levels are kept at a minimum. Subsequently, when the end results must be made audible, visible, or stored, signal levels can be brought up from their pico-volt amplitudes to that required.

Thin-film storage elements are formed by depositing an alloy of magnetic material (such as nickel and iron) on a glass substrate to a thickness of approximately 2000 angstrom units. (One angstrom unit = $10^{-8}$ centimeter.) During the depositing process, the material is subjected to a magnetic field and hence the thin-film elements become magnetized and retain such magnetism because of their

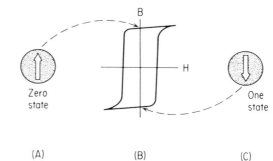

**Fig. 7-24. Thin-film storage states.**

Zero state

B

H

One state

(A)                    (B)                    (C)

ferromagnetic properties. The direction of magnetism is referred to as the *easy*, or *preferred*, magnetism because of the high residual rententivity of the magnetism characteristic of materials producing the rectangular hysteresis loop (as shown earlier in Fig. 7-12). Thus, the thin-film deposit has the ability to represent either 0 or 1, depending on the north-south or south-north direction of easy magnetism. This is shown in Fig. 7-24, where the zero direction of the magnetism shown at *A* represents the upper residual-magnetism point on the hysteresis curve at *B*, and the 1 direction of the magnetism shown at *C* represents the lower residual point.

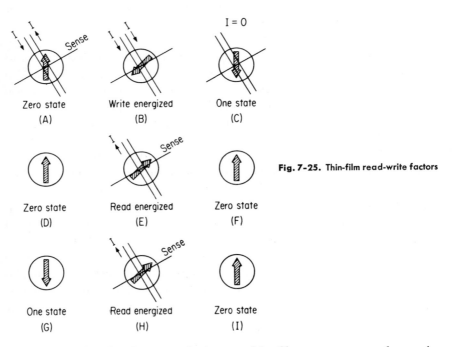

Fig. 7-25. Thin-film read-write factors

The read-write factors relating to thin-film storage are shown in Fig. 7-25. The read-write and sense lines are also formed by micro-miniaturization processes and overlay the thin-film spot as shown at A. When currents in the digit lines are opposing, as shown at A a logic 0 is written (or retained) in that particular spot. For changing the 0 state to a 1 state, currents through the digit lines coincide and cause the core magnetism to shift to a position approximately perpendicular to the digit write lines, as shown at B. Upon termination of the writing currents, the magnetic dipole shifts to the nearest residual-magnetic position. For the conditions shown at A and B, the nearest residual point would be the 1 state shown at C.

Only one line need be energized for read-out purposes. This is done by causing current to flow in one line with a polarity opposite to the write currents. If a read current occurs while the thin-film spot is in the 0 state shown at D, the dipole shifts clockwise toward the sense wire as shown at E. Upon termination of the read current, the magnetic dipole returns to the nearest residual-magnetism position again, which in this case is 0. Since no complete reversal of state has occurred, no signal is felt in the sense wire.

If the thin-film spot is in the 1 state shown at 7-25G, the read current causes the dipole to shift to the saturation level for the current polarity used as shown at H, and this is the same position as E. In consequence, upon the termination of the read current, the dipole shifts to the nearest position, which is 0. Since this has been a complete reversal of magnetic state, an output signal is produced in the sense (read-out) line.

The read-out is destructive and, for information retention, re-circulation is required. Nondestructive thin-film storage can be fabricated however, though the process is more complex. Two thin-film spots are used, one formed of high-coercive material for retention, and the second spot of low-coercive material for read-out.

## Cryogenic Thin Film

Whereas the access time of thin-film storage can be held to less than a few microseconds, if more rapid switching is required, cryogenic principles may be employed. With cryogenic thin-film storage, the bit capacity is also increased to a considerable extent. The operating apparatus required, however, is more complex because of the necessity for coolant devices and the special fabrication techniques which must be employed.

The term cryogenics comes from the Greek word meaning "icy cold" and it relates to the science involving temperatures below approximately $-300\,°F$. Cryogenic temperatures affect the resistance values of conductors. At normal temperatures the molecular movement in matter is continuous and takes the form of an endless vibratory type of motion. In most conductors the molecular movement increases with heat and decreases as temperatures drop. The molecular movement is related to the resistivity of a material and such movement normally interferes with electric current flow. At $-459.72°F$ such molecular movement ceases (though electron spin around the nucleus of the atom still continues). Thus, as the temperature is reduced in metals, resistance decreases until finally the metals become *super-conductive* and consume no electric power during current circulation.

In ordinary metals, superconductivity during cryogenic temperatures can be nullified by a magnetic field, and such a field can be used to cause a superconductor to become an ordinary conductor with resistive charactetistics. Thus, in computer storage elements operated at cryogenic temperatures, switching operations in read, write, sense, etc., can be performed by magnetic field applications. Since the super-conductivity states are sharp, access time can be in fractional micro-seconds. Storage capacities in excess of 15,000 bits have been obtained from a 2-inch square plane consisting of the superconducting thin film, drive lines, a sense line, and the substrate.

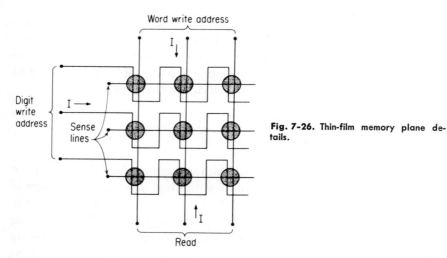

Fig. 7-26. Thin-film memory plane details.

Thin film is fabricated into multiple-unit frames, such as those used in ferrite-core storage, for both the normal-temperature memory units and the cryogenic type. A typical plane section is shown in Fig. 7-26, with operational characteristics as described earlier for the single thin-film spot. For writing, as shown here, the word- and bit-address currents flow in the same direction. For reading, a single current opposite in polarity to the write currents is used. Only a reversal of the thin-film spot from 1 to 0 causes a read-out signal from the sense wire.

## Twister Storage

The original twister element consisted of a twisted wire under torsion; hence the term twister was applied to this device. Eventually the method of construction took the form shown in A of Fig. 7-27. Here, a spiral magnetic ribbon is wound around a thin copper wire. The ribbon material has a rectangular hysteresis loop as in the other storages devices discussed, hence it has an easy direction of magnetism, as shown by the arrows in A. Hence, the twister has operational characteristics similar to those of the thin-film storage in which the writing of a 1 rotates the magnetic dipole 180°.

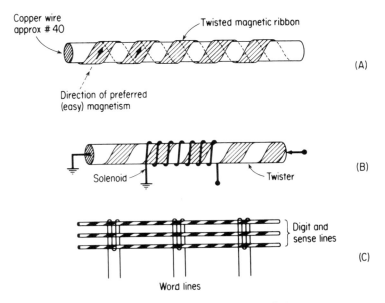

**Fig. 7-27. Construction of twister storage device.**

A solenoid is wrapped around the twister as shown in B. When a current is passed through the center wire of the twister at the same time that a current is made to flow in the solenoid, the combined magnetic fields reverse the magnetic state and a 1 is stored. Since the magnetic ribbon is not a closed loop as is a ferrite core, only the area under the solenoid is energized to the 1 state during writing. The wire core of the twister produces a circumferential field when current flows through it, and, with the correct polarity current in the solenoid, an axial magnetic field is created. The combination reverses the magnetic dipole area.

For read-out, a voltage is applied to the solenoid that creates a current flow opposite in polarity to that used for write purposes. Sufficient current is caused to flow so that the magnetic fields produced will reverse the magnetic state of the area in which a 1 has been written. During magnetic dipole reversal, the changing flux induces a voltage in the center conductor of the twister, and the resultant current flow is sensed as the read-out signal. Switching time is less than 0.5 microsecond. In such a storage system, a number of twisters can pass through a solenoid, and a number of such solenoids are spaced along the length of the twisters as shown in C of Fig. 7-27. Thus, each solenoid represents the address of a single word, and each twister threading through the solenoid contains one bit (1 or 0) of the word in that address.

The basic twister is destructive, and content is lost during read-out and must be recirculated if it is to be retained. The twister storage can, however, be designed to function as a nondestructive memory by modifying it so the magnetic state returns to its original position after the read-out solenoid current is terminated. One method which has been employed is to place a small permanent magnet in the twister-solenoid storage area. The magnetic field of the magnet, since it is permanent, returns the twister flux to its original magnetic direction after read-out. The magnets are mounted on a thin aluminum card and placed over each storage area of the twister.

A later development by Bell Telephone Laboratories is a twister using two magnetic tapes, one over the other, and each wound in a spiral wrapping. Since one magnetic tape is placed over the other, the term *piggyback* twister has been applied to this method. One of the magnetic spiral ribbons is used for information storage and the other to sense the stored information. Thus, the system retains the information during read-out. The read-cycle access time is approximately 5 microseconds.

## Laminated-Ferrite Storage

A storage system formed by a laminating process is a development of Radio Corporation of America (RCA). The method permits economical fabrication of a microminiature memory plane, yet one having high storage capabilities. The manufacturing technique for the laminated-ferrite storage produces monolithic ferrite sheets having embedded conductors separated by an insulating ferrite material. Basically, the process starts with a glass substrate upon which conductive strips of metallic paste are formed. A composition of ferrite material with binder is next spread over the substrate and permitted to dry. When the solid sheet thus formed is peeled off the substrate, it contains the conductive strips. Two such sheets are placed one over the other, with another similar sheet (but without conductive strips) between the two acting as a spacer. The outer sheets have the conductive strips at right angles, as shown in Fig. 7-28.

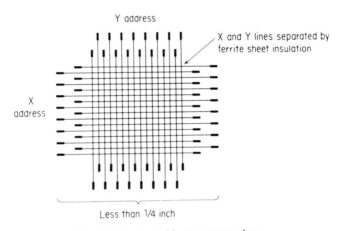

**Fig. 7-28. Laminated-ferrite storage plane.**

The triple-deck stack is laminated, and tiny holes punched at appropriate places for making external contact to the active components within the laminated unit. The laminate thickness is approximately 5 mils (0.005 inch), with conducting spacings of approximately 10 mils. With closer conductor spacings, the bit content can be increased for a given size sheet, or much smaller units can be produced for a given number of bits. Address and sensing procedures are similar to those described earlier for ferrite storage systems. Read-write cycle times are around 100 nanoseconds when driving currents are several hundred milliamperes. With lower driver currents, the read-write time rates are lower.

## Other Storage Systems

There are additional storage systems which have had practical applications, and others which are in the development stage but have shown promise when prototypes have been tested in laboratories. Design engineers are constantly striving for storage systems combining some or all of the following advantages:

   High storage capability
   Rapid write and access time
   Nondestructive characteristics
   Space saving (microminiaturized)
   Economical operation and manufacture
   Minimal temperature and minimal stray field effects

The ease with which a new storage system can be adapted to an existing computer is also a factor, since this contributes to its versatility. Thus, a new memory can be employed to extend the external storage capacity, or it can be added for use as an auxiliary (sometimes termed *scratch-pad*) type of storage to augment the existing storage facilities of an older computer.

## Optoelectronic Storage

By combining optical and electronic sciences, practical computer storage systems can be devised for increasing bit capacity and access time. Since the development of semiconductor devices capable of emitting and sensing light, miniaturization has been achieved in this field.

Optical signals have a wavelength range from approximately 9000 Angstrom units (infrared) to 2000 Angstrom units (ultraviolet). [1 Angstrom unit ($\text{Å}$) = 0.1 millimicron = $10^{-8}$ centimeter.] The optical range is preferable for optoelectronic storage systems to wavelengths above or below the range given. As light frequency is raised, the light photons have increased energy and the energy is easily absorbed by materials, as exemplified by the penetrating power of X rays. Such absorption produces signal attenuation. Toward the lower-frequency infrared regions, heat generation causes signal attenuation and component cooling is necessitated.

Optoelectronic storage devices are capable of storing millions of bits in very small surface-area units, with access times in milliseconds, and with nondestructive read-out characteristics. Since light photons have a neutral electric charge, electrical isolation is achieved easily. Because of the parallel propagation characteristics of light, more closely spaced signal paths are possible without cross interference of one signal with another.

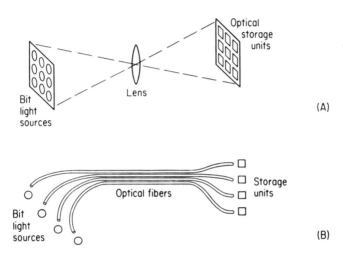

**Fig. 7-29. Photoelectronic storage.**

A basic optoelectronic storage system is illustrated in A of Fig. 7-29. Here, solid-state light sources generate the bit-state light. A lens focuses the light beams on the optical storage plane containing light storage units. Individual optoelectronic detectors are used for sensing whether the storage bit area contains a 1 or a 0. A variety of solid-state light sources are available, including the p-n semi-conductor types manufactured by combining gallium arsenide with gallium phosphide. Some are small enough to permit several hundred to be mounted on a 2-inch square board. Other types include the electroluminescent devices, light-emitting tunnel diodes, and other similar units.

Miniature solid-state sensors of the silicon-junction (p-n) variety are cf two basic types, photovoltaic and photoconductive. The photovoltaic types are transducers, since they convert light energy directly into electric energy and require no bias potential for operation. The photoconductive, on the other hand, require a voltage source, and they alter circuit resistance in proportion to the light striking them.

The optical storage unit in A of Fig. 7-29 may consist of a photographic-emulsion mask which stores bits by transparent and opaque areas. Information is read out by directing light on the entire mask face and employing photosensitive detectors at each storage area. A dark area passes no light and the photodetector produces no signal, representing the 0 state. When light passes through an area, a signal is produced from the photocell to indicate the sensing of a 1 bit.

Conventional photographic emulsions form optoelectronic storage of the nondestructive type with permanent (nonerasable) characteristics. Reversible films, however, are also used. Photochromic film (reversible) can provide a darkened area by light exposure in the ultraviolet region and thus store a 1 representation. When this same area is then exposed to light in the infrared region, the darkened area reverses to its original state to represent the 0 state.

Optical fiber may be used to steer the bit light signals to the storage units as shown in B of Fig. 7-29. Such optical fibers are of plastic with an extremely smooth exterior. When light enters one end, it travels the length of the flexible fiber rod and is emitted at the other end with a minimum of radiation loss. Because of the smooth exterior, light within the fiber is reflected from the inside walls in mirror fashion. Such optical fibers thus permit the directing of light beams along any desired bend, and bundles of such fibers are used for channeling individual light signals. Since the fiber rods at the ends of the bundles can be spread out as desired, crowding of the light-source units can be avoided and circuitous paths employed if necessary.

## Grid-Slot Ferrite

Another form of storage with ferrite consists of using a base plate composed of ferrite material and cutting rows of slots across the plate and also cutting additional rows perpendicualr to the first. The result is the formation of a number of equally spaced rectangular ferrite posts. These give a waffle-iron type of appearance, hence this storage system has been termed a waffle-iron storage system. Read-write and sense wires are threaded between the posts, and operation is similar to the ferrite-core storage discussed earlier.

## Woven-Screen Storage

Woven-screen storage systems contain interlaced magnetically surfaced wires which have the appearance of webbing or conventional wire screens in miniature form. One vertical and one horizontal wire of each sector is used for $X$ and $Y$ address purposes, another wire for inhibit purposes, and one wire for sensing the stored information. Half-set currents at the intersection of two read-write wires magnetize the area to write 1 in a fashion similar to the ferrite-core storage system. Average access time is approximately 10 microseconds.

## Organic Diode Storage

Evaporated organic diodes formed in arrays on flexible substrates are also employed for storage devices. A dye compound, such as the organic semiconductor copper phthalocyanine is used in a vacuum evaporation process. This forms the center layer of a three-layer diode One outer layer becomes the diode anode and the other, the diode cathode. This system has been used by RCA in an *associative* memory system, using 4-inch plastic cards. The diodes make up a matrix system into which information is written in punched-card fashion. A punched hole opens one of the diode anode lines for the storing of the bit information. On read-out, a signal pulse is sent into the desired address-bit lines, and the entire information on the card is read out by the sense signals procured. This storage method permits address searching of an entire batch of stacked cards (without card removal) and also reading out of the required associated information in signal pulse form.

## PROBLEMS

**1.** What is meant by *access time?*

**2.** Define the terms *internal storage* and *external storage.*

**3.** Define the terms *destructive* and *nondestructive read-out.*

**4.** Define the terms *word, address,* and *mode of access.*

**5.** What is meant by *random-access memory?*

**6.** Describe the method by which digital information is stored on magnetic tape.

**7.** In magnetic-tape recording, how is the information starting point located?

**8.** Describe the method by which digital information is stored on magnetic drums.

**9.** How is the information for a particular address on a drum located for read-out purposes?

**10.** Describe how digital information is stored on disks.

**11.** Describe in what manner a ferrite core stores a 0 or 1 representation.

**12.** How is a particular core in a ferrite memory plane located for read-out purposes?

**13.** How may parallel read-write operations be performed with ferrite-core storage?

**14.** What is the primary advantage of the transfluxer over the single-aperture ferrite core?

**15.** Describe how single and multiaperture cores may be used to form logic circuits.

**16.** Draw a five-core, ferrite-ring shift register to show performance of right to left shifting of a binary bit.

**17.** How are thin-film storage elements formed?

**18.** What is meant by the *preferred*, or *easy*, direction of magnetism?

**19.** In what manner does thin-film storage distinguish between a 0-bit representation and a 1-bit state?

**20.** What temperatures are involved in *cryogenics?*

**21.** What effect do cryogenic temperatures have on the resistance of some metals?

**22.** Describe the principles of twister storage.

**23.** Draw a twister storage showing five word solenoids and six digit lines.

**24.** Describe the basic principles of laminated-ferrite storage.

**25.** What qualities should an ideal storage system possess?

**26.** What type of storage is sometimes referred to as a *scratch-pad* memory?

**27.** In optoelectronic storage, why is the photographic spectrum preferable to one with wavelengths above or below this span?

**28.** What are the differences between the photovoltaic and the photo-conductive solid-state light sensors?

**29.** How are optical fibers used in optoelectronic storage devices?

**30.** Describe how a grid-slot ferrite storage device is formed.

# INPUT AND
# OUTPUT DEVICES

**8**

**Introduction.** A digital computer, to perform its required operations properly, must be instructed regarding the sequential steps to be taken. Also, the data to be processed must be inserted in a form compatible with the computer's binary code system. After the acquisition phase has been completed and the computer has obtained the desired end result by the various sorting, classifying, or computing procedures, some means must be provided for producing this information in either visual display or printed form. Thus, various input and output devices must be used for information exchange between the operating personnel and the computer. Computers used for data processing such as inventory control, payroll, accounting, and other such activities usually require numerous input and output devices. Computers used for computations in scientific problem solving need relatively fewer input-output units.

Direct or indirect methods can be used for input-output communication with the computer. For direct input, the instructions and data to be processed can be applied with an electric typewriter or push-button controls. Since this is a slow procedure compared with the computer's inherently rapid processes, such piecemeal data insertion is only used on special occasions when it is necessary to correct program errors (debugging) or to test programs. Other direct methods of operational personnel and computer communication include the use of the various switches and push-buttons on the control panel of the computer console. With these, direct manual control is possible for starting and stopping the computer, transferring data, clearing registers, overriding errors, and performing other operations. Indirect input-output methods include the use of paper tape, magnetic tape, magnetic drums, punched cards, printers, alphanumeric display tubes, and similar devices.

The selection of a particular input-output medium depends on the factors of cost, speed, utility, and desired flexibility. Punched cards represent the earliest form of data storage and are, with punched paper tape, the least costly input item. Punched cards are easily prepared and can store up to 80 character columns of information. Access time is slow compared with other input devices, and special processing equipment is required. Stored information is permanent and visible and follows a fixed format that differs from the computer language.

Paper tape is punched in machine-language form and stored data length is not limited to the 80 columns in cards. Access time is more rapid than for cards (though exceeded by that for magnetic tape). Processing equipment generally is less costly than that required for punched cards.

Magnetic tape and its associated devices are more costly than paper tape and punched cards. Access time for magnetic tape is, however, far superior to that for paper tape or punched cards. Thus, while magnetic tape provides an excellent auxiliary storage system for the primary computer storage, cards and paper tape are more widely used for input systems because of their lower cost.

## Input-Output Terminology

In addition to *direct* and *indirect* input-output designations, the terms *on line* and *off line* are also used. The on-line equipment channels coded data directly into or out of the computer. Such devices, according to instructions previously programmed, are controlled by the gate and switching systems of the computer. The off-line (also called *peripheral*) units are used by the operating personnel to write or punch data manually for subsequent processing or storage by the computer. A block diagram of the various on-line and off-line devices is shown in Fig. 8-1. The individual units are discussed more fully later in this chapter.

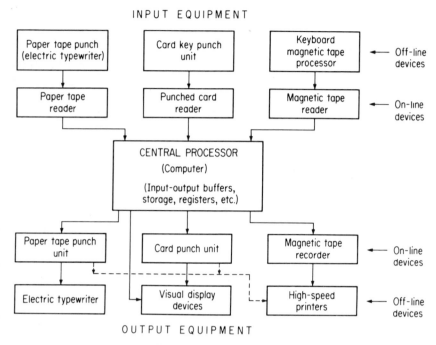

INPUT EQUIPMENT

OUTPUT EQUIPMENT

**Fig. 8-1.** Input-output system.

*Real-time* operation of a computer is that in which the computer solves problems as rapidly as they occur so that the calculated results can be employed immediately to correct and guide the operation being sensed.

Analog to digital conversion is one example (see Chapter 5, Gray Code). Industrial machine control by computers is another example, where the sensing of variables (error signals) causes the computer to calculate (from the information received) the corrective signals which must be generated. Missile and satellite tracking involves the continuous processing of information by the computer for operation in a real-time mode.

The *buffers* referred to in Fig. 8-1 are intermediate systems between the on-line equipment and the central processor (computer) for data-synchronization purposes at input and output. Thus, the input buffers link the slow-speed mechanical devices to the high-speed computer circuitry and synchronize the data signals with the internal computer timing. Such buffers usually contain temporary-storage shift registers for converting data transfer time. Thus, the shift register can

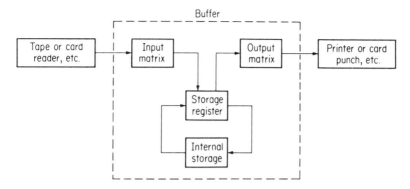

**Fig. 8-2.** Buffer sections.

accept data in serial form and read them out in high-speed parallel form. The process is reversed in the output buffers. The basic block diagram of a typical buffer is shown in Fig. 8-2.

*Encoders and decoders* are diode matrix systems for conversion of base 10 data to binary or of binary to base 10. These are explained in greater detail later. Converters are devices for converting one type of stored information to another, such as translating the data on punched cards to magnetic tape. Converters are also available to change magnetic-tape data to card punch or tape punch information or to convert paper tape to punched cards, etc.

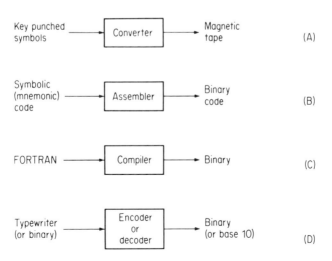

**Fig. 8-3.** Conversion devices.

As shown in Fig. 8-3, two other devices are also encountered in digital computer systems: assemblers and compilers. As explained in the next chapter, assemblers accept *mnemonic* instructional codes such as ADD (for addition), LDA (load accumulator), SUB, MUL, etc., and convert them to the binary machine language. Thus, an assembler is an automatic coding device that translates a symbolic code instruction into one recognizable and acceptable to the computer. The compiler is a more complex device than the assembler and accepts a problem or mathematical expression in basic form and translates it into a group of machine-coded instructions. Such program languages include FORTRAN, ALGOL, and COBOL. These terms are *acronyms*, since they are made up of initial letters or syllables of the consecutive words describing the system: FORTRAN (*FOR*mula *TRAN*slator), ALGOL (*ALG*ebraic-*O*riented *L*anguage), and COBOL (*CO*mmon *B*usiness-*O*riented *L*anguage).

Essentially, the assemblers and compilers are special computer *programs* which are unified with read and write units to perform the type of translation functions just described.

*Alphanumeric*, as the term implies, refers to a combination of alphabetic and numeric representations. Though the internal language of a computer is numeric, using binary bits, groups of such bits are selected in specific order to identify an alphabetic character. This process is applied to punched cards, paper tape, typewriter output, etc., as discussed later in this chapter. For the punched cards an added hole is punched to identify an alphabetic character represented by a number. Thus, a card has alphanumeric characteristics and can accommodate both numbers and letters.

Paper tape, punched by a special machine having a standard typewriter keyboard, uses the binary notation 001 for 1, 010 for 2, etc. For alphabetic representations, however, an additional binary number is placed to the left to identify the alphabetical character. Initially, A is given the binary 001 representation, B the binary 010, C the binary 011, etc., in consecutive order. With the added numbers, A becomes 1100 001, B is 1100 010, C is 1110 011, etc. The complete coding is shown later in Fig. 8-6.

Since identifying binary numbers (or card punching) are used for the alphabetical characters, they can be intermixed with number representations. Card readers and encoders permit storage of alphanumeric data and upon information retrieval the coded characters are decoded by matrix circuitry and printed, typed out, or displayed, in proper form.

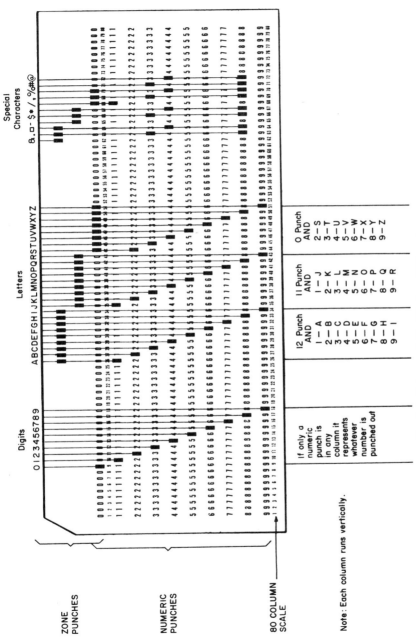

Fig. 8-4. Alphanumeric identification of IBM card.

215

## Punched Cards

Information is stored on a card by punching holes in certain parts of the card which correspond to the data bit which is to be recorded. The cards are punched by inserting them into appropriate key-punch machines and depressing the necessary keys. A representative card, shown in Fig. 8-4, measures $3\frac{1}{4}$ by $7\frac{3}{8}$ inches. The rectangular holes are punched according to the alphanumerical code shown. This is a standard IBM card and code, though sometimes it is referred to as the Hollerith card, so named after Herman Hollerith, who adapted the original Babbage punched-card concept in 1880 while an employee of the U.S. Census Bureau.

As shown in Fig. 8-4, there are 12 holes (bits) that can be punched in the vertical plane, 10 in the 0 to 9 positions, and two additional positions above the 0 row. The upper two rows are designated as 11 and 12, which in combination with the 0 row are referred to as *zones*. There are 80 columns horizontally, setting the limit of the number of bits which can be punched on one card. Numbers are punched in whatever sequence necessary, without any other identifying punch. Alphabetic characters, however, are accompanied by a zone punch as well as a numeric punch. For the special characters shown (& . □ - $ * / , % # @), three punches are necessary. In some data-processing applications the cards are printed with vertical dividing lines. The areas thus formed are referred to as *fields*, each of which holds a specific portion of the information punched (name, address, etc.).

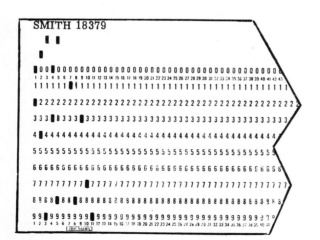

Fig. 8-5. Sample name and number punching.

An illustration of alphanumeric punching of a name and identifying number is shown in Fig. 8-5. For the first letter of the name, the S is identified by a 0 punch and a 2 punch, as shown. The letter M requires an 11-zone punch as well as a 4 punch, while the letter I is identified by a 12-zone punch and a 9 punch, etc. As mentioned, the card can be partitioned by vertical line separations, one holding the full name, another the social security number, address, and other information.

The punched card reader senses the information contained on a card by either using wire feeler brushes which make electrical contact through the holes or by photocells which are activated by light passing through the holes. The sensing procedures thus parallel the method used for the encoder disk described in Chapter 5 and illustrated in Fig. 5-2. Reading speeds up to 2000 cards per minute are possible with some card readers. The key-punching operation is, of necessity, slower, and in manual operations the number of cards punched in a given time depends on the proficiency of the operator. Key punching of cards under the control of the central processor may attain speeds of 250 cards per minute.

Corner cuts on punched cards may be at the upper right or upper left, depending on the card identity. Thus, the cut for a particular card type will permit proper card stacking and assurance that all in the stack are facing the proper direction. Colored cards or stripes may also be used to identify certain stored information categories.


## Paper Tape

Paper tape, like cards, may be prepared manually with electric typewriters equipped for the process, or they may be punched under the control of the central processor. Also, as with the paper cards, reading may be by wire feelers making electric contact through the perforations or by photocell sensing of light through the apertures of the tape. Often the punch and read functions are performed by a single compact machine. Reading speeds may be over 1500 bits per second, and write speeds, to over 100 bits per second.

The recommended standard paper-tape coding is shown in Fig. 8-6. Here, eight channels are employed, using a binary-coded process, with the absence of a hole representing 0 and a punched hole indicating 1. Each alphabetical or numerical character contains an

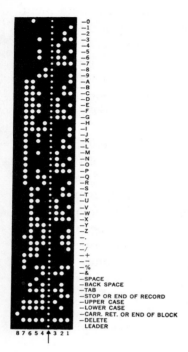

**Fig. 8-6. Standard eight-channel paper tape code.**

odd number of 1 bits, hence the number of digits for each character (code group) has a self-contained odd-parity bit check. Consequently, any even-digit read-out, such as 00101 011, would indicate an error. The sprocket holes are the smaller holes running lengthwise through the tape, between the third bit channel from the right and the fourth bit channel, marked by the arrow at the bottom of the tape illustration in Fig. 8-6. Such a tape can be reinserted into the electric typewriter to retype the information contained on it, since carriage return, upper and lower case, etc., are coded on the tape during the initial typing.

The paper tapes are stored in reels in similar fashion to magnetic tape. Unlike magnetic tape, however, paper tapes cannot be erased and reused. If necessary, however, tape splices can be made and sections deleted or added.

## Electric Typewriter

As shown in Fig. 8-1, electric typewriters are used as off-line equipment for paper tape preparation manually. Such electric typewriters have been modified and auxiliary equipment (tape perforators and readers) added for use as both input and output units in a computer. On-line operation could be performed, though the comparatively slow write process compared with the computer's internal speed of operation limits such use, as mentioned in the Introduction to this chapter. For on-line operation, encoder matrix systems are employed to produce a binary output in parallel form, as shown in Fig. 8-7. The diode-matrix binary encoder shown has a pulse source which is triggered to produce a single pulse output such as is procured from a single-shot multivibrator (see Chapter 1). If, for instance, the 5 key is depressed, the pulse generated would pass through the diodes and enter the first

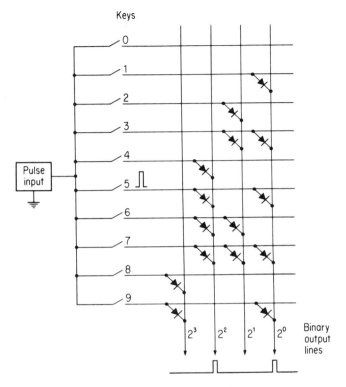

**Fig. 8-7.** Diode matrix binary encoder.

and third vertical lines from the right, as shown, producing the parallel binary output number 0101. Similarly, a pulse entering any of the other horizontal lines would produce a binary output corresponding to the base-10 digit selected. Since the diodes conduct in a single direction only, they block the signals from entering other number lines. Thus, the polarity of the signal entering any vertical line is such that it encounters an open circuit for any of the other diodes connected to the particular line.

An electric typewriter which has been widely used in data processing and as an off-line input-output device for computers is the Flexowriter shown in Fig. 8-8. During manual typing of a document (on a standard typewriter keyboard), it can punch a tape or edge-punch cards to store the data being typed. Standard 1-inch tape is used, and the punching code is an eight-unit type (see Fig. 8-6). The prepared tape may be used for computer input and output, for tape-

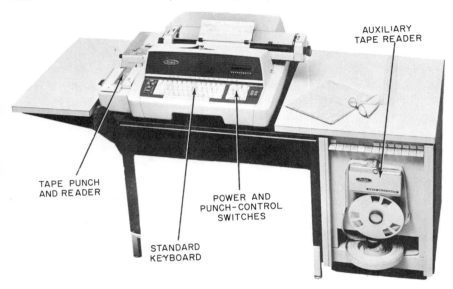

AUXILIARY
TAPE READER

TAPE PUNCH
AND READER

POWER AND
PUNCH-CONTROL
SWITCHES

STANDARD
KEYBOARD

**Fig. 8-8.** Flexowriter model 2201 with Selectadata reader. (Courtesy, Friden, Inc.)

to-card conversion, for conversion to other code structures if desired, and for similar applications. Since the code is of an odd-parity type, the Flexowriter circuitry is so designed that only valid codes are punched (1, 3, 5, or 7 holes in a group). Thus, if some malfunction occurs and the machine attempts to punch an even-digit code, the keyboard will lock and all machine operations are stopped. This error detection prevents the accidental manual operation of more than one key lever at any time. Hence, punchings cannot be overlapped. After lock, normal operation is restored by a manual control switch.

Standard equipment is a reader and punch for tape only. An edge-punched card reader and/or punch can be installed in place of the standard unit. Edge-punched cards are encoded along one or two edges of a standard-size card with the same eight-channel code used for paper tape. An auxiliary unit, the Model 2216 card-punch control, permits the linkage of the machine with a Hollerith-coded key punch to permit such punched cards to be produced.

The Model 2201 Flexowriter shown in Fig. 8-8 has power- and punch-control switches positioned to the right of the manual keyboard and additional control keys at the left. The last control tape feed, the starting and stopping of tape or card reading, and the punch-print or -nonprint function. The switches to the right turn power on and off, control auxiliary equipment, cause the read process to stop automatically after the code is read, and other similar machine functions. In Fig. 8-8 the unit at the lower right is the Selectadata reader, which is an auxiliary tape-reading unit containing its own unwinder and take-up reel. This unit has the ability to search through a tape at the rate of 50 codes per second and select certain pre-specified data. (Reading speed of the Model 2201 is 680 codes per minute, and automatic typing is at a rate in excess of 135 five-letter words per minute.)

## *Character-Recognition Devices*

In computer-related data-processing for banks, savings and loan institutions, and other such organizations, automatic character-reading devices are extensively employed to automate accounting and computing procedures. Characters are printed with an ink containing ferromagnetic materials and thus lend themselves to magnetic-ink character recognition (MICR). The magnetic base material is of the iron-oxide type used in magnetic tapes. The characters have a standard configuration which makes them recognizable to humans and at the same time provides significant difference in the signals produced from read heads for interpretation by electronic circuitry. The character shapes are illustrated in Fig. 8-9.

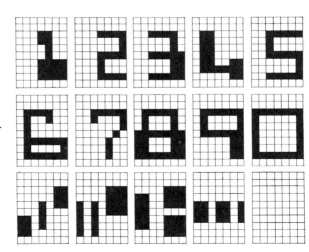

**Fig. 8-9.** Magnetic ink characters.

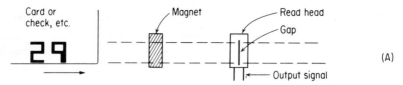

**Fig. 8-10. Magnetic ink character recognition (MICR).**

The basic read operation is shown in A of Fig. 8-10. The check or card is held by the reading equipment and slid past a permanent magnet which magnetically energizes the ferromagnetic materials in the imprinted characters. The check then passes over a reading head that has a read gap slightly higher than the magnetized characters. As a character passes the read head, signals are produced at the output which are proportional to the magnetic density variations in the character. The output signals are fed to matrix decoding and logic circuits which interpret the numerical value or representation of the character. For each character, the magnetic density for a given area depends on the number of horizontal or vertical magnetized imprints. The 0 character in B, for instance, has one vertical (magnetized) area passing over the head initially. As the magnetized area approaches the gap, a positive polarity signal will be produced, and as the area leaves the gap another signal of opposite polarity is developed. For the central portion of the number there is no *change* in magnetic intensity, and signal amplitude drops to a steady-state level. For the vertical area at the end of the character, another positive to negative signal polarity change occurs, producing the waveform shown. Other characters produce signals which differ in a manner dependent on the character shape, as shown for the 6 in B. The decoding networks are designed to recognize the signal configurations and register the number value applying to a particular character.

Instead of the single-gap head shown in A of Fig. 8-10, one IBM system uses a multigap head capable of sensing 30 separate, scanned areas. The output signals are applied to a flip-flop matrix system. As individual signals reach various flip-flop stages they are triggered to the 1 state, while those receiving no signals remain in the 0 state. The representative number is thus temporarily stored and may be decoded as required.

## Optical Methods

Checks, credit cards, and other such items are also identified by optical scanner devices. These units can scan ordinary printing and writing by scanners, sense the information by photocells, and encode the electrical signal into the representative characters. Several basic methods for optical scanning have been developed and are already widely used. Other processes are under experimental development and show promise for simplifying the operation and increasing reading speeds.

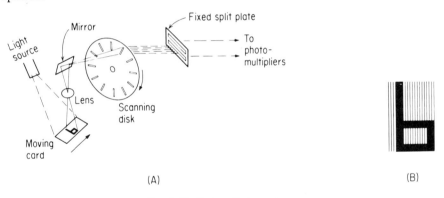

(A)                                        (B)

**Fig. 8-11.** Basic optical scanning.

One basic system, shown in Fig. 8-11, uses a scanning disk with a number of slits around the edge. The card or document to be read is placed in the scanning machine and moved to the reading position. The illuminated card or document is scanned horizontally as it passes under the sensing area. Images are focused on the revolving disk by the lens-mirror system, and, here, the rotating slits in the disk and the fixed-slit plate produce vertical scanning. Two beams are produced which are directed to two photomultiplier tubes for increasing the image signal strength. Thus, the result is a sectional scanning process as shown in B for the number 6.

The signal waveforms which are produced are channeled to logic circuits designed to sense the over-all character shape by determining which significant areas produce signal outputs. Matrix and matching circuits verify the character identification and produce an output indicating the number scanned. This basic method has been widely used by the Farrington Manufacturing Company in their reading machines.

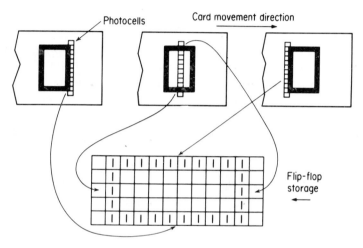

**Fig. 8-12.** Photocell-storage matrix character recognition.

Another optical scanning method is that employed by Rabinow Electronics, Incorporated. The basic system is illustrated in Fig. 8-12 and consists of a vertical row of 12 photocells. As the illuminated document moves across the scanning area, timing circuits select output signals from the row of photocells for five separate horizontal areas of the character. The output signals from the photocells are sent to a flip-flop type of storage register containing 60 stages, as shown.

Three positions of the number 0 are shown in Fig. 8-12 for reference. As the horizontal section of the rectangular 0 reaches the row of photocells, each activated cell develops a signal which is fed to the bottom row of flip-flop stages shown. Successive samplings involve only two of the photocells shown for the center position, and these signals cause the flip-flop stages at the right and left to be triggered to the 1 state. The final scan shown at the upper right of Fig. 8-12 again involves 10 photocells, as was the case in the first scan; hence this final scan sets the upper flip-flop stages into the 1 state. Now, all the

1-state flip-flop stages in this register cause the group to assume a numerical 0 representation.

The output lines of flip-flop circuits are connected to matrix decoding systems for character identification. As in most optical scanning systems, every segment of a character need not be scanned perfectly for proper recognition. In Fig. 8-12, for instance, if one or two stages are incorrectly set, proper character recognition will still be the end result.

Instead of the stationary light source shown in Fig. 8-11, a moving light, focused to a pinpoint, can scan the document to be read. In such an instance the document can be stationary. The Philco-Ford Corporation uses such a system. The scanning tube is of the cathode-ray type operating in what is termed the *flying-spot scanner* principle. A small cathode-ray tube emits a high-intensity light when the internal electron beam strikes the phosphur faceplate. Thus, a brilliant spot is obtained and focused on the material to be read. The spot is made to move across the screen repeatedly, with each rescan moved downward slightly until the entire reading area has been covered. High-speed scanning is possible with this method (up to 2000 characters per second), in a $7\frac{1}{2}$- by 13-inch area. The information read is translated into computer language and can be put into storage, displayed, or processed as required.

The Farrington Manufacturing Company employs an oscillating mirror for scan movement in one of their optical reading devices. A stationary light source is used, and a document can be scanned by the oscillating light beam reflected by the vibrating mirror.

## Decoder Matrix

Because flip-flop registers store numbers in binary form, some means must be employed for converting the binary representation to a base-10 equivalent for read-out using visual display tubes, printers, typewriters, card and tape punch, etc. The diode-matrix read-out decoder shown in Fig. 8-13 serves this purpose by providing a means for sensing the base-10 equivalent of the binary number stored in the flip-flop stages. Note that, for the first flip-flop stage at the right, the diodes are connected alternately between the vertical and horizontal lines. For the second stage, however, the diodes are connected in pairs. For the third stage, they are in groups of four, while, for the fourth stage

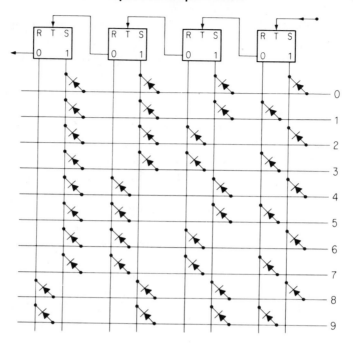

**Fig. 8-13.** Diode matrix read-out system (decoder).

they are in groups of eight. Thus, the base-2 place value of 8-4-2-1 is in evidence by the diode matrix arrangement.

As shown, the vertical lines are connected to the 0 and 1 output terminals of the flip-flop stages. For purposes of analysis, assume each stage is in the 0 state and that a negative polarity exists at each 0-output line and a positive polarity is present at each 1-output line. Thus, since all the diodes in the *horizontal* (zero-output) line directly below the flip-flop stages are connected to positive terminals, no diode on this line will conduct because of the reverse-bias connection. Thus, a count detection of zero output prevails for the matrix. During the time the four stages are all in a 0 state, there will always be one or more diodes connected to the negative (0-output) terminal of one of the flip-flop stages in *every horizontal line except the zero line.*

This can be more clearly understood if we assume the horizontal matrix output lines are connected to *inhibiting* gates as shown in A of Fig. 8-14. For the horizontal line marked 0 no diode conducts, hence *no inhibiting function exists.* Consequently, an output is produced from this upper *inhibitor* circuit for actuating a print-out or visual indicator

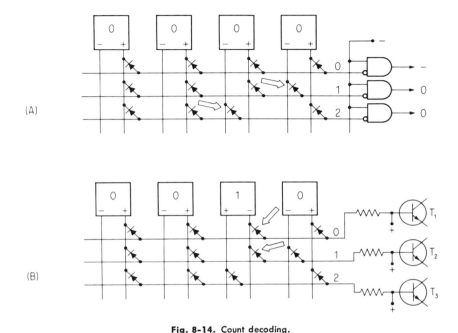

**Fig. 8-14. Count decoding.**

device. Note, however, that in succeeding horizontal lines below the 0 line, some diodes conduct and hence initiate an inhibiting action which prevents an output signal from appearing from the *inhibiting* gates. (The conducting diodes are referenced by the arrows pointing toward them.)

In practical circuitry, transistor drivers are used for applying signals to indicating devices, as shown in B. Here, assume the transistors are properly biased and normally conduct. For the stages shown in B, the count of 2 is stored, which produces signal polarities from the second-place flip-flop which are opposite to the signal polarities prevailing at the other three flip-flop stages. Now, conducting diodes will be found in both the 0 and 1 lines, as shown by the arrows. In the horizontal line marked 2, however, there is no diode conduction, hence the transistor base emitter potentials are unaffected and conduction continues. In the 0 and 1 lines, however, the diodes conduct and apply potentials to the transistor base circuits to cut off these transistors. Hence, for any number appearing in the decade counter, only one output transistor will conduct to initiate an indicating device for that particular number.

Special-purpose tubes are available which dispense with diode-transistor decoder networks by performing their functions by internal beam-switching procedures. A typical tube of this type is shown in Fig. 8-15, which is the Beam-X Switch tube of the Burroughs Corp. As shown in Fig. 8-16, the tube accepts binary-coded decimal data from a flip-flop counter and converts them to signals of decimal form available from 10 output lines. In the tube's internal decoding process, an electron beam is formed from the cathode to any digit-count position and switched sequentially to produce an output current for operation of indicator tubes or a printer. A cascade output pulse is also available for driving succeeding decade units when such tubes are used for decade counting. Such tubes are also available to handle the Gray code or others. Decoding time for the tube is 10 microseconds.

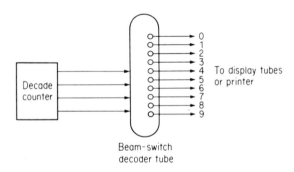

**Fig. 8-16.** Beam-switch decoding.

**Fig. 8-15.** Burroughs Corporation Beam-X Switch tube.

## Visual Read-out Devices

There are a number of devices which can be used for visual read-out from a digital computer. Some contain groups of neon bulbs which are connected to circuitry that selects only certain bulbs when a specific number is to be displayed. Thus, the bulbs selected will glow and form the number shape to indicate the character. Other devices include gas-filled tubes with cathodes shaped in the form of numbers or letters, cathode-ray tubes for large-scale display, units with perforated plates so placed that numbers or letters can be formed by selecting light emission through appropriate slots, and indicators using incandescent bulbs illuminating alphanumeric display surfaces.

Many display devices consist of small units which are placed side-by-side in in-line fashion for obtaining the maximum numerical value desired. One such unit, the Numerik Indicator manufactured by General Radio Company, is shown in Fig. 8-17. The type IND-0300 has a window size of $\frac{3}{4}$ by $\frac{15}{16}$ inch, with unit dimensions of 1 inch wide, 2 inches high, and $2\frac{1}{2}$ inches deep, including terminals.

For the unit shown, 10 incandescent bulbs are used, each of which introduces its light at one end of a thin acrylic-plastic strip. When a

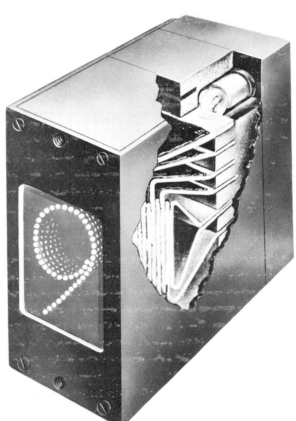

**Fig. 8-17.** GR numeric indicator. Courtesy, General Radio Co.

particular bulb is energized to display a number, its light is conducted by the plastic strip to the display surface consisting of sheets of plastic dimpled with numerals. The result is a bright display of closely spaced dots in the form of the numeral or symbol being read out.

**Fig. 8-18.** Nixie tubes. Courtesy, Burroughs Corp.

Gas-tube display devices of varying sizes are shown in Fig. 8-18. These glow tubes, manufactured by the Burroughs Corporation, are called Nixies and are available in either numeric or alphanumeric con-

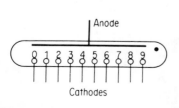

**Fig. 8-19.** Nixie tube symbol.

figurations. These cold-cathode tubes have individual cathodes shaped in the form of numbers or letters of the alphabet. Figure 8-19 shows the numeric type. When a negative voltage is applied to a selected cathode, the potential difference between the negative cathode and the common anode causes gas ionization around the selected cathode. In consequence the visible glow during ionization around the cathode forms the desired number. Display size varies with tubes, some producing a character height of less than $\frac{1}{2}$ inch, with others providing a 2-inch display.

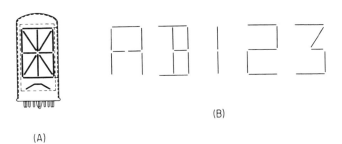

(B)

(A)

**Fig. 8-20. Alphanumeric Nixie.**

Another type of read-out indicator tube is the Alpha-Numeric Nixie shown in Fig. 8-20. The tube consists of a number of straight-line cathode segments, as shown in A, mounted in a rectangular-shaped glass envelope. A character is formed when negative potentials are applied to the cathode structures required to form the number or letter. The negative cathode with respect to the positive anode establishes a potential difference and causes ionization. The result is a red neon glow easily visible. The manner in which this tube shapes letters and numbers is shown in B of Fig. 8-20 where *A*, *B*, 1, 2, and 3 are shown. Note that only the appropriate cathodes glow that are necessary to produce the formation desired.

**Fig. 8-21.** Burroughs Corp. Pixie tube.

**Fig. 8-22.** Pixie display of independent bits.

The Burroughs Corporation's Pixie tube, shown in Fig. 8-21, contains 10 glow position cathodes spaced 36° apart. Each cathode becomes visible through perforations which are numerically shaped. These perforations are formed in a plate positioned above the cathode structures and serve to provide a visible numeric indication when potentials exist between particular cathodes and the anode structure. This tube is useful for counting displays or for indicating the status of computer equipment. It has the ability to display one number or groups of numbers simultaneously, as shown in Fig. 8-22. The tube shown in Fig. 8-21 is less than an inch in diameter.

**Fig. 8-23.** Amperex biquinary decade counter and display tube.

Package units and modules are often used which have counter or decoding circuits matched to indicating tubes. A typical example shown in Fig. 8-23 is the Amperex Electronic Corporation's biquinary-decade counter BQDC-100. This counter uses a combination of

binary and quinary circuits and requires no decoding matrix for direct
digital read-out display on the indicator tube. A carry signal is generated by this unit when triggered from 9 to 0 for driving a succeeding
counter of this type. A conversion matrix and Bi-Qui Driver DP101
by the same company is shown in Fig. 8-24. This has a conversion
matrix for decoding binary-coded decimal codes and includes a driver
for the biquinary indicator tube shown. Error-detection is built in
because in any failure, two numerals within the single tube will be
visible simultaneously. (See Chapter 5 for reference to the biquinary
code.)

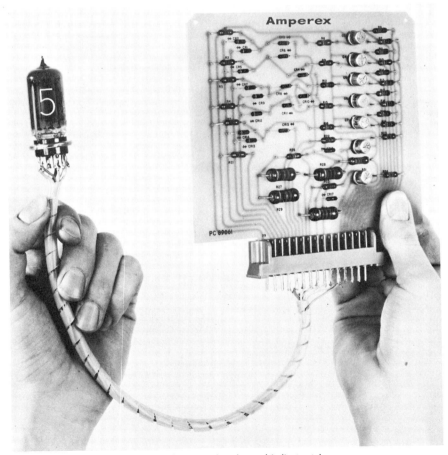

**Fig. 8-24.** Amperex decoder and indicator tube.

**Fig. 8-25.** Raytheon DIDS-500 display system.

Several companies manufacture large-screen display devices capable of alphanumeric representation of multiline characters. One such device is the Digital Information Display System, DIDS-500, of the Raytheon Company. The screen and control console are shown in Fig. 8-25. This unit is housed in a cabinet $4\frac{1}{2}$ feet high, 3 feet wide, and 2 feet deep. As shown, a standard typewriter keyboard is provided so the operator can prepare permanent typed records of data and transfer it into or out of storage. This unit is adaptable for linkage with a digital computer and is capable of translating digitized binary data from the computer's storage onto the 16-inch display screen for immediate visual inspection.

The DIDS-500 also permits split-screen display of information, such as using part of the screen for existing data and another portion for new entries. It has a buffer core storage of 4096 nine-bit words. The screen can display 34 lines of 80 characters per line. As shown in Fig. 8-25, various status indicators are present on the front panel as well as program controls for initiating various programs and subroutines stored in the computer.

Display cabinets with storage capabilities and some logic-circuit characteristics are well suited as remote consoles in computer *time-sharing* systems. This subject is discussed in Chapter 10.

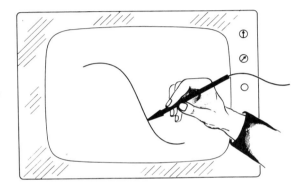

**Fig. 8-26.** Data alteration with light pen.

With a specially designed computer-oriented display screen it is possible to alter the displayed data with a *light pen*, as shown in Fig. 8-26. When this pen is brought near the faceplate of the display screen, the emitted light is capable of adding or modifying the represented data. The internal scanning by the electron beam of the display tube senses the changes made by the light pen, and the new data is assimilated by the computer storage. Alphanumeric changes can be made as well as alterations in graphic displays. With this type of screen a sketch or graph can be placed on the display surface for assimilation by the computer. With proper programming, the computer can reshape the drawings into standard graphic representations if desired. Deletions or additions, if made, will be used by the computer to calculate end results (areas, volumes, stresses and strains, etc.).

## Printers

Printers for digital computers are housed in desk-size consoles and are capable of complete alphanumerical printing on continuous paper feed. In addition, standard characters such as $, #, %, &, etc., are present for use as required. Some printers have a line capacity in excess of 125 characters and are capable of printing over 500 lines per minute in single or double spacing. Thus, large sheets can be printed in only a few seconds.

The basic operating principles of two types are illustrated in Fig. 8-27. In A is shown a metal print cylinder that contains the alphanumerical and special characters. Often a single line will have a triple content of the full characters, that is, three alphabets, three 0 to 9 sections, plus special characters. Circumferentially, the triple content is repeated in the form shown in the figure.

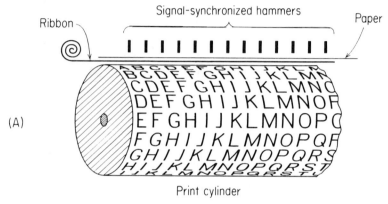

(A)

Print cylinder

**Fig. 8-27. High-speed printer principles.**

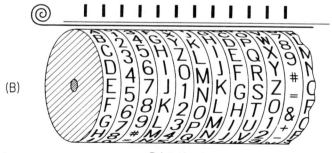

(B)

Print wheels

Hammers are spaced above the paper and ribbon areas, with each hammer placed directly in position over one character segment of the print cylinder. The cylinder is rotated at high speeds, and the hammers are actuated by synchronization with the output signals from the computer. Thus, when a particular hammer mechanism receives the appropriate signal, it presses down with a rapid motion that forces the ink-impregnated ribbon over the paper and thus prints the selected character. The synchronization is such that the hammer is actuated only when directly over the letter to be printed. Since any particular hammer has a selection of the complete set alphanumeric characters and because the characters are repeated around the cylinder circumference, only a fractional-second of delay is encountered before the printing occurs.

Another type, also using the hammer principle, is shown in B of Fig. 8-27. Here, however, individual wheels are used, and as many as 120 may be placed side by side as shown. Each wheel contains all the alphanumeric characters plus a blank space. The individual wheel positions are synchronized with the computer-storage bit identification If, for instance, an A is to be printed at the extreme left on the paper, the first wheel would be positioned to place an A under the ribbon-hammer-paper area and the hammer blow would print the character.

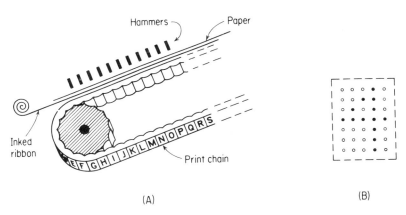

(A)                                            (B)

**Fig. 8-28. Chain and styli printing.**

In A of Fig. 8-28 is shown a chain type of printer which has been widely used by IBM. Here, five chain sections are linked together, each containing the complete set of alphanumeric characters, plus special notations. Electromechanical synchronization is used to position the required character under the hammer for printing the character at the particular place on the line.

In B is shown a character-printing section which uses multistyli wire segments arranged in five-unit by seven-unit rows in matrix fashion. To form a character, certain wires in the matrix are pushed down against the paper and ink ribbon to form a dotted outline of the character. Individual wire selection is under the control of an electro-mechanical network which is guided by the code representation of the character to be printed.

The wire-matrix printing system is also employed in other types of printers. One type operates on electrostatic principles (Burroughs' S-203 Printer) in which the selected wire styli have a high voltage applied to them which causes an arcing between the wire pins and adjacent metal bars. Special plastic-coated paper is used, and the electrostatic arc fields in the wire matrix transfer to the paper, setting up a pattern of the character to be printed. The paper is then advanced to an ink chamber where the charged areas of the paper attract the powdered ink and thus form the printed character. The paper then passes over a heat roller to fix the print and prevent smudging.

Another use of the wire matrix is in the thermal printing process. Here, signals from the computer are used to heat the selected styli which form the character to be printed. The hot styli then darken appropriate portions of heat-sensitive paper to form the character.

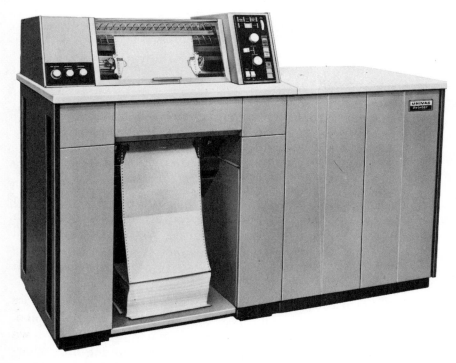

**Fig. 8-29.** UNIVAC III high-speed printer. Courtesy, UNIVAC division of Sperry-Rand Corp.

A typical high-speed printer is shown in Fig. 8-29. This is the UNIVAC III unit (UNIVAC Division of Sperry-Rand Corporation) which is capable of printing up to 55,000 lines per hour. One line of print utilizes 128 characters. As shown at the lower left, folded perforated paper is used which is fed upwards to the printing mechanism. The edge perforations are engaged by sprockets for continuous feeding of the paper.

As mentioned earlier, the electric typewriter used for input is also used as an output printer. Under the control of the computer, it can type out information at a rate dependent on its mechanical speed.

A complete digital computer, with peripheral input and output equipment is shown in Fig. 8-30. This is the IBM Computing System, which consists of the central processor, the printer, paper-tape reader and punch, card reader and punch, and a plotter.

**Fig. 8-30. IBM 1130 computing system.**

As shown in Fig. 8-30 the stand at the extreme left holds the plotter on the top shelf and the paper-tape reader and paper-tape punch on the lower shelf. The reader processes eight-channel punched paper tape at the rate of 14.8 characters per second. The punch also operates at the same speed. The second unit from the left is the card reader and punch console. Model 7 reads 400 cards per minute and punches 160 columns per second.

Next is shown the IBM 1131 Processor, Model 1. This computer is designed for use in engineering and research laboratories and for commercial business operations. It has three standard index registers and ten basic computer registers for arithmetic operations and control of logical functions. A SELECTRIC typewriter provides console output at an automatic rate of 15.5 characters per second.

The 1132 printer is shown at the right. This provides for high-speed, on-line printing at a rate up to 80 alphanumeric or 110 numeric lines per minute. It uses 48 character-set wheels and 120 print-line positions horizontally spaced 10 characters per inch. The printer operates under stored program control.

## PROBLEMS

1. What are the factors which determine whether punched cards, paper tape, or magnetic tape shall be used as input devices to a computer?

2. Define the terms *on-line* and *off-line* devices.

3. What is meant by the term *real time?*

4. What are buffers used for between input and the central processor?

5. What functions are performed by encoders and decoders?

6. Explain how alphanumeric information is recorded on punched cards.

7. What method is employed for error detection in punched paper tape?

8. Reproduce the encoder shown in Fig. 8-7, and indicate the diodes involved for a read-out of the binary number 0110.

9. What is meant by MICR, and what is the process involved?

10. Describe the basic principles of one type of optical scanning.

11. Reproduce the encoder matrix shown in Fig. 8-13, and encircle all diodes which are in the conducting state at the time number 7 is being read out.

12. Briefly explain the function of a Nixie tube.

13. Briefly explain the function of a Pixie tube.

14. For the indicator tube shown in Fig. 8-20, show the manner in which this tube would display the letters K, M, X, and W as well as the numbers 4, 5, and 9 by drawing straight-line segments for the shape to be indicated.

15. Explain the basic operation of printers that use rotating cylinders.

# PROGRAMMING
# FUNDAMENTALS

**9**

**Introduction.** When a simple problem such as $8 + 4$ is to be added on an ordinary desk adding machine, the 8 key is depressed, followed by the $+$ key. Now, the number 8 has been literally stored in the machine. Next, the 4 key is pushed, again followed by the $+$ key, and now the machine holds the 8 and 4, awaiting further commands. If the *total* key is now pushed down, the machine performs the necessary addition and displays or prints out the answer. The digital computer, even though much more versatile in its ability to store vast data, solve complex problems, and perform decision-type operations, must also first be fed the data to be processed as well as the sequential instructions for the procedures involved. Also the computer must be told *where* to procure the information to be processed, so it can seek out the data word from the storage address designated at the time required. The complete instructions and appropriate data addresses form what is known as a *program*. Thus, a program tells the machine *what* to do, *how* to do it, and *where* to find the data to be acted on during execution of the program.

Effective digital computer programming necessitates the preparation of an orderly sequence of steps adapted to the computer's capabilities of data manipulation, storage capacity, and functional design. Some programs may be short, others quite lengthy, but all follow the general format dictated by the characteristics of the computer for which they are written.

**241**

## Program Types

The philosophy of programming is the same for all computers, but instruction flexibility, codes, and related matters differ to some extent for the various computers. Also, the program structure is, of necessity, related to the type of problem to be solved or the procedures to be undertaken for accomplishing particular tasks such as sorting, classifying, and storing data. Thus, essential differences prevail for programs in scientific problem solving, general arithmetical calculations, industrial control by computers, or data processing of business operations. For any one of these categories, a particular program written by one programmer, may differ to some extent from that written by another. One reason for the difference is that a computer's operational flexibility may permit a considerable variation in the instructional sequence for solving a particular problem or producing an end result in data processing. Similarly, one programmer may be more adept in setting up a particular program by recognizing certain short-cut procedures. Hence, his program may be much shorter than another, even though both perform the same tasks and are equally valid. Since, however, the rental costs of an expensive computer may be high or the usage demands of an owned computer may be approaching capacity, the shorter program is particularly advantageous.

Thus, while program organization may vary somewhat among different programmers, the basic approach remains the same for achieving the end result. Program types differ in major areas with the nature of the tasks to be performed. In the programming of scientific mathematic problems, for instance, the problem or mathematical equation must be set up in proper form and then translated into the language of the computer. Some simplification may also be required before it can be handled by the computer. In complex or lengthy problems, flow charts (described later) are prepared, which illustate in graphic form the sequential steps necessary for final solutions. Such flow charts aid in program preparation because they help simplify the problem by indicating the repetitive phases (iterations), where the process must be halted and returned to an earlier phase (loops and transfers), and similar factors.

After finishing the flow chart, machine-language coded instructions are prepared and storage addresses referenced at appropriate places in the program for detailed, step-by-step instructions for the computer to follow. Time-saving subroutines, automatic-coding procedures, and other techniques are employed where possible to shorten both program preparation time and computer operational time. Finally, the completed program is entered into the computer, either on a trial run for ascertaining its effectiveness or validity, or as a final program to be processed by the computer.

Trial runs of a program are sometimes necessary because the instructional complexity may be such that a careful inspection of the program may not indicate certain errors or certain operational procedures that are not compatible with the computer's design. In such instances the program may be run with selected and tentative data to ascertain what faults exist in execution. Corrective procedures (referred to as *debugging*) are then undertaken, and after checks and changes have been made, additional trial runs may be necessary before the program will do the job for which it is set up.

Real-time operations (see Chapter 8, Input-output Terminology) also require careful program preparation to assure proper end results. Since the environmental changes sensed must be acted on by the computer, the program type must be such that the computer can modify its operational processes accordingly. Here, in addition to the mathematical procedures involved, a number of so-called decision commands, or instructions, must be included to take into consideration all variance eventualities.

In electronic data processing (EDP), the program type is one which is concerned only with basic mathematical calculations but must be directed toward compiling, classifying, filing (storage), and similar procedures. The classification procedures involve transcribing the data fed to the computer for purposes of record keeping, processing the data, and performing related bookkeeping type of functions. Since inventories, payrolls, magazine subscriptions, etc., are involved, the storage capabilities (and hence storage addresses) are much greater than those for general-purpose computers solving mathematical and scientific problems.

For data-processing programming, it is necessary to prepare initially a complete procedural prospectus of the business operations which are to be undertaken by the computer. Again, as for complex mathematical problems, a flow chart is prepared for aid in visualizing the over-all operational scope. Changes and debugging procedures may also be necessary to modify the bookkeeping structure to conform to the computer's method of processing the data. Program loops (discussed later) are more frequently used for identical processing of numerous accounts (payables, receivables, payrolls, inventory control, tabulation, deductions, etc.). A typical example is that of maintaining magazine subscription lists, where, in some instances, over 15,000,000 subscribers may be listed. Here, the computer program must be such that there is automatic cancellation of expired subscriptions, insertion of new ones, sensing of pending expiration dates, notification of pending expiration of subscription, classification of subscribers geographically to meet postal regulations, and periodic printing of labels.

Another example of the programming routines necessary in data processing is that of payroll computations. In payroll check preparation the computer must, for a particular employee, print the gross pay, deduct such items as withholding tax, social security, unemployment compensation, hospitilization, etc. The net pay must also be printed on the employee's statement. A paycheck can then be printed, listing the net pay, employe's name, address, etc.

### Flow Charting

A flow chart is prepared by drawing a series of interconnected blocks, circles, or other shapes, to identify a sequential set of operations for the logical conclusion of a data-processing or mathematical problem. Hence, the flow chart presents a graphic illustration of the manner in which the program should be constructed. Once the flow chart organization appears complete, the actual computer program is written with a sequence and step function coinciding with the flow chart. As mentioned earlier, the flow chart thus expedites the setting up of the problem so that its particular pecularities can be studied and modified as needed for conversion to a program that is acceptable to the computer.

In data processing, a systems chart is sometimes prepared by business management for presenting graphically the over-all bookkeeping structure within the organization. Such a chart shows the data flow and its inter-relationship with the various departments or branches of the total organization. From such a systems chart, a programming flow chart can be prepared for adapting the entire system to one compatible with the computer's mode of operation.

Various symbols are employed by programmers for preparation of the flow chart, though there is no set standard relating a particular symbol to a specific operation. Hence, flow charts prepared by some programmers will differ in symbol usage from those prepared by others. Basically, however, the general preparation factors are common, as are many of the symbols employed. Hence, the selection of certain symbols over others is not the important factor; rather, the primary purpose is to prepare a graphic guide for the programmer to expedite the proper coding of the instructions for the computer.

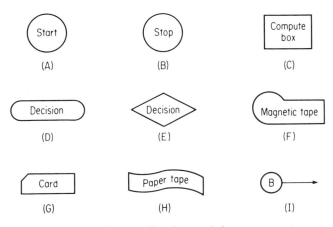

**Fig. 9-1.** Flow chart symbols.

Typical of the symbols often used are those shown in Fig. 9-1. Circles are used to indicate program start and stop points, as shown at A and B. Arithmetic operations are indicated by a rectangle, and sometimes referred to as a computing box, as shown at C. When a computer decision or conditional choice instruction is to be represented, a truncated ellipse as shown at D or the isosceles-related symbol shown at E is used. These are sometimes referred to as decision boxes, because they indicate the computer must ascertain the *yes* or *no* condition and act accordingly. Magnetic tape is sometimes symbolized as shown at F, and a punched card, as at G. Paper tape may be represented as shown at H.

The symbols are connected by arrows to indicate the data flow in the sequence desired. A small circle, as shown at I, is often used to identify (by letters of numbers) common transfers to some point in the flow chart, as illustrated later. On occasion, the small circles are omitted in favor of dashed lines for showing interconnections or return data flow.

Generally, only a single line is shown entering a symbol box, with the arrowhead indicating the line termination. If two lines are to enter a single box symbol, they are first joined, though this is not an inflexible rule and some programming personnel may draw two lines entering.

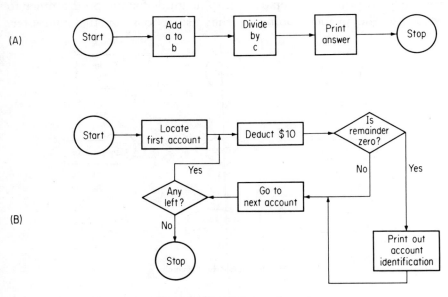

**Fig. 9-2. Flow chart examples.**

Some representative flow charting is shown in Fig. 9-2. In A, the simple problem $(a + b)/c$ is illustrated. The start operation is indicated by a circle, with an arrow leading into the compute box to indicate the addition of $a + b$. From this box another arrow leads into another compute box to indicate the division process. The program ends with a stop instruction, again symbolized by a circle.

A more involved flow chart is shown in B. Here, the problem charted could refer to a charge-account operation, a time-payment arrangement on stocks or other merchandise, or the purchase of shares in a building and loan operation. A number of accounts exist, which must be placed in the computer's storage for processing. The accounts represent a time payment of $10 per month on items purchased at various intervals. Thus, each account balance may be different from the others, or identical to some accounts. Assume we wish to ascertain which accounts will be paid up at the next monthly payment.

For the computer to perform this function, it must seek out each account sequentially and deduct $10 from it to ascertain if such a deduction results in zero (paid up). If a zero results, we want this fact printed out, after which the computer is to process the next account in a similar manner until all are sampled. If the $10 deduction does not result in a zero balance, no print-out is to occur and the computer is to continue with the next account. If the account listing is exhausted, the computer is to stop.

From the flow chart shown in B, you will notice that these sequential operations are indicated using appropriate symbols. After the start of the computation, the first account must be found and the deduction made. Now, a decision box is shown indicating that either a *yes* or *no* output will be obtained. For a *yes* output a compute-box print command is shown, while for a *no* output the computer is directed to continue the progressive operations on successive accounts. For each account sampled (except the first), another decision box indicates the necessity for sensing if the account file has been exhausted. If this is so, the computer is issued a stop command; otherwise it is to continue.

A flow chart showing common branching for a *yes* operation is shown in Fig. 9-3. Here, the flow chart represents the sequential operations to solve the equation $a^2 + b \cdot c = y$. In addition, we want the computer to act on the following instruction: "If any product or sum within the equation exceeds an assigned $x$ value during computation, stop operation; otherwise, continue." Note that a *yes* resultant from the decision box connects to a small circle with an $A$ in it, representing a common connection with the stop command. This method illustrates how long interconnecting lines can be eliminated when setting up the flow chart. The numerical value assigned to $x$ could be placed in a particular storage location of the computer, and, after the execution of each arithmetic operation, the resultant would be compared in value with the $X$ value to ascertain whether or not the computation sum or product exceeds the assigned $x$ value.

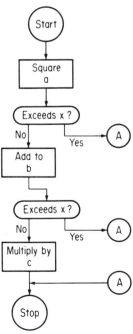

**Fig. 9-3.**      Representative equation flow chart.

The flow charts shown are representative of the procedures employed. Flow charts and computer programs may, of course, be much longer and more elaborate, depending on the nature of the problem or the extent of data processing to be employed. As illustrated, the flow charts may be drawn either horizontally or vertically, depending on the method which proves to be most convenient to indicate progressive data flow.

## Program Codes

Since the computer functions in binary form, this is known as the *machine language*. Hence, any instructions or address of storage locations must be in binary form in the central processor (internal computer circuitry). When data words are to be stored, they are placed in storage in binary form, and the address which indicates the location of a specific word is also in pure binary form. Storage locations may start at a zero address and range in consecutive numerical order to the limit of the computer's storage capacity. The computer is also designed, however, so that when a binary number is placed in a specific register, certain *and* gates will open and other circuit functions will be initiated to perform such tasks as taking data from storage and placing it in a register, adding other data to this, or performing other functions as desired.

Thus, an octal number such as 43 (binary 100011) may be designed as an instruction to the computer to load the contents of a certain storage location into the accumulator register. To perform this function, however, the storage address must also be given so the computer will know what circuits must close to abstract the required data from storage. Thus, another binary number is involved, that of the storage address. In computer programming notation, the storage address is usually placed to the right of the instruction number. Hence, if the storage location desired is 150, for instance, the first binary number notated would be the *instruction code* and the second, the memory address:

| *Octal* | | *Binary equivalent* | |
|---|---|---|---|
| *Instruction Code* | *Memory Address* | *Instruction Code* | *Memory Address* |
| 43 | 150 | 100011 | 001101000 |

Thus, if these numbers apply to a particular instruction and address for a certain computer, the numbers would be entered in proper fashion and the computer's start button depressed. Now, the accumulator would first be cleared, the data which is stored at memory address 150 would be copied into the accumulator register, and the computer would await further instructions. If another instructional code binary number is now entered, accompanied by the appropriate storage address, certain storage data would be added to the contents of the accumulator, or subtracted, etc. Some type of register is always involved in calculation, shifting, and other processes, since these functions cannot be performed in storage.

In programming, the basic binary machine language for the instructional code is used primarily for program debugging, or when program modification and checking procedures are necessary. For primary programming purposes, several other programming languages may be used. One of these is a symbolic machine language known as the *mnemonic code*. Here, three or more letters are used to symbolize the instruction to be performed, such as LDA (*LoaD* the *A*ccumulator), or simply ADD for addition. Thus, the programmer uses an instructional code constructed from English-language symbols instead of binary, and programming procedures are simplified to some extent. For the example shown earlier, the load instruction and address would be stated as

LDA 150 = load the accumulator with the data found in storage location 150, clearing the accumulator before loading

With such a mnemonic instructional code, a special unit called an assembler is used to translate the LDA symbolic code into appropriate binary form acceptable to the computer (see Fig. 8-3 and related discussions). Similarly, other mnemonic instructions such as ADD, SUB, MNI (manual input), etc., are translated by the assembler into their equivalent binary form. This process can be considered as a form of automatic coding, because the assembler handles the binary coding automatically.

In some computers, still higher-level programming languages are utilized which are closely allied to ordinary English programming language as well as that of the basic language of mathematics. As mentioned in Chapter 8, such systems are called FORTRAN (*FOR*mula *TRAN*slator), COBOL (*CO*mmon *B*usiness-*O*riented *Lan*-

guage), and ALGOL (*ALG*ebraic-*O*riented *L*anguage). With these systems, a compiler is used which translates a single common-language expression into a *series* of machine-language instructions.

The FORTRAN system was developed by IBM and first used in 1957 in its 704 computer. Since then this type of programming has been widely adopted by other computer manufacturers.

In FORTRAN, the mathematical equation

$$Y = \frac{a+b}{c}x$$

would be notated as

$$Y = ((A + B)/C)*X$$

Except for the use of capital letters and the asterisk * for multiplication, the statement of the equation is straightforward and closely resembles the basic mathematical language. (Additional data on FORTRAN will be found in Chapter 10.)

## *Data-Interchange Circuitry*

For a computer to execute the instructions comprising a program, there must be considerable data interchange between computer circuits. Some of these flow linkages are illustrated in Fig. 9-4. The exchange register (sometimes designated as the X register) is the central routing section which communicates between storage and the calculation circuits. The program-address register is used for locating the particular instruction to be executed. The instruction register holds the binary number representing the code of the instruction to be performed. The quotient register is used for division (see Chapter 6), and the accumulator holds various data for addition, subtraction, and multiplication processes, as well as sums, products, etc. Clock timing and control circuits regulate pulse gating, shifting, and other related functions. (Reference should be made to Chapters 4 and 6 for gating, shifting, data transfer between registers, and other information applying to data interchange between circuits.)

The index, or counting register as it is sometimes called, has a number of important functions in a modern computer. In one application it is set to count the number of steps to be performed in a pro-

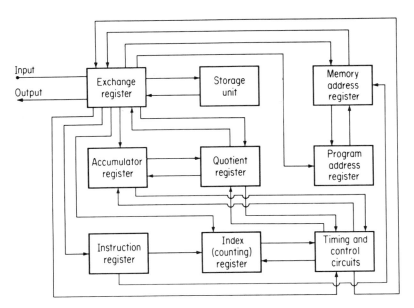

**Fig. 9-4. Data interchange of computer.**

gram loop. These repetitive operations will be performed for as many times as indicated by the index register. This register can also regulate the number of shifts to be executed, the number of words to be placed into internal storage from peripheral equipment, and the modification of program instructions as required. In practical applications, the computer program must have the proper commands to load the index register with the necessary count representation and to initiate the counting process when needed.

The basic data-interchange circuits shown in Fig. 9-4 may vary somewhat from one computer to another, though essentially similar data-flow procedures are followed in each. Some computers may have more than one index or counting register, plus several other registers to supplement the ones shown for added flexibility. In all instances, timing and control circuits must activate the acquistion and execution phases of the program and select the data to be processed. Thus, to execute a program, the instruction (coded in binary machine language) plus the operand address must be identified as dictated by the program. The procedure indicated by each instruction code must be executed by the computer before the next instruction is acquired and acted on.

In a stored-program type of computer, the program instructions are stored in memory and, upon command, the instruction code is routed (through the exchange register) to the instruction register. The instruction, by opening various *and* gates and establishing closed-circuit routes, actually performs several tasks. It may initially clear the accumulator; then bring from storage certain data, and place them in the accumulator. The control and index registers then advance the program register to the next instruction address and thus sequence the program steps automatically. If the next instruction is an ADD, for instance, immediately followed by a storage address, the data in the address indicated are withdrawn, routed through the exchange register, and added to the contents of the accumulator register. The sum will now remain in the accumulator register, awaiting the next ininstruction. The program register is again automatically advanced to the next instruction address to indicate the new instruction. The clock pulses fed to the control circuits automatically time and initiate the sequence of instruction execution and progressive advances to the next operational instruction of the stored program. The index register also initiates the transfer of the operand address from the instruction register to the memory address register. It is thus an identification of where the data are stored to which the instruction applies.

While such routing is complex, the reasons for data exchange between the registers will be clearer after a study of the programming examples given in the next chapter. The basic routing processes may be better understood at this time, however, by inspection of the illustrated processes in Fig. 9-5. Here, assume that a simple problem has been programmed for adding 330 to 50 with a print-out of the sum. Initially, the addend (330) is placed in memory, and, for purposes of illustration, assume this storage location is 200. The augend (50) is placed in storage location 201. Now the computer has been supplied with the data to be processed and awaits the instructions on how this must be done.

Assume we are going to feed the instructions into the computer manually. The first step is an instructional command such as LDA 200, which, when decoded by the computer, states that the accumulator is to be cleared and the data stored in memory address 200 are to be placed into the accumulator register. The sequential steps are shown in A. Initially, the exchange register decodes the instructions, and the timing control system sends a clearing pulse to all the flip-flop stages of the accumulator register and clears them. The second step

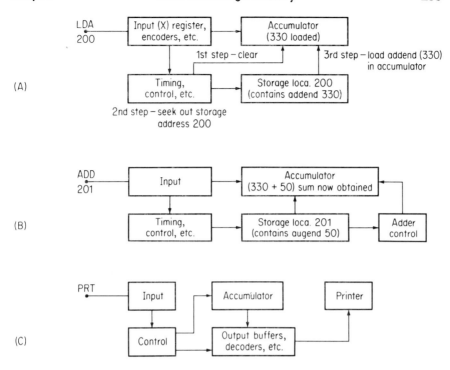

**Fig. 9-5.** Operational sequence for simple addition.

consists of seeking out the storage address 200 which was part of the instructional command LDA 200. Thus, storage location 200 is found by the computer and the data (330 in this instance) transferred to the accumulator register. The instruction has now been executed and the computer awaits the next command.

Next, the additional instructional command, plus the operand address, is entered: ADD 201. When this is decoded by the computer, the data in storage location 201 are read into the accumulator, and the adder control produces the sum of the number already in the accumulator plus that procured from storage. The sum remains in the accumulator, and the computer again awaits the next instruction.

The next instruction PRT tells the computer to print out the data in the accumulator. Hence, the binary sum in the accumulator is decoded into equivalent base-10 form and transferred through the on-line equipment to the printer. The accumulator is cleared of the data it held, though the original numbers 330 and 50 will still be in memory if the storage characteristics are of the nondestructive type. The storage locations can be cleared on command or cleared by rewriting data over the previous material.

For a basic subtraction process the operational procedures are similar, with the minuend extracted from storage and placed in the accumulator. Next, the subtrahend is found, from the storage address given with the subtract instruction, and subtracted from the number held by the accumulator. The remainder is then retained by the accumulator register until the next instruction is executed (transferred, added to another sum, printed out, etc.). For division and multiplication, the process is somewhat more complex, as described in Chapter 6 and illustrated in Figs. 6-13 to 6-19.

## PROBLEMS

1. How do the instructions which are given to a computer compare, basically, with the operation of a desk calculator?

2. Why may a program prepared by one person differ from that prepared by another for the same problem?

3. What are the basic steps necessary in programming?

4. What are some of the operations involved in data processing?

5. What are the advantages of preparing a flow chart prior to writing a computer program?

6. Prepare a representative flow chart for the following problem: A number of charge accounts are stored in a computer, and it is desired to ascertain which exceed $200. The identification for each which exceeds $200 is to be printed out.

7. Prepare a flow chart for the following problem: $n + m = x$. If the sum $x$ exceeds a value designated as $z$, stop the computer; otherwise continue with $x - y$, and print out the answer, ending with a stop command.

8. Prepare a flow chart for the following:

   $\dfrac{a \cdot b \cdot c}{d}$   (all positive numbers). If any part of the equation exceeds a value designated as $x$, stop; otherwise, continue.

9. Explain what is meant by a code such as LDA 300.

10. When is an assembler unit used?

11. When is a compiler used?

**12.** How were the terms FORTRAN, COBOL, and ALGOL derived?

**13.** What is the general function of an exchange register?

**14.** What is the purpose of a quotient register?

**15.** What is the purpose of a program-address register?

**16.** What are some of the tasks performed by the index register?

**17.** Why are the multiply and divide operations more complex than the add and subtract?

**18.** In addition and subtraction, where are the answers generally located?

# PROGRAMMING
# PROCEDURES

**10**

**Introduction.** Modern digital computers have a wide range of operational abilities that permit them to be programmed to execute an extensive array of mathematical equations and problems or perform tasks involving industrial control, data processing, and the interpretation of statistical data. To have these inherent abilities, digital computers are so designed that they can modify their own instructions if the need arises, can perform a decision type of operation; transfer operation to another portion of a program if required, and repeat certain phases of a program upon command. In addition, their high operational speed and interface with so much peripheral equipment (scanners, typewriters, printers, card readers, tape readers, and other related units) greatly facilitate data loading and unloading and provide a high degree of versatility.

Hence, for effective programming, not only must one be aware of the particular potentialities of a computer, but he should be able to utilize them to best advantage. In programming mathematical equations, for instance, the algorithm (the method of calculating by use of a particular notation) may differ considerably from that used in conventional arithmetic. This is so because the computer's inherent speed may be substituted for standard solving methods as the most suitable in a given circumstance. If, for instance, we were to solve the simple equation $1200 - 2x = 0$, we would not assign $x$ a 1 value and keep increasing it progressively, one digit at a time, until we arrived at the solution. For us it is a tedious and time-wasting procedure, but for a computer, working at microsecond speeds, it is frequently found useful in certain equation algorithms.

Similarly, in business data processing, repetitive samplings of stored accounts or statistical data can be used effectively with accuracy and speeds far exceeding older methods. Also, the extensive listings on file in some business enterprises can be searched at will by the computer and specific data unloaded and processed periodically, as required, on command by an appropriate program related to the business activities.

While extensive programming examples involving higher mathematics and data processing would require a text devoted exclusively to this specialized subject, some aspects and samples of symbolic language (mnemonic), FORTRAN, and COBOL programming are included in this chapter. Such material will enable the reader to become familiar with the basic concepts and procedures involved. A bibliography has been included at the end of the chapter for reference to more advanced and detailed coverage of the various areas of computer programming.


### Instruction Format

In Chapter 9 the two basic essentials of an instructional format were discussed, the first consisting of the instruction code which specifies what is to be done, and the second consisting of a code which represents the location (address) of the data to be processed. This is a commonly used type of instructional format and is known as the *single-address* type. Thus, the LDA 100 instruction mentioned in Chapter 9 consists of the left member, which is the *operation code*, and the right member, which is the *operand address*.

Some computers have used a *two-address* system, wherein the left member is the operation code, the second part is the operand address, and the third part is the address of the next instruction to be executed. The initial operation sequence follows that of the single-address format. Initially the operation code (specifying add, subtract, etc.) causes the data to be abstracted from the memory location specified. Such data may be placed in an accumulator register and the necessary calculation process performed. Next, the storage location of the next address is found and the instructions contained therein decoded and executed. The new instruction would contain the operand address also for procuring the necessary data to be processed.

A *three-address* system may contain the operation code, two separate operand addresses, and a third address indicating the location of the next instruction. In some three-address systems the third address specifies the storage location to which the results of the operations are to be transferred. In such instances, the address for the next instruction is found by automatically taking the next instructional address in storage sequence.

In the *four-address* system the first part is again the operation code. This is followed by the two operand addresses of two data words to be processed (the multiplier and the multiplicand, for instance). The third address is the storage location to which the computation result is to be sent, and the fourth address is the location of the next instructional code. The four-address type was used in some of the earlier computers. It entailed the use of more registers than the one- or two-address systems.

## Instruction Types

The various instructional commands used in a computer perform a number of special tasks. One instruction will cause a register to be loaded, another will initiate an arithmetic operation, while another may perform data transfer between storage and registers. Others permit certain decisions to be made relating to the data status at a specific program point, and operation to branch to other portions of the program as required. Instructional commands are also used to procure input data, print out computed results, stop operations, or repeat certain program operations a specified number of times (or until a preselected end result is obtained). Some of these instruction operations may also be omitted by the computer in decision portions of the program, as discussed more fully later.

One instructional command often used in computer programs is the *branch* operation. This command is also known as *transfer*, or *jump*. As these terms imply, the command will cause the computer to interrupt a sequential series of steps and branch to another section of the program. The branch operation may be *conditional*; that is, the branch is only to be executed *if* a certain set of conditions prevail at that part of the program where the branch command is inserted. An *uncon-*

*ditional branch* is also used and causes the computer to transfer to a certain program position regardless of the conditions which prevail at the time the unconditional branch is reached during the program.

The conditional branch involves a decision operation on the part of the computer, and a basic form is shown in Fig. 10-1 (see also Figs. 9-2 and 9-3). The flow chart in Fig. 10-1 is for the equation $n + (x - y)^2$, and the program can be used repeatedly for various values of $n$, $x$, and $y$. Normally the flow chart could be straightforward and drawn in sequential steps if the value of $x$ will never be equal to $y$. If we suspect, however, that the $x$ and $y$ values may, on occasion, be equal, we can introduce a branch command and save a number of program steps each time this condition occurs. Thus, a decision box is indicated immediately after the start to ascer-

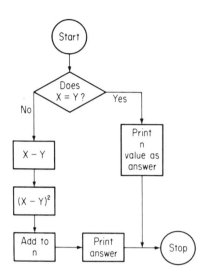

Fig. 10-1. Basic branch operation.

tain if $x$ is equal to $y$. If not, the $y$ is subtracted from the $x$ and the resultant squared and added to $n$ as shown. If, however, $x$ is equal to

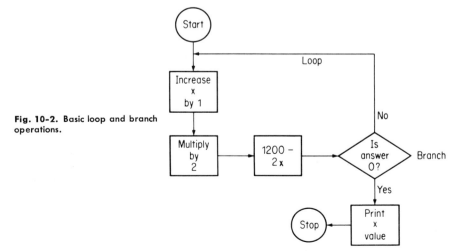

Fig. 10-2. Basic loop and branch operations.

*y*, a branch instruction is used to by-pass all the other steps and print out *n* as the answer to the problem.

Branch instructions sometimes involve a transfer to some previous point in the program so that certain sections can be repeated a number of times. Such a transfer is referred to as a *loop* and is illustrated in Fig. 10-2. Here, the simple equation $1200 - 2x = 0$ is shown in flow-chart form. While this problem could be solved by division, the algorithm shown is often used in programming certain equations or portions of certain lengthy problems. As shown, *x* is repeatedly increased by 1, multiplied by 2, and subtracted from 1200, until the computer ascertains that the resultant is equal to 0. Therefore, the branch instruction involves a loop to the start of the program until the *x* value has been obtained. When this occurs, the branch is to the print instruction and program halt command.

Independent branch and loop operations are shown in Fig. 10-3. Here a flow chart is shown for the basic operations involved in the data processing of magazine subscriptions. Each time the magazines are sent to the subscribers, the computer is to initiate the printing of the appropriate address label, reduce the subscription account by 1, and repeat the process for each subscription on file (in the storage of the computer). Since the various subscriptions expire at different times, the computer must also ascertain which accounts expire with the current publication and remove these from the records.

As shown in Fig. 10-3, the first subscription account is located and immediately tested to see if it is an expired account. If not, a label is printed and the account is reduced by 1. Now the next subscription account is located, and an *unconditional branch* loop brings the instruction sequence back

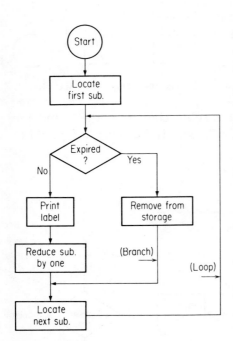

**Fig. 10-3. Independent branch and loop operations.**

to the decision box for testing whether or not the subscription has expired. The loop repeats the entire operation until an *end* indication (end of file) is sensed in the subscription storage.

When an expiration is sensed, a branch occurs, the account is removed from the storage file, and the branch continues the program by locating the next subscription account. Similar branch and loop processes are used for payroll computations, inventory control, and other data processing, as well as in many mathematical problem-solving programs. For the latter, the number of times the loop repeats a certain portion of the equation may be established by the decision process or by presetting the index register to the number of iterations to be performed.

Other instructional commands have been mentioned earlier and include *clear a register, load a register from memory, transfer the contents of*

**Fig. 10-4.** Central processor control panel of Philco 1000 computer system.

*one register to another* (or to storage), *stop operation*, etc. Switches on the operating console of the computer often provide manual control of certain program processes for data insertion under certain conditions, for by-passing programmed stop commands, for starting the program over again, and for program modification as required.

The console also has *overflow* lights to indicate some error condition in the program or a calculation result which produces a number of such proportions that it is beyond the storage capabilities of a particular register. (Overflow was also discussed at the end of Chapter 4 as well as in Chapter 6, in the section on Dividers.) The number of bits per word for a particular computer must be known to avoid overflow conditions. The overflow indications on the console are, however, useful in program debugging to indicate errors in magnitude or incorrect program loops, etc.

Console switch and indicating device layouts differ for the various computers, though the basic manual control functions are present in all units. Typical of the variety of controls which may be present is the control panel shown in Fig 10-4 for the central processor of the Philco-Ford 1000 computer system. Indicator lights for the instruction register are centrally located. At the left are jump, store, and display switches. At the right are on-off switches. At bottom left are the automatic-load switches (rectangular plastic push-switches which light up when depressed), and at the lower right, the processor halt and continue switches.

## Mnemonic-Code Programming

In program debugging or manual loading procedures where binary (or octal) coding is employed, the system might be considered as the basic (and original) method employed for instructing the computer and entering the data to be processed. This is essentially a low-level type of programming. When mnemonic codes are used the programming can be considered as medium-level. The abbreviations ADD, SUB, etc., are not machine languages but help the operator remember the instructional meanings. This *aid-to-memory* aspect is the reason this coding is called *mnemonic*. Such a code is, however, not a mathematical one (as FORTRAN is), and hence the programming of equations with it necessitates the spelling out of the sequence of operations which must be performed and the decisions, branches, and loops to be executed. Also, the mnemonic is not a business-oriented language (such as COBOL), and again, if used in data processing, step-by-step procedures must be programmed.

Mnemonic-code programming, where each sequential step must be listed, is sometimes known as *microprogramming*. FORTRAN, COBOL, and other such systems, where one instruction is converted into a group of machine-language instructions, is often referred to as *macroprogramming*.

As previously mentioned, when mnemonic codes are used, an assembler translating system converts the code to the appropriate binary machine language. Assume, for instance, that a particular digital computer uses a one-address instructional word length of 24 bits. Here, 9 bits may be assigned for the instruction code and 15 bits for the address, and a load command might be

$$\text{LDA} \qquad 327$$

The mnemonic code LDA would be translated by the assembler into the equivalent octal number. If, for instance, this happened to be octal 16, the assembler would produce the following (instruction code $16_8$ and address $327_8$):

```
000 001 110 000 000 011 010 111    binary (octal grouping)
( 0   1   6 )     ( 3   2   7 )   octal
```

The address only indicates the storage location to which the instruction applies. The data to be processed (addend, multiplicand, etc.) must still be stored in the address indicated, as explained more fully later. For purposes of illustrating basic programming procedures using mnemonic coding, the octal representations for ADD, MPY, etc., will be omitted in these discussions. Addresses, however, will be shown in octal coding.

The octal numbers representative of the mnemonic codes vary for the different computers, as do some of the mnemonic alphabetical designations. The LDA instruction, for instance, could have an octal value of 20 for one computer or 36 for another. Similarly, multiply MPY might have a MUL designation, the stop command STP might be indicated as halt HLT. Such differences, however, do not alter the basic programming procedures.

A composite code listing follows for reference purposes to illustrate the basic concepts of computer programming. For the larger computers, such a list would contain many more codes to perform specific or specialized program operations and provide added flexibility to programming. A sufficient number of codes are shown, however, to provide the reader with a fundamental understanding of applications to programming.

| *Instruction Code (Mnemonic)* | *Function* |
|---|---|
| LDA$_d$ | Clear the accumulator. Load into the accumulator the contents of storage address designated (d). Memory data is not affected and is retained. |
| ADD$_d$ | Add to the contents of the accumulator the contents of storage address designated (d). Leave the sum in the accumulator. |
| SUB$_d$ | Subtract the contents of storage address designated from contents of accumulator. Leave remainder in accumulator. |
| DIV$_d$ | Divide the contents of accumulator by contents of storage address designated. Leave quotient in Q register, remainder in A register. |
| MPY$_d$ | Multiply the contents of accumulator by contents of storage address designated. Leave product in accumulator. |
| STA$_d$ | Store contents of accumulator at memory address designated. |
| STQ$_d$ | Store contents of quotient register at memory address designated. |
| STP$_d$ | Stop program execution. Jump to address designated if start button on console is depressed. |
| CLR$_d$ | Clear contents of storage address designated. |
| BRP$_d$ | Branch to address designated if the contents of accumulator are positive; otherwise continue normal sequence of instructions (conditional jump). |
| BRN$_d$ | Branch to address designated if the contents of accumulator are negative; otherwise continue instruction sequence (conditional jump). |

| *Instruction Code (Mnemonic)* | *Function* |
|---|---|
| $BRZ_d$ | Branch to address designated if the contents of accumulator are zero; otherwise continue instruction sequence (conditional jump). |
| $BRU_d$ | Branch to address designated (unconditional jump). |
| CHS | Change the sign of the accumulator contents. |
| $SRA_n$ | Shift the accumulator contents right n places. |
| $SLA_n$ | Shift the accumulator contents left n places. |
| $SLQ_n$ | Shift the quotient register contents left n places. |
| $SRQ_n$ | Shift the quotient register contents right n places. |
| $LIR_n$ | Load the index register to a count value of n. |
| XCH | Exchange the contents and signs of the A and Q registers. |
| $INT_n$ | Load input data procured from tape. Load consecutively, starting at storage location n until the END instruction is reached on tape (or as designated by the index register). |
| PFA | Print out contents of accumulator register. |
| SQA | Square the contents of the accumulator. |
| $ADT_d$ | Add 1 to contents of memory address designated. |
| $SUF_d$ | Subtract 1 from contents of memory address designated. |

With many computers, the branch instructions will cause the computer to stop if the jump switch on the console is set. When the start button is depressed, the jump command is executed and the program sequence is interrupted for branching to the designated address.

## Program Examples

The instructional codes increase in proportion to the number of active registers employed in a specific computer. Other commands may include the addition of 1 (increment of 1) to the contents of a register or the contents of a certain storage address. Similarly, an instruction may specify that 1 be subtracted from the contents of a register. Reciprocal divide may also be included, where the contents of a storage location are divided by the contents of a register. Another instruction useful in some arithmetical programming is the *load negative* command, where the accumulator is cleared initially and the contents of the storage address designated is subtracted from the zero value of the accumulator.

As an initial illustration of programming using the code list given, assume the following problem is to be programmed:

$$\frac{27 + 15}{2} \quad \text{(print out answers)}$$

The data involved in the equation must be stored so the computer can call on it as required. The address selection is left to the programmer and may be influenced by the fact that some storage locations have information in them. Assume we selected storage location 30 as the starting point for the data to be placed in memory. Thus,

| *Memory Address* | *Data* |
|---|---|
| 30 | 27 |
| 31 | 15 |
| 32 | 2 |

If the memory address register is set initially at storage location 30, it will automatically sequence to the next location as each data word is inserted.

With the data to be processed now stored in the locations specified, we are ready to program. The initial instruction should clear the accumulator and load the first data word into it. Next, the addition is undertaken, followed by the division. Finally, the results are printed out. From an inspection of the code list given earlier, the following mnemonic designations are indicated.

| *Instruction* | *Address* | *Remarks* |
|---|---|---|
| LDA | 30 | Clear A register and place data in address 30 into it. |
| ADD | 31 | Add contents of storage address 31 to contents of accumulator. |

| Instruction | Address | Remarks |
|---|---|---|
| DIV | 32 | Divide contents of accumulator by contents of storage address given. |
| XCH | | Exchange A and Q contents. |
| PFA | | Print answer from accumulator. |

The exchange step was necessary, since the list of codes does not indicate a print-out instruction from the quotient register. Thus, since the division process resulted in the quotient remaining in the Q register, the A and Q contents were exchanged so the answer could be printed from the accumulator. Since the XCH and PFA instructions involved no stored-data retrieval, no addresses follow the instruction codes.

Once the data have been entered into memory and the program written, the program itself is stored in the computer's memory so the computer can execute it upon command without having to wait as each instruction is fed to it. This program storage is typical for the stored-program type of computer (see Chapter 9).

Thus, the foregoing program would be stored consecutively and could, as the following example shows, start with storage location 000:

| Program Address | Instruction | Data Address |
|---|---|---|
| 000 | LDA | 30 |
| 001 | ADD | 31 |
| 002 | DIV | 32 |
| 003 | XCH | |
| 004 | PFA | |

Now, if the program-address register is set to 000 and the start switch depressed, the computer would execute the program and print out the answer. The program could be repeated every time the program address is set at 000 and the start switch depressed. Thus, different data could be placed in storage locations 30, 31, and 32 and processed by the same program. When no longer needed, storage locations indicated would be cleared, or new material would be read over the old and thus replace it.

The program-address register would not have to be set manually to the program start if a stop-jump (STP) command is used:

| | | |
|---|---|---|
| 000 | LDA | 30 |
| 001 | ADD | 31 |
| 002 | DIV | 32 |
| 003 | XCH | 00 |
| 004 | PFA | 00 |
| 005 | STP | 00 |

With the addition of the stop instruction, the program would halt after print out. If the start switch is then depressed, the program would jump to address 000 and be repeated automatically. (Refer to the STP code function given earlier.)

The use of the branch-zero code $BRZ_d$ is shown below, using the equation given in flow-chart form in Fig. 10-1.

*Data Storage*

| Address | Data |
|---|---|
| 300 | x |
| 301 | y |
| 302 | n |

Program, for equation $n + (x - y)^2$, print out answer:

| Program Address (octal) | Instruc-tion | Data Address | Remarks |
|---|---|---|---|
| 000 | LDA | 300 | Clear accumulator, load x. |
| 001 | SUB | 301 | x − y in accumulator. |
| 002 | BRZ | 007 | If zero, branch to address 007. |
| 003 | SQA | . . . | (x − y)² in accumulator. |
| 004 | ADD | 302 | Add n to accumulator contents. |
| 005 | PFA | . . . | Print answer. |
| 006 | STP | 000 | |
| 007 | LDA | 302 | Load n in accumulator. |
| 010 | PFA | . . . | Print out n value. |
| 011 | STP | 000 | |

Note that the $BRZ_d$ instruction given in the code list causes a branch to be performed *if* the content value of the accumulator is equal to zero. The branch causes a jump to the program address 007, which has the LDA command to load the accumulator with the *n* value. The next instruction causes a print-out of this *n* value. If, however, the BRZ decision operation indicates that the subtraction $x - y$ does not yield a zero, the instruction sequence is continued with a *square* command and an *add* to equate the entire problem. The computer then prints out the answer and stops at program address 006. If the start switch is depressed, the branch is to 000 for a repeat of the entire program.

In some computer trainers, the design is such that a separate program address is used for the instruction word as well as the data address. Again, however, the program address register would sequence automatically to the next octal number each time an entry is made. Hence, once the program address register is set for the program start, the instruction word is entered, followed by the data address, and the program register advances automatically. For individual program addresses for the instruction word and the data address, the program given earlier would appear as:

|     |     |     |
|-----|-----|-----|
| 000 | LDA | 30  |
| 002 | ADD | 31  |
| 004 | DIV | 32  |
| 006 | XCH | 00  |
| 010 | PFA | 00  |
| 012 | STP | 00  |

In this program, the LDA is loaded into program address 000 and the latter sequences to the 001 address to accept the data address 30. Next, the program register sequences to 002 for the ADD instruction, etc. We could have stored the entire program at a starting address of 050, or at any other storage address which does not conflict with the data addresses. In any case the program-address register must be set to the starting address of the stored program for computations to begin.

The programming of a basic data-processing procedure follows along the same lines. If, for instance, the charge account example given in Chapter 9 were to be programmed, the sequence would be as shown in Fig. 9-2. Assume that each account has a balance related to multiples of 10 and that $10 are paid off each month. Which accounts will be paid up next?

With an expanded code list, print-out commands of account numbers (or names and addresses) would be executed. For the code list given earlier, however, we will identify a particular account by reference to the memory address of the data to locate the paid-up accounts. Thus, when a paid-up account is sensed by the computer, the branch command will cause the computer to halt its program sequence and the memory register will display the account on the console.

Assume the accounts start with memory address 100. Thus, the account in storage 100 may have a $90 balance, in 101 a $50 balance, in 102 a $20 balance, in 103 a $200 balance, etc. The program will be of a branch-loop nature, repeating the processes for each account, as shown by the flow chart in Fig. 9-2. Storage location 77 contains the $10 reference for use with the program.

| *Octal Program Address* | *Instruction* | *Memory Address* | |
|---|---|---|---|
| 00 | LDA | 100 | 1st account in A register. |
| 01 | SUB | 77 | Deduct $10. |
| 02 | BRZ | 03 | If 0, stop. |
| 03 | LDA | 101 | |
| 04 | SUB | 77 | |
| 05 | BRZ | 06 | |
| 06 | LDA | 102 | |

etc.

The program is continued until all the accounts have been located and processed. With the branch (jump) switch set (on the console), the computer will stop at each BRZ portion of the program and display the account number if the $10 deduction resulted in 0. Upon resetting the switch the branch is to the next account which is then loaded into the accumulator. If the account is not paid up, no program halt is executed and the instructional sequence is continued.

In the foregoing we had an assigned value of $10 which was used as the decision reference by the computer. A similar condition also occurs for the equation shown in flow-chart form in Fig. 9-3:

$$a^2 + b \cdot c = y$$     (If any product or sum exceeds an assigned $x$ value, stop operation; otherwise, continue.)

For this equation, we can use the BRP instruction which executes a branch if the number in the accumulator has a positive value. Thus, we can subtract $x$ from any value to be tested and, if a positive remainder is produced, the number under test must exceed the $x$ value. If a negative remainder is produced (or a zero), the $x$ value has not been exceeded and the program continues.

Initially, the data is stored, and as an arbitrary storage location, we shall start with 150:

> a    in storage address 150
> b    in storage address 151
> c    in storage address 152
> x    in storage address 153

| Program Address (Octal) | Instruction | Data Memory Address | |
|---|---|---|---|
| 50 | LDA | 150 | Loads a into accumulator. |
| 51 | MUL | 150 | $a^2$; The SQA instruction could also have been used. |
| 52 | SUB | 153 | $a^2 - x$ |
| 53 | BRP | 062 | Branch to 062 if positive. |
| 54 | ADD | 153 | Restores $a^2$. |
| 55 | ADD | 151 | $a^2 + b$ |
| 56 | SUB | 153 | Testing if x is exceeded. |
| 57 | BRP | 063 | Branch if positive. |
| 60 | ADD | 153 | Restores $a^2 + b$. |
| 61 | MPY | 152 | $(a^2 + b) \cdot c$; y in accumulator. |
| 62 | STP | 050 | |

At program address 61 the last part of the equation has been executed. Since the program comes to a stop after this operation, there is no need to include the branch instruction. Also, since our program started at program address 50 (octal), the STP code is referenced to 050 to repeat the program if the start switch is depressed.

In programming, the limitations of a particular code list and computer must be kept in mind. For the brief code list we are using in these examples, only two registers (A and Q) are indicated. Since the accumulator register must be used for calculations, it may be necessary to store part of an equation to complete another. This occurs for the the following example:

$$\frac{a + b + c}{a^2 \cdot d} \quad \text{(store answer)}$$

Here, if we execute the upper member of the equation, we would have to remove it from the accumulator before we could perform the lower half. Also, since the DIV code only permits us to divide the contents of the accumulator by the contents of a storage address designated, it would save program steps if we ended up with the sum of $a + b + c$ in the accumulator and $a^2 \cdot d$ in storage. Thus, the following program steps are indicated, with the initial program focused on the execution of the $a^2 \cdot d$ portion of the equation.

| Storage | Data |
|---------|------|
| 200 | a |
| 201 | b |
| 202 | c |
| 203 | d |
| 204 | (Answer) |

| Program Address | Instruction | Data Address | |
|---------|---------|---------|---|
| 20 | LDA | 200 | a in accumulator. |
| 21 | SQA | . . . | $a^2$ |
| 22 | MPY | 203 | $a^2 \cdot d$ |
| 23 | STA | 205 | $a^2 \cdot d$ stored in location 205. |
| 24 | LDA | 200 | a in accumulator. |
| 25 | ADD | 201 | $a + b$ |
| 26 | ADD | 202 | $a + b + c$ |
| 27 | DIV | 205 | |
| 30 | STQ | 204 | Store answer in location 204. |
| 31 | STP | 020 | |

The foregoing programs have been fairly short, since the problems involved have been of a basic type. For complex problems and data processing, programs become quite lengthy and may take considerable time to set down, both in flow-chart form and in program write-up. Payrolls for large companies, magazine subscription processing for popular publications, and inventory control involving numerous accounts and warehouses may entail dozens of sequential programming steps for only one phase of operation.

As an example, assume a wholesale house has five warehouses, which we shall identify as $A$, $B$, $C$, $D$, and $E$. The first four ($A$, $B$, $C$, $D$) can hold only a maximum of 20,000 items, but the fifth (warehouse $E$) is a central warehouse which can hold 200,000 items and which is used as an overflow for the first four. If a shipment of 100,000 new items has been received it is necessary for the computer to indicate how many items must be placed in $A$, $B$, $C$, and $D$ to fill them to capacity. Also, the computer must indicate how many items in excess of the quantity needed by warehouses $A$, $B$, $C$, and $D$ must be shipped to the central warehouse $E$.

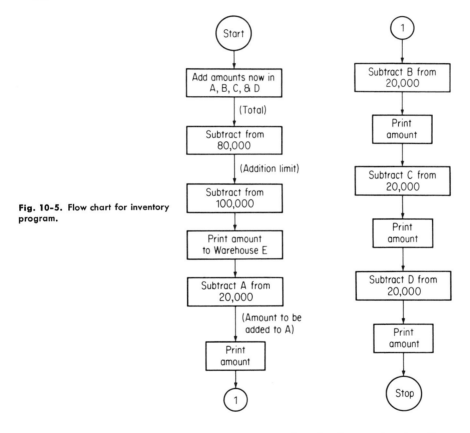

**Fig. 10-5.** Flow chart for inventory program.

One method of logic sequence processing is shown in the flow chart of Fig. 10-5. Initially, the amounts now in warehouses $A$, $B$, $C$, and $D$ are added to find the total on hand. This total is subtracted from 80,000 (the total capacity of the four) to find how many items must be added to fill these up. Now, the total amount needed for $A$, $B$, $C$, and $D$ is subtracted from the amount shipped (100,000) to ascertain the surplus which are to be routed to warehouse $E$.

Next, the quantity now in $A$ is subtracted from 20,000 (the maximum) to find out how many must be added to warehouse $A$ to reach its capacity. The amount is printed out as shown by the flowchart sequence. Next, the current amount stored in the $B$ warehouse is subtracted from 20,000 to find out how many items must be added to $B$ to reach its capacity. Similar procedures are undertaken for the other warehouses.

This flow chart is straightforward (without branching), though other logic sequences could be used. It can be seen, however, that, *if a few dozen warehouses were involved*, the program would be increased proportionally. In programming this flow chart, the reference quantities 20,000 (the maximum for a single warehouse) and 80,000 (the maximum for the combined capacity of $A$, $B$, $C$, and $D$) are stored in separate storage locations. Also, the amount of items in the current shipment must be stored as a reference. The amount of items now stored in each warehouse ($A$, $B$, $C$, and $D$) are given storage locations also, as shown below. The storage addresses are chosen as desired.

| Memory Address | Data |
|---|---|
| 75 | 100,000 |
| 76 | 20,000 |
| 77 | 80,000 |
| 100 | Quantity in A warehouse |
| 101 | Quantity in B warehouse |
| 102 | Quantity in C warehouse |
| 103 | Quantity in D warehouse |

| Program Address | Instruction | Data Address | |
|---|---|---|---|
| 001 | LDA | 100 | Quantity in A in accumulator. |
| 002 | ADD | 101 | |
| 003 | ADD | 102 | |
| 004 | ADD | 103 | Total currently in A, B, C, and D. |
| 005 | STA | 104 | Total placed in temporary storage. |
| 006 | LDA | 77 | Maximum A, B, C, D capacity in accumulator |
| 007 | SUB | 104 | Maximum capacity minus current quantity. |
| etc. | STA | 104 | Amount needed for maximum capacity in storage 104. |

| Program Address | Instruction | Data Address | |
|---|---|---|---|
| | LDA | 75 | Current shipment (100,000) in accumulator. |
| | SUB | 104 | Current shipment minus amount needed. |
| | PFA | . . . | Print amount to be shipped to warehouse E. |
| | LDA | 76 | Individual warehouse capacity in accumulator. |
| | SUB | 100 | Maximum minus present quantity of A warehouse. |
| | PFA | . . . | Print amount to be placed in warehouse A. |
| | LDA | 76 | 20,000 |
| | SUB | 101 | 20,000 less present quantity of B warehouse. |
| | PFA | . . . | Print amount to be placed in warehouse B. |
| | LDA | 76 | 20,000 in accumulator. |
| | SUB | 102 | |
| | PFA | | Print amount to be placed in warehouse C. |
| | LDA | 76 | |
| | SUB | 103 | |
| | PFA | | |
| | STP | 001 | |

At the eighth step the storage location could have been 105 or any other address desired. While storage location 104 was used in step 5, the contents were employed in step 7 and no longer needed the location. During step 8, the writing of new information over the old obliterates the original contents. (Flip-flop registers are automatically cleared by the LDA instruction.)

## Subroutines

There are many occasions when a specific program is repeatedly required at various intervals. The inventory program of Fig. 10-5, for instance, would be required every time a new shipment arrived in order to make proper allocations to the various warehouses. Also, in mathematical programs, the occasion often arises for extracting square roots, finding the roots of a quartic (fourth degree equation), obtaining roots of quadratics, etc. Hence, to eliminate the necessity of rewriting such programs each time they are required, each program of this type is permanently stored and so identified that it can be reused or inserted into a new program as required. Permanently stored programs which are to be inserted into new programs are called *sub-*

*routines*, since they are intended for use with a primary routine (program) and thus to save programming time.

Subroutines can be stored on magnetic tape, paper tape, magnetic drums, punched cards, or other storage media. A variety of subroutines are usually obtainable in prepared form from computer manufacturers for use with their equipment. Most large-scale computer centers in industry or business have a *library of subroutines* for payroll procedures, inventory control, charge accounts, mathematical equations, and other often used programs. As the need arises, new subroutines are formulated or purhased outright when available.

Most computer manufacturers also have available primary programs (routines) for often-used mathematical processes or business procedures. Such routines, subroutines, and other program data, are usually referred to as *software*, to distinguish such available material from the chips, modules, and other circuit components known as computer *hardware*.

Where the subroutine is stored and the ease with which it can be linked with a primary program (routine) are factors which relate to the design of the computer system. Basically, to perform a subroutine, the computer must interrupt its primary program, branch to the subroutine, and upon completion branch back again to the main program and resume the sequence of operations where the interruption occurred. To do this, the instruction address stored in the program register must be removed and stored in another location while the subroutine is being performed. Upon completion, the main program addresses are reinserted into the program register so the normal sequence of instructions can be processed.

One method for doing this is to insert into the program register the address of the subroutine instruction. This causes the subroutine to execute sequential program steps until the subroutine is completed, at which time another branch instruction (as part of the subroutine) transfers control back to the primary program. Also, provisions are made to permit the programmer to insert the necessary data with which the subroutine is concerned. Thus, the programmer must be acquainted with the nature of the subroutine linkage so he can readily adapt it to a particular program. In additon, he should understand the branch commands necessary for insertion of the subroutine, the storage space occupied by the subroutine, and how much data can be handled by it before overflow occurs.

Index registers may also be used for expediting subroutine linkage. The branch command to the subroutine is accompanied by an index-register set instruction, indicating the number of steps involved in the subroutine.

## Square-Root Subroutine

To indicate the basic principles involved in subroutine programming, a typical square-root subroutine will be discussed using the program codes previously listed. This will also illustrate another application of the special algorithms used in computer programming involving basic mathematical equations.

In setting up a subroutine for extracting square roots, several methods may be employed which are more suitable to a digital computer and hence more efficient than the ordinary methods used in basic arithmetic. One method could consist of dividing the number for which a root is to be obtained by 2 and having the computer check for equality between the divisor and the quotient:

$$\text{Problem:} \quad \sqrt{16}$$
$$\text{First step:} \quad \tfrac{16}{2} = 8$$
$$\text{Equality?} \quad 2 \text{ versus } 8$$

If the computer senses that no equality exists, the quotient is again divided by 2 and the divisor is multiplied by 2 and the results again tested for equality:

$$\text{Second step:} \quad \tfrac{8}{2} = 4$$
$$2 \times 2 = 4$$
$$\text{Equality?} \quad 4 \text{ versus } 4$$

Since equality has been achieved, the square root is 4. For this method, however, provisions must be made for instances when the divisor magnitude over-runs the quotient and for handling remainders when perfect squares are not present. The method is, however, programmable and has been used.

Another method consists of subtracting successive odd integers until a zero (or a negative) number results. The number of steps required to reach 0 is the square root. The procedure is based on the fact that the sum of successive odd integers equals their square, $n_1$, $n_2$, $n_3$, ..., $n = n^2$, and the number of integers involved equals the square root:

$$\left.\begin{array}{r} 1 \\ 3 \\ 5 \\ 7 \\ 9 \\ +11 \\ \hline 36 \end{array}\right\} n \;=\; 6 \\ \phantom{36}\;=\; n^2$$

The logic of this is apparent from inspection of Fig. 10-6. In A, to form a square for the open circle, *three* must be added, as shown by the shaded circles. To *four*, $(2 \times 2)$ an additional *five* must be added to form the next perfect square, $3 \times 3$. As shown in C, *seven* must be added to form the square $4 \times 4$; and for a $5 \times 5$ square, *nine* must then be added, as shown in D by the shaded circles, etc. Thus, to extract square roots, we will reverse the process and then subtract successive odd integers:

$$\begin{array}{r} \sqrt{49} \\ -\;1 \\ \hline 48 \\ -\;3 \\ \hline 45 \\ -\;5 \\ \hline 40 \\ -\;7 \\ \hline 33 \\ -\;9 \\ \hline 24 \\ -11 \\ \hline 13 \\ -13 \\ \hline 00 \end{array}$$

Since the total number of steps required to reach zero is 7, the square root of 49 is indicated. Because, however, perfect squares are not always in order, the computer is asked to repeat the subtractions until a negative number is obtained, at which time the square root will be equal to the number of steps minus 1. In flow-chart form this is set down as shown in Fig. 10-7. Here, by iteration, the algorithm is simple and readily programmed.

**Fig. 10-6.** $N^2$ logic.

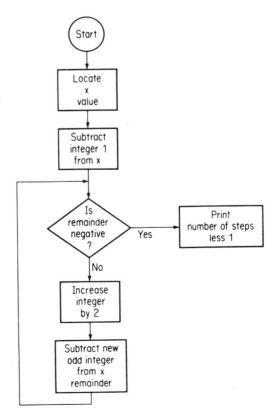

**Fig. 10-7.** Flow chart for square root.

Using this odd-integer subtraction method and the coding previously given, we should initially select storage locations for the program steps involved. First, we must provide a storage location for the number from which the square root is to be extracted. Next, we must provide storage locations for the first odd integer 1 and for the number by which the integer is to be successively increased, 2. In addition, we must make provisions for counting the number of steps involved by storing an integer 1 to represent the start of the count. Designating the number as $x$ ($\sqrt{x}$) and starting at storage location 500 we have

x in storage location 500
1 in storage location 501
2 in storage location 502

The program may now be stated as follows:

| Program Address | Code | Data Address | |
|---|---|---|---|
| 1000 | LDA | 501 | Clear accumulator and load 1 |
| 1001 | STA | 503 | Set "no. of steps" count to 1 |
| 1002 | LDA | 500 | Place x in accumulator |
| 1003 | SUB | 501 | Substract odd integer from x |
| 1004 | BRN | 1022 | If negative, branch to 1022 |
| 1005 | STA | 500 | Place new x value in 500 |
| 1006 | ADT | 503 | Add 1 to "no. of steps" count |
| 1007 | LDA | 501 | Clear accumulator and load 1 |
| 1010 | ADD | 502 | Increment of 2 (new odd integer) |
| 1011 | STA | 504 | Place new odd integer in 504 |
| 1012 | LDA | 500 | Place new x value in accumulator |
| 1013 | SUB | 504 | Subtract odd integer from x |
| 1014 | BRN | 1022 | If negative, branch to 1022 |
| 1015 | STA | 500 | Place new x value in 500 |
| 1016 | ADT | 503 | Add 1 to "no. of steps" count |
| 1017 | LDA | 504 | Place new odd integer in accumulator |
| 1020 | ADD | 502 | Increment of 2 (new odd integer) |
| 1021 | BRU | 1011 | Branch for iteration |
| 1022 | SUF | 503 | Subtract 1 from "no. of steps" |
| 1023 | BRU | n | Return to original program address n |

Storage location 503 is used to count the number of steps (subtractions of odd integers). Initially this memory is set at 1 to obliterate any square root number left in this place from previous usage of the subroutine. After the initial sampling, the new odd integers are placed in storage 504, so that the integer 1 is kept in storage 501 for subsequent use of the subroutine. Thus, to rerun the program, only the new value of x need be placed in storage 500.

Note the iterative branch loop from program address 1021 for successive subtraction of odd integers. When results produce a negative answer at program address 1014, the square root is stored in address 503 for use by the primary program as required.

To illustrate the usage of the subroutine now permanently stored in memory address 1000, assume we are to program the simple problem

$$486 \times \frac{\sqrt{7056}}{4} \quad \text{(print answer)}$$

The multiplier 486 is placed in storage 466 the divisor, in 467; and the 7056 value, in storage location 500. The program, calling on the subroutine for the square root, is

| 50 | LDA | 466  | Load 486 into accumulator.              |
|----|-----|------|-----------------------------------------|
| 51 | BRU | 1000 | Branch to subroutine.                   |
| 52 | MUL | 503  | Multiply 486 by square root of 7056.    |
| 53 | DIV | 467  | Divide by 4.                            |
| 54 | XCH |      | Place answer in accumulator.            |
| 55 | PFA |      | Print answer from accumulator.          |
| 56 | STP | 050  |                                         |

The instruction XCH (fifth step) is necessary since our restricted code list does not provide for a print-out from the quotient register. Thus, after a division process, if subsequent instructions relate to the accumulator, the quotient register contents must be placed in the accumulator. This can be done by reading the quotient register into storage and then reading it into the accumulator, or by the exchange instruction (which saves some steps).

In the subroutine-linkage method illustrated, the subroutine ends with a branch instruction which returns control to the primary program. In the example shown, the program address 052 in the primary program would have to be referenced in the data-address portion of the subroutine program address 1023 for the square root subroutine shown earlier.

## Fixed and Floating Point

In programming, consideration must be given to the method employed in a particular digital computer for the handling of fractional numbers and the identification of the decimal (radix) point. These factors may be more clearly understood by identifying the basic characteristics of a register. If a register, for instance, has a maximum capacity of 16 bits, the first register at the left represents the *sign* (see Chapter 2) and the registers to the right hold the *magnitude bits*, with the least significant bit at the extreme right:

$$S \; x \; x \; x \; x \; x \; x \; x \; x \; x \; x \; x \; x \; x \; x \; x$$

If we place the number $9_{10}$ in this register, the binary equivalent 1001 would be positioned

$$S \; 0 \; 0 \; 0 \; 0 \; 0 \; 0 \; 0 \; 0 \; 0 \; 0 \; 0 \; 1 \; 0 \; 0 \; 1$$

Here, the radix (binary) point is understood to be at the extreme right, 1001. to represent a whole number. Assume, however, we wish to place $9\frac{5}{8}$ into this register. The binary equivalent is 1001.101, and our radix point has now shifted three places left. With this number in the register, we would have no visible identifying means for ascertaining the true location of the radix point, since the number could be binary 1001101, or 10.01101, or any other number containing the same bits with a differently positioned radix:

$$S \; 0 \; 0 \; 0 \; 0 \; 0 \; 0 \; 0 \; 1 \; 0 \; 0 \; 1 \; 1 \; 0 \; 1$$

In binary-coded decimal form the same problem exists, since the radix point will also assume different positions for combinations of whole and fractional numbers. Thus, if we initially place 623 in decade counters or storage, and later 4.9826, the alignment will be

623
4.9826

One solution would be to add as many zeros to the whole number as needed to align the radix points,

623.0000
4.9826

This would complicate the read-in programming, however, and a more convenient method is to operate the computer as a *fractional machine* in which all numbers are in fractional form (positive or negative). Since, however, the true values may be whole numbers or fractions, some means must be employed to maintain identification of the radix point. There are two basic methods for handling radix-point identification. One is the *fixed-point* type where the programmer maintains records of the radix point locations. The other process is the *floating-point* method where the computer handles the radix-point location automatically. The floating-point method finds extensive applications in complex arithmetic programming, while data-processing programming procedures find that the fixed-point type is more appropriate.

In fixed-point arithmetic, the identification of the radix-point location is done by what is termed the *scale factor*. This is based on either powers of 10 (for decimal computers) or powers of 2 for binary operations (see Chapter 2). The following illustrations, again using a 16-bit word, will help make clear the fixed-point operation. If we wish to place 5.75 in the register, the binary equivalent is 101.11 ($5\frac{3}{4}$). Assume this appears as:

| S | 0 | 0 | 0 | 0 | 0 | 0 | 0 | 0 | 0 | 0 | 1 | 0 | 1 | 1 | 1 | 1 |

In fractional representation, the number in the register is

$$+.000000000010111$$

For a representation of the true value of this number, the binary point would have to be moved to the right 13 places. Hence, the *scale factor for this number is* $2^{13}$, since the number would have to be multiplied by $2^{13}$ to have a 101.11 value. Had the binary representation been $+.000101110000000$, the scale factor would have been $2^6$, since the binary point would have to be shifted 6 places to the right to produce the true number 101.11. If the scale factor is a negative power of 2, the binary point is moved to the left for the number of places indicated by the exponent. For instance if the following number has a scale factor of $2^{-3}$, the true number is 0.00011:

$$+.110000000000000$$

Had the sign bit been a 1 (to indicate a negative number) the true value would have been −0.00011.

In fixed-point techniques the programmer must keep an accurate record of the scale factors and make sure the computations do not produce number magnitudes in excess of the machine's capabilities, otherwise overflow will occur. Similarly, number positioning to the far right must take into consideration the possibility of loss in precision. (See Chapter 1, Digital versus Analog.)

When scaling is used, appropriate right and left shifting is used for proper alignment of the radix point in computations, because the exponents must be identical for addition and subtraction. For multiplication the exponents have to be added, and for division the exponents must be subtracted. Appropriate codes are furnished to perform the degree of shifting required, as shown in the mnemonic listing given earlier in this chapter.

A computer designed for *floating-point* operation automatically maintains identification of the radix point of the various numbers (integers and fractions) handled. It does this by keeping track of the mantissa (such as the 101 in $101 \times 2^3$) as well as the exponent (the 3 in $2^3$). At the conclusion of a computation, the radix point will automatically be placed in the proper position in the quotient, remainder, product, or sum. For floating-point operation, additional circuits are necessary in the computer to handle the process.

In a computer using the floating-point system, some of the word bits are used to express the exponent besides those normally used for the mantissa. (The exponent may be called the *characteristic* and the mantissa the *fraction* by some computer manufacturers.) With a 36-bit word, the allocation (including sign bit) may be as follows:

| S | 8 bits | 27 bits |
|---|--------|---------|

Exponent (characteristic)     Mantissa (fraction)

In the floating-point system additional instructional codes are used to perform the operations. The mnemonic code FMU_d, for instance, is used to multiply the number in the accumulator (in floating-point manner) by the number in the memory address designated. Similarly, FDV_d is the floating-point divide instruction, FAD_d is the add code, and FSU_d the subtract command.

## *FORTRAN*

In the programming procedures previously discussed, it was necessary to spell out each sequential step which the computer must undertake to perform the operations required. Also the symbolic language is more closely related to that of the machine than to the mathematics or data-processing language. With the introduction of FORTRAN by IBM in 1957, a computer programming language became available which was mathematically oriented, using a notation closely related to basic algebraic expressions. With FORTRAN, the programmer codes a problem by writing a series of basic FORTRAN-language statements. These are, in turn, translated into appropriate computer commands by the compiler system. One simple statement may be interpreted into an algebraic equation, another may be a decision instruction, and some specify the handling of input or output data, etc.

The compiler is a FORTRAN programming system which not only translates the basic series of FORTRAN statements into an intermediate language, but also processes the latter to form the necessary machine language. The compiler program which undertakes the translation is written and oriented to the particular computer with which it is to be used.

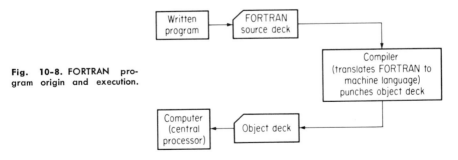

**Fig. 10-8. FORTRAN program origin and execution.**

The general sequence of FORTRAN programming and program processing is shown in Fig. 10-8. As for any lengthy or complex programs, a flow chart would be prepared initially to outline the sequence of steps which are to be undertaken. The program is then written in FORTRAN language on a program sheet. A keypunch machine is then used to punch the information contained in each program statement into a card. The complete deck of cards is known as the *source deck*. The source deck is next translated by the compiler system, which consists of a specially prepared program containing numerous instructions for converting the source deck FORTRAN language to machine language. Thus, the source deck is read by the compiler and its program processed by the computer. Another set of cards is now punched, known as the *object deck*. It is this object deck which is finally loaded into the computer for execution of the program originally written. At the same time additional cards are loaded which contain the data to be processed.

In some computer systems the object deck may be written on magnetic tape instead of punched in cards. The tape is then read by the computer and the program executed. Some compiler systems have provisions for printing out the source and object programs for use by the programmer in debugging and program modification procedures. As with some assemblers, the compilers also are designed to indicate instructional errors in the written program and will print out indications of certain symbol omissions or other violations of programming rules.

While a complete description of the FORTRAN programming of various mathematical equations is too lengthy to discuss here, some aspects are given to indicate the general features of the system. Since its introduction FORTRAN has gone through several modification phases for improving the format. Roman numerals are used to designate successive types. Thus, FORTRAN I is the predecessor of FORTRAN IV, etc.

The symbols for arithmetic operations in FORTRAN language are

|  |  |
|---|---|
| * | Multiply |
| ** | Exponentiation |
| / | Divide |
| + | Add |
| − | Subtract |

Capital letters are used to indicate variable quantities, and an equation is written on a single line. If more than one operation symbol appears between two variables, parentheses are used between the operation symbols. For any single-line equation there must be an equal number of right and left parentheses, or the compiler will be unable to interpret the logic and will print out an error message indicating the need for program debugging.

As in the symbolic-code programming discussed earlier in this chapter, equations can be programmed in generalized form ($a + b$, etc.) and different data used for the arithmetic symbols as needed. Specific values (5 + 28, etc.) can, of course, also be used initially. If, for instance, we wish to program $y = a + b^2$, the FORTRAN expression is

$$A + B**2$$

If, however, $a$ represents a known value of 286 and $b$ a value of 97.5, the statement becomes

$$286 + 97.5**2$$

Note that the exponent is not raised but instead is preceded by a double asterisk to indicate its function. The following illustrates the use of both the multiplication and exponent symbols:

In equation form:          $ax^2 + bx + c$
FORTRAN statement:     A*X**2 + B*X + C

Use of the division symbol plus the parentheses is indicated in programming the following:

In equation form:          $\dfrac{a + b}{c}$

FORTRAN statement:     (A + B)/C

The following equation uses several of the symbols in the single-line statement, ending with a double parenthesis to maintain equality in the number of right and left parentheses used:

In equation form:          $\dfrac{a \cdot b}{c^3 + \dfrac{d}{x - y}}$

FORTRAN statement:     (A*B)/(C**3 + D/(X − Y))

Symbols for other arithmetic functions are also provided, as the following (FORTRAN IV) list indicates:

*FORTRAN IV*

| | |
|---|---|
| Sine | SIN |
| Cosine | COS |
| Square root | SQRT |
| Logarithm base $e$ | ALOG |
| Logarithm base 10 | ALOG 10 |

Thus, for the expression $y = \sin(x)$, where $x$ is the angle expressed in radians, the FORTRAN expression is

$$Y = SIN\ (X)$$

Use of the square root expression is shown in the following, where the root of the quadratic equation is programmed. The root of the quadratic equation $ax^2 + bx + c = 0$ is given by the formula:

$$x = \frac{-b + \sqrt{b^2 - 4ac}}{2a}$$

In FORTRAN the expression for this formula is

$$X = (-B + SQRT\ (B**2 - 4.\ *A*C))/(2.*A)$$

The equal sign in the FORTRAN expression shown above acts as an instructional code to the computer to perform the operations indicated to the right of the equal sign and to replace the left member (the X) with the computed resultant. Thus, the equal sign has a different operational meaning than it has in basic mathematical computations where it denotes equality between the left and right members of the equation. This can be more clearly understood by inspection of the expression for $x = x \cdot 46.6 + c$ which is not valid as a mathematical equation since $x$ cannot be equal to itself if it is multiplied by 46.6 and has an additional value represented by $c$ added to it. Assume, however, that $x$ is stored in memory location $n_1$, 46.6 in location $n_2$, and $c$ in storage $n_3$. The FORTRAN expression is

$$X = X*46.6 + C$$

The computer will process this in the following sequence:

1. The value of X is taken from storage $n_1$ and placed in the accumulator.
2. The X is multiplied by 46.6 from storage location $n_2$.
3. The value of C from storage location $n_3$ is added to the contents of the accumulator.
4. The new value of X is stored in storage location $n_1$ to replace the original value at this memory address.

In addition to the arithmetic commands, a variety of other instructions are available for programming purposes, so that start and stop commands can be issued, branching and looping undertaken when required, and reading or printing procedures executed. Typical FORTRAN symbols of this type include:

| | |
|---|---|
| READ n | Causes card reading of listed values according to the stated arrangement of data given. |
| PRINT n | Causes printing of listed values according to the statement arrangement. |
| READ (i, X) | Causes reading of data specified by the X listing from a unit designated by i. |
| STOP | Halts the program. |
| END | Used as the last statement of a program to indicate to the compiler the program conclusion. |
| WRITE (i) | Causes the writing of listed data on a unit designated by i. |
| GO TO n | A transfer command which branches to statement n. |
| IF (L) s | A decision instruction. If logical expression (L) is true, statement s is to be executed, otherwise go to statement immediately following IF. |
| PAUSE | A halt command which causes the computer to stop. If the start switch is depressed the program sequence following the PAUSE command will be continued. |
| FORMAT | This statement is followed by alphanumeric specifications of the manner in which the data are arranged on cards or other such media. |

Using the foregoing to write a complete program in FORTRAN for the simple equation $y = ax^2$, we have

```
    READ 1, A, X
    Y = A*X**2
    PRINT 2, Y, X
    STOP
  1 FORMAT (2F10.0)
  2 FORMAT (2F14.4)
    END
```

In the foregoing the fifth and sixth statements are numbered for identifying the data arrangement to be read by the first statement, as well as that for the print reference in the third statement. Though each statement could be numbered, usually only those statements which will be referenced in the program are assigned numbers (placed at the left, as shown). Statement numbers need not be consecutive, nor must they start at 1. Thus, the first and third statements could have been READ 20, A, X and PRINT 21, Y, X. In this instance the fifth and sixth statements would be: 20 FORMAT (2F10.0) and 21 FORMAT (2F14.4).

Thus, the READ symbol indicates the numerical values of A and X are to be read from the input punched card, in the arrangement indicated by the numerically referenced FORMAT. Thus, for the program shown, the fifth statement indicates 2 values are involved and each occupies 10 columns on the input data card. The sixth statement indicates the spacing (14 spaces) and the decimal places to be printed (4) in addition to the numbers to the left of the decimal (radix) point.

The second statement is the FORTRAN expression for the equation to be processed, followed by the third statement which indicates what quantities are to be printed out. The fourth statement, STOP, brings the computer to a halt after execution of the print instruction. The END statement is always last and signifies the last card has been read and hence halts the compiling process.

As another example, the following programs the equation given in the FORTRAN expression indicated by the second statement. The first and third statements are referenced to the formats numbered 10 and 11 as shown.

```
   READ 10, A, B, C, X
   Y = (A + B)/C*X**3
   PRINT 11, Y
   STOP
10 FORMAT (4F10.0)
11 FORMAT (1F14.4)
   END
```

## COBOL

In 1959 the U.S. Defense Department instigated the formation of a committee composed of both government and computer company representatives. This committee was charged with the task of developing a common language code for data processing for use with any computer. The result of this committee's work was the development of COBOL which could be used with any computer having a COBOL compiler for translating this basic language into that recognizable by the computer.

COBOL uses our basic English language to express the sequential operations which the computer must undertake to execute a given program. Hence, COBOL is written with letters, numbers, and punctuation marks, all of which make up meaningful words, sentences, and paragraphs. Just as the English language has rules of grammar, so COBOL has a set of rules which must be followed for proper program execution. Once written, the COBOL program can be read by a non-programmer and the data-processing sequence easily understood and followed. Because specific rules must be followed in writing COBOL, however, the untrained person could not write such a program. For instance, the verb PERFORM is valid, but *execute* is not. Similarly, COMPUTE is acceptable, but *calculate* cannot be used. In sequence control verbs, ALTER must be used instead of *change*, etc.

As mentioned earlier in this chapter for the mnemonic code, a computer recognizes an instruction code (in binary form) as a command to perform a certain operation, such as add, multiply, etc. Thus, an instructional code can be compared to a verb in the English language, since either expresses an action to be taken. Similarly, the nouns in the English language represent the data to be processed by the verbs. Thus, by using verbs, nouns, conjunctions, and other parts of speech, the COBOL language is formed and translated by the compiling program into machine-acceptable instructions and data names. If, for instance, the computer is to *compute* the *annual* sum paid *in salaries*, the COBOL statement would be COMPUTE ANNUAL IN SALARIES = 12*MONTHLY PAY. (As in FORTRAN, the asterisk * indicates multiplication.)

### Program Verbs

The program verbs used in COBOL for input and output functions are OPEN, READ, WRITE, CLOSE, ACCEPT, and DISPLAY. The OPEN statement is used to process one or more files (identified stored data) of the computer. The OPEN verb must be followed by a

modifying statement (input or output), such as OPEN INPUT
PAYROLL-FILE. Once the OPEN command has been written, the
READ or WRITE commands may follow: READ PAYROLL-FILE
or WRITE SALARY-RECORD. (Hyphenated words are part of the
same modifying statement.)

Data manipulation verbs are MOVE and EXAMINE. The
MOVE statement is used for interchange of data from one computer
section or unit to another. The EXAMINE verb permits the inspection of data stored in the computer.

Arithmetic verbs are ADD, SUBTRACT, MULTIPLY, DI-
VIDE, and COMPUTE. The COMPUTE verb permits the programmer to include equation statements when such are necessary in
the data-processing procedures. In addition to the arithmetic operation verbs, the characters +, −, *, and / are also used, as in FOR-
TRAN, for addition, subtraction, multiplication, and division.

Additional verbs are used for sequence control, and these are GO
TO, ALTER, PERFORM, and STOP. These statements permit
branching and the execution of program modifications as dictated by
the nature of the data processing being programmed. Included may
be such statements as GO TO REORDER-ROUTINE; DISPLAY
MESSAGE ON PRINTER; STOP.

### COBOL Program Divisions

There are four basic divisions of a COBOL program, the Identification Division, Environment Division, Data Division, and Procedure Division. The first three, as the terms imply, identify the program and equipment, describe the nature and source of the data, and
the methods to be used for the data-processing procedures. The
Procedure Division contains the sequential steps comprising the data-
processing program.

The *Identification Division* is made up of sentences and paragraphs
composed of:

Program ID     program name (*must* be used)
Author     name identification (optional)
Installation     (optional)
Date written and compiled     (optional)
Security     (optional)
Remarks     (optional)

As indicated, only the Program ID must be included in the Identification Division, and it should identify the source and object of the program. Since the writing of COBOL produces an easily read program, the optional subdivisions are used only if additional explanations are required, and their inclusion does not affect the program structure as executed by the compiler.

The *Environment Division* of COBOL has two subdivisions, the *configuration* section and the *input-output* sections. The configuration section identifies the computer which compiles the program (source computer) and the computer which will execute the program (object computer). Both such references may, of course, apply to a single computer. The input-output sections identify the type of input and output equipment to be used for the file references in the program. Thus, the Environment Division is composed of sentences and paragraphs composed of:

    Configuration section
        Source computer (name)
        Object computer (name)
    Input-output section
        File control. Select....
    Input-output control. Apply....

The file control selects the particular file specified, and the input-output control indicates the particular input and output procedures to be followed.

The *Data Division* has three sections:

    File section
    Working-storage section
    Constant section

The file section identifies the manner in which the data are recorded in the file storage, whether or not the file has label records, the names of the records making up the complete file, the number of characters in each record, the decimal location, etc. Entries are made to describe the file records, and identifying numbers (02, 03, 04, etc.) are assigned, as shown later in the program example. The entries consist of independent clauses, and a special one, called a *picture* clause, is used to denote operational signs, decimal point, item unit magnitude, and classification.

Special characters are included in a picture clause to denote certain conditions. The number 9 denotes one numeric character position, and several 9's would be used to indicate unit magnitude. If a payroll program, for instance, contains the statement EMPLOYEE NO PICTURE IS 99999, it would indicate that a maximum of five character positions are involved, such as 38931, for a particular employee's identification number.

A capital-letter V denotes the decimal point position. Thus, if a statement reads GROSS PICTURE IS 99999V99, it indicates a numeric value such as 25387.64. If an S is used, it indicates an operational sign. Thus, S999V99 could indicate −432.67, or −929.33, etc.

Use of the capital letter A denotes the character position is alphabetic only. Thus, AAAA in the picture clause indicates that four letters are contained in the file position identified. The letter X denotes alphanumeric. Thus, XXXXXX in a picture clause could indicate the alphanumeric expression 121AB5, or 9742J9, etc. The character Z indicates zero for a given character position. Use of the letter Z suppresses zeros to the left of significant bits and replaces them by blanks. Hence, when the significant bits are printed, the undesired zeros will not appear. The code ZZZ9V99 for a file record containing 0000.28, for instance, produces a print-out of 0.28.

The working-storage section of the Data Division indicates temporary-storage locations during processing. The constant section identifies named items having a fixed unit-value magnitude and also indicates the specific values.

The *Procedure Division* of COBOL is used by the programmer to spell out the sequential processes to be applied to the data in the Data Division. Again, basic English words are used to form sentences and paragraphs outlining the program execution.

## COBOL Programming

In writing a COBOL program, identifying numbers are used for each of the program steps written on a program sheet. Thus, 010010 could start the program, and the first three bits (010) would identify the program page number, and the second three bits (again 010), the number of a line on page 10. Similarly, 010090 indicates page 10, line 90, etc. To permit insertions and program modifications, numbers may increase by 10 as shown later.

For complex inventory, payroll, or other business procedures, the setting up of a program in COBOL should be preceded by a flow chart of the entire operation. This chart then serves as a guide for setting up the sequential steps necessary for processing the data as required, in similar fashion to other programming procedures discussed earlier.

A typical payroll program would start with the Identification Division, written in capital letters, and would end each statement with a period:

```
001010    IDENTIFICATION DIVISION.
001020    PROGRAM-ID. PAYROLL CALCULATION.
001030    ENVIRONMENT DIVISION.
001040    CONFIGURATION SECTION.
001050    SOURCE-COMPUTER. IBM 1401.
001060    OBJECT-COMPUTER. IBM 1401.
001070    INPUT-OUTPUT SECTION.
001080    FILE-CONTROL. SELECT PAYROLL-FILE
              ASSIGN TO i.
```

In the last statement, at step 001080, the *i* portion would indicate the location where the processed payroll information is to be filed. If any specific input and output procedures are to be followed, these would also be identified. The data Division would be next, and like the Identification Division, the specific division must be listed:

```
001090    DATA DIVISION.
001100    FILE SECTION.
001110    FD  PAYROLL-FILE.
001120        LABEL RECORDS ARE OMITTED.
001130        DATA RECORD IS PAYROLL.
001140    01  PAYROLL.
```

In step 001110 the FD must always precede a file description entry. Note also that the *working-storage section* was omitted. Had it been necessary to include this, it would have been step 001140, followed by a description of storage locations which temporarily hold intermediate results.

The 01 preceding the PAYROLL indicates that the succeeding statements describe the payroll record. These descriptions will have level numbers of 02 to indicate subdivisions of 01 PAYROLL. Included, could be the following:

```
001150    02  EMPLOYEE-NO PICTURE IS 999999.
001160    02  NAME PICTURE IS X(30).
001170    02  EXEMPTIONS PICTURE IS 9.
```

In step 001160 the X(30) listing is used to avoid writing 30 X characters. Following step 001170, other appropriate items (withholding tax, gross, etc.) would also be entered in succession, preceded by the 02 level number. After all entries have been included under the file section, the Procedure Division would follow, to end the program. As other divisions, the Procedure Division must be listed:

```
001180    PROCEDURE DIVISION.
001190    START. OPEN OUTPUT PAYROLL-FILE.
001200    READ-IN. READ PAYROLL-FILE RECORD.
002010    COMPUTE WITHHOLDING-TAX.
```

The procedures would continue, entry by entry, for sequential processing of the necessary steps required in the payroll computation, ending with CLOSE-FILES. CLOSE PAYROLL-FILE. STOP 99.

## ALGOL, PL/I, etc.

Another computer language which permits the writing of a program in basic mathematical equation form is ALGOL. This was developed by an international committee and has found greater applications in Europe than in the United States. Since it can be used to express mathematical and scientific problems by using the symbols and terms of such problems, it is closely allied to FORTRAN.

Comparison of ALGOL with the earlier versions of FORTRAN (I and II) indicates greater versatility for ALGOL, though FORTRAN II embraced some of the notational advantages found in ALGOL. With the advent of FORTRAN IV, the essential differences have become minor, since FORTRAN IV now permits multiple entries to subroutines and additional features provide added flexibility. Committees of program engineers have been actively engaged in improving the automatic-programming features of FORTRAN, COBOL, and ALGOL in an effort toward the development of a universal computer language retaining the most advantageous characteristics of each, plus the additional factor of simplification which will ultimately accrue. One result of such committee activity is the

PL/I (program language 1) introduced by IBM early in 1966. The PL/I has retained some of the best features of FORTRAN, ALGOL, and COBOL, and is intended to be a universal-type language. It has been designed to provide greater flexibility and simpler programming procedures than FORTRAN. As with other high-level languages, a compiling program must be employed for conversion of the language to that acceptable by the computer.

Some special-purpose languages have also been used on occasion, such as MAD (Michigan Algorithm Decoder) used in certain time-sharing systems, and JOVIAL (Jules' Own Version of International Algebraic Language) which has found some applications in the military. The most widely-used languages, however, have been those discussed earlier and reference should be made to the bibliography at the end of this chapter for extensive coverage of the programming principles involved.

## *Time-Sharing Systems*

When the operational demands on a computer are high, a number of written programs (software) may be on the waiting list to be processed. In the meantime, the computer handles each program assigned to it in sequence—a method also termed *batch processing*. If some of the programs held in abeyance are priority types, the system has disadvantages which may be costly and time consuming. When a program is finally entered into the computer, it may be rejected because of program faults, incomplete data, etc. Thus, the waiting time was wasted and the program must be debugged and again placed in order on the waiting list.

Another method for expediting the handling of many programs is that known as *time sharing*. In this system special remote units are used as shown in Fig. 10-9. These may consist of interfaced (compatible) devices which can relay the program information to the central processor. Teletypewriters may also be used or computerized cathode-ray tube display systems of the type described in Chapter 8. Essentially, in time-sharing systems, the programs are handled in *parallel* rather than in the sequential method used in batch processing. A stored *supervisory program* in the main computer functions, as the name implies, as a supervising control center for gathering data from the remote units at appropriate intervals so that program material of all sorts can be in-

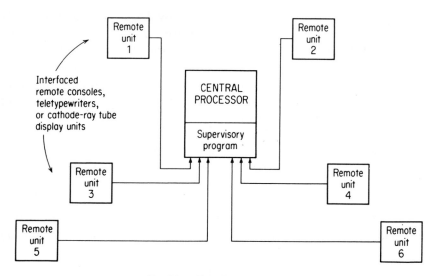

**Fig. 10-9.** Time-sharing system.

terlaced and handled in the most expeditious manner. Thus, the supervisory program constantly *monitors* the flow of program material, data, and input and output processes to and from the remote units. Since it acts as an intermediary between the computer and the remote user, it will give immediate indication of program faults and eliminate delays.

As mentioned earlier, in a stored-program computer the written program is entered into the computer's storage before the program is executed. If a number of programs are stored in a computer at one time, the term *multiprogramming* is applied. The term refers to both the batch processing and the time sharing, though in the latter the program loading is from remote units. For either system, only one program (or program segment) is run at any one time, though the supervisory control may interrupt a program, place the tentative results in storage, and execute another program if the need arises.

Time-sharing systems differ from the *multiprocessing* systems in which two or three computers may operate independently of each other but have common access to the storage facilities of each. Multiprocessing, however, overlaps the time-sharing area when the display type of consoles are used that have storage facilities, logic circuitry, and some calculation characteristics and interacting control between remote units and the central processor.

The storage requirements for time-sharing systems are large, since the supervisory program takes up considerable storage space to hold the control-sequence information it requires. If, for instance, the computer has a storage capacity of 100,000 words, half of this memory maybe taken up by the supervisory program. Rapid-access primary storage, such as ferrite cores, are used in addition to the auxiliary storage systems using magnetic drums or magnetic discs. Storage capacities of millions of characters are necessary in addition to the stored programs obtained from the remote units, since subroutines take up space, as do the compiler programs for translating FOR-TRAN or other high-level languages into machine language.

The operational characteristics of time-sharing systems are varied and depend on the nature of the problems, their length, and particular priority over others. One method is to allocate a specific time for each program as a maximum. If the program is executed before that time, the computer's supervisory control prints or displays the answers and seeks out the next program. If, however, the solutions are not obtained in the time allocated, the supervisory control interrupts the program, stores the program and results, and starts operations on the next program. At some later time the interrupted program is again activated and the process completed.

A variation of this method is to have no time allocation, and process each program to completion. The supervisory control, after the completion of one program, ascertains which stored program has been received before the others in storage, and permits the central processor to execute this program next. Thus, each stored program which has been obtained from the remote units, is executed in the order in which it has been received.

The supervisory program can, of course, be designed to accept programs in the order of highest priority. If desired, the sequence can be such that the supervisory control selects, from storage, those programs which are the shortest for initial execution, saving for last the more lengthy ones. Because many programs of the problem type are executed within a few milliseconds or minutes, the solutions are obtained at the remote units shortly after the programs are entered. Thus, all the short-time programs are executed quickly and the computer does not have too many on the waiting list.

In time-sharing computer systems, a special coded password is often allocated to each user. This password must be furnished to the computer at the start of the program so the machine can identify the personnel and verify permission to run a program. This procedure prevents access to classified information in storage and also avoids the accidental alteration of private data held in memory. Each user may also be allocated a specific memory capacity. When the password is given to the computer, the machine will indicate the total storage capacity available to the user, or that amount still remaining after certain data have been stored from earlier programs.

## Bibliography

The material in Chapters 9 and 10 provides a foundation for computer programming by discussing and illustrating basic concepts and the techniques involved for the several program languages. Programming aspects of FORTRAN and COBOL are more involved and extensive than could be detailed in the space provided in this text. Hence, for a comprehensive survey of programming procedures, reference should be made to one or more of the following publications.

Awad, Elias M., *Business Data Processing*. Englewood Cliffs, N. J.: Prentice-Hall, Inc., 1965.

Cutler, Donald I., *Introduction to Computer Programming*. Englewood Cliffs, N. J.: Prentice-Hall, Inc., 1964.

Dimitry, Donald L., and Mott, Thomas H., Jr., *Introduction to FORTRAN IV Programming*. New York: Holt, Rinehart and Winston, Inc., 1966.

Galler, Bernard F., *The Language of Computers*. New York: McGraw-Hill Book Company, Inc., 1962.

Golden, James T., *FORTRAN IV Programming and Computing*. Englewood Cliffs, N. J.: Prentice-Hall, Inc., 1965.

Hull, Thomas E., *Introduction to Computing*. Englewood Cliffs, N. J.: Prentice-Hall, Inc., 1966.

McCracken, Daniel D., and Dorn, William S., *Numerical Methods and FORTRAN Programming*. New York: John Wiley & Sons, Inc., 1964.

Swallow, Kenneth P., and Price, Wilson T., *Elements of Computer Programming*. New York: Holt, Rinehart and Winston, Inc., 1965.

Weinberg, Gerald M. *PL/I Programming Primer*. New York: McGraw-Hill Book Company, Inc., 1966.

# PROBLEMS

**1.** How does a single-address computer differ from a two-address type?

**2.** Explain the difference between a conditional and an unconditional branch.

**3.** Show, by flow-chart diagram, a basic transfer operation.

**4.** Explain what is meant by *mnemonic code*.

**5.** Using the mnemonic-code listing given in this chapter, program the following equation, starting with program address 20 and data-storage address 200:

$$Y = \frac{a^2 + b}{c} \quad \text{(print out answer)}$$

**6.** Using the mnemonic code, program the following equation. Assume the values have been stored in the following locations: $a$ in storage 300, $b$ in storage 301, $c$ in 302, and $d$ in 303. Storage location 304 is reserved for the answer $Y$.

$$Y = \frac{(a + b)^2}{c - d} \quad \text{(store answer)}$$

**7.** Using the mnemonic code, program the following:

$a + b^2 + c = Y$     (If any produce or sum exceeds an assigned $X$ value stop; otherwise continue until $Y$ is in accumulator.)

Assign storage addresses as required.

**8.** Program the two equations:

$$a^2 + b^2 = X \quad \text{and} \quad c \cdot b^2 = Y$$

Then,

$$Y \cdot X = Z \quad \text{(store } Z \text{ in location 207)}$$

Initially place $a$ in 200, $b$ in 201, and $c$ in 202. Start with program address 030.

**9.** Modify and rewrite the warehouse program given on page 274 to include three additional warehouses $E$, $F$, and $G$. Assign storage 105 to $E$, 106 to $F$, and 107 to $G$. Again print out amounts to be placed in each warehouse, etc.

**10.** Explain what is meant by a *subroutine*.

**11.** Using the subroutine procedures detailed in this chapter, program the following:

$$Y = 2866 + \frac{\sqrt{27225}}{15} \quad \text{(store } Y \text{ in location 650)}$$

**12.** How does floating-point operation differ from fixed-point operation?

**13.** In what manner does a computer using floating-point operation identify exponent values?

**14.** How does FORTRAN differ from mnemonic programming?

**15.** What is the difference between the source deck and the object deck in FORTRAN?

**16.** In FORTRAN programming, how are instructional errors indicated by the computer?

**17.** Write the FORTRAN expression for $a/(x - y)$.

**18.** Write the FORTRAN expression for $ax + bx + y^2$.

**19.** Write the FORTRAN expression for the following equation:

$$\frac{a - b}{x/(y + z)}$$

**20.** List and explain several program verbs used in COBOL.

**21.** In the Identification Division of a COBOL program, which subdivisions are optional?

**22.** What is the purpose of the configuration section of the Environment Division of COBOL?

**23.** What sections comprise the Data Division of a COBOL program?

**24.** What is meant by a *picture clause* in COBOL?

**25.** Explain how the capital letters V, S, X, and Z are used in COBOL program writing.

**26.** Explain the function of the Procedure Division in COBOL programming.

**27.** Why is it advisable to have identifying numbers of COBOL expressions progress in steps of 10?

**28.** Of what significance is the 01 in the COBOL expression 001140 01 PAYROLL?

**29.** Of what significance is the 02 in the COBOL expression 001170 02 EXEMPTION PICTURE IS 9?

**30.** How is ALGOL similar to FORTRAN?

**31.** How does a computer *time-sharing* system operate?

**32.** What are the differences between *multiprogramming* and *multiprocessing?*

**33.** What type of units may be used as the remote devices in the time-sharing systems?

**34.** Why must there be greater storage facilities in the time-sharing systems?

# ANALOG
# COMPUTER
# PRINCIPLES

**11**

**Introduction.** Some of the factors relating to analog computers, plus basic differences between it and the digital computer, have already been discussed in Chapter 1 (Analog versus Digital). Essentially, the analog computer operates in a parallel mode, that is, all variables entered into the machine are acted on *simultaneously* during the computation. Thus, it differs from the digital computer where programs of problems or data processing are handled in step-by-step fashion. The analog computer is adapted to perform the functions of summation, multiplication, and division of variables, integration with respect to time, and other problems related to the calculus.

By restating the physical system equations or utilizing special sensing devices, the analog functions can be modified or programmed so they are acceptable to the digital computer circuitry. Some aspect of this has already been covered in Chapter 5 in the section on the Gray Code. Such a union between the analog computer and the digital machine is known as a *hybrid computing system*. In addition to such hybrid systems, which couple the analog to the digital, special digitized analog computers are used which have some of the functional characteristics of the digital built in, such as storage capacity and the ability of iteration (repetition of a computing process). The basic analog circuitry, however, differs considerably from that of the digital computer, and the fundamental principles involved are covered in this chapter.

## Analog Computer Factors

The basic analog computer is made up of a number of computational circuits which act as building blocks, or modules. Only a few basic types are involved, but, as in a digital computer, the circuitry is repeated for a sufficient number of times to perform the tasks required. Each building block is capable of performing a certain mathematical operation and recognizes quantities as specific voltage levels. The components of the analog machine are connected (patched) to relate to the problem to be solved. Voltage variations, representative of the quantities to be processed, are usually between $+100$ and $-100$. All the analog machine variables are *scaled* to fall within the specific range for which the computer has been designed. Thus, a variable which may range from 0 to 1000 could be represented by an actual voltage range of 0.1 to $+100$ volts. In such an instance, a unit value of 1 is represented by 0.1 volt, and the 1000 value, by $+100$ volts. Thus, temperature, mileage, displacement, or other physical variables are scaled to fall within the voltage variation for which the machine was designed.

The basic analog computer components and circuits are potentiometers, amplifiers, multipliers, and function generators. In setting up the problem to be solved, interconnections are made on the machine's *patch panel*. In most instances the panel can be removed for convenience in programming. With several patch panels, the computer can be used to solve other problems while some patch panels are being programmed. Once a problem is solved, the answer appears as a steady-state voltage on a panel meter or is a varying value which can be sensed and applied to X-Y plotters or strip-chart recorders.

A typical patch panel and indicator meter are shown in the analog computer illustrated in Fig. 11-1. This is the *Pace* TR-20 analog computer of Electronic Associates, Incorporated. Like modern digital computers, this is a transistorized machine. It has an amplifier computing accuracy of 0.01 per cent. Color-coded patching modules and accessories are used to promote programming efficiency. A null type of voltmeter is used for direct reading, or precision null reading.

**Fig. 11-1.** Pace TR-20 analog computer.

## Plotters and Recorders

The X-Y plotter is essentially an electronic graphing device capable of plotting the results of two variables under the control of an analog computer. In one type, the chart, mounted on rollers, is capable of moving up or down, depending on the polarity and amplitudes of the signals (variables) applied to the vertical movement mechanism. The writing pen can also respond to positive or negative signals (variables), and its movement is either to the left or right. Thus, the plotting process is under the control of one signal representing the $X$ axis and another representing the $Y$ axis of a graph. In another type the recording pen moves along a straight arm to plot $X$ values, and the arm itself moves vertically to graph the $Y$ values.

In the strip-chart recorder, a roll of paper is moved at a constant speed under the recording pen. The pen moves to the left or right in proportion to the applied voltages. Thus, the pen graphs the computer voltages as a function of time (the movement of the pen). The general appearance of the strip-chart recorder is shown in Fig. 11-2.

**Fig. 11-2.** Strip-chart recorder. Courtesy, Leeds-Northrup.

## Arithmetic Operations

The operational characteristics of an analog computer can be more easily understood by first investigating the arithmetic operations which can be performed by passive resistive networks. If the resistors used have linear functions (that is, current through the unit changes in proportion to the voltage across it), accurate addition, multiplication, division, and subtraction can be performed.

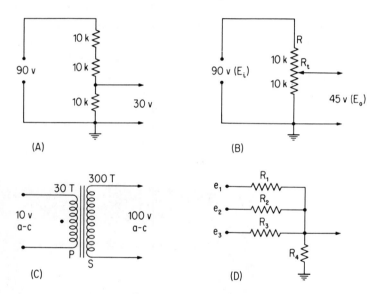

**Fig. 11-3.** Passive circuits.

A voltage-divider circuit, as the name implies, will perform division processes. Typical of the function is the divider network shown in A of Fig. 11-3. Here, equal-value (10K-ohm) resistors are used, with the output obtained from the bottom resistor. Hence, a division by 3 is obtained for any signal voltage applied to the input. Similarly, a potentiometer can be used as shown in B. Assuming a linear change, the dial of the potentiometer can be calibrated to indicate the coefficient of division. If the coefficient potentiometer is set for half its resistance, as shown, the result of the division is, of course, an output voltage one-half that of the input.

The signal-voltage output can be expressed in equation form as

$$E_o = IR_t = \frac{E_i}{R}R_t$$

where $E_o$ is the output voltage,

   $E_i$ is the input voltage,

   $R$  is the total resistance, and

   $R_t$ is the resistance of the tapped section to ground.

From the foregoing it is evident that the output voltage is the product of the input voltage multiplied by the fraction of the total resistance tapped off. Hence, such a circuit provides *multiplication* by a fraction, or *division* by a constant coefficient.

A transformer, as shown in C of Fig. 11-3, exhibits multiplication characteristics because of the voltage step-up procured if the secondary has more turns of wire than the primary. Since the voltage ratio between primary and secondary $E_p/E_s$ equals the turns ratio $N_p/N_s$, the amount of voltage step-up depends on the turns ratio. Thus, if the primary has 30 turns of wire, as indicated, and the secondary, 300 turns, a 10 to 1 voltage increase (multiplication by 10) is obtained.

In analog computers a resistor circuit such as shown in D performs additive functions. This type of circuit is known as a *summing network* and can add either positive or negative numbers (represented by positive or negative signal voltages applied to the input terminals.) The operation of this circuit can best be understood by analyzing, initially, a two-input circuit of this type, as shown in A of Fig. 11-4.

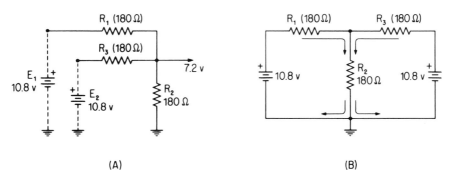

(A)                                              (B)

**Fig. 11-4. Summing network**

Here we are representing the input signals by fixed-value voltages from batteries, as shown by the broken lines. Thus, the circuit is equivalent to one having two independent voltage sources, with the current for each flowing through the common series resistor $R_2$ and branching into individual paths through $R_1$ and $R_3$. The circuit can be rearranged as shown in B, which is a familiar network often used to study Kirchhoff's laws. The voltage-drop effect of the branch currents through $R_2$ can be solved by standard Kirchhoff's law procedures. If we start with $R_1$ and proceed in the direction shown by the arrows, we obtain

$$180I_1 + 180I_2 = 10.8 \text{ volts}$$

Since $I_1 = I_2 - I_3$, the equation can be rewritten as follows to eliminate the $I_1$:

$$180I_2 - 180I_3 + 180I_2 = 10.8 \text{ volts}$$

Collecting terms, we get

$$360I_2 - 180I_3 = 10.8 \text{ volts}$$

This forms the first equation of the simultaneous equations. Adding this to the values obtained from the circuit for the second simultaneous equation, we have

$$
\begin{aligned}
360I_2 - 180I_3 &= 10.8 \text{ volts} \\
180I_2 + 180I_3 &= 10.8 \text{ volts} \\
\hline
540I_2 \phantom{- 180I_3} &= 21.6 \text{ volts}
\end{aligned}
$$

Hence,

$$21.6/540 = 0.04 \text{ ampere}$$

Voltage across $R_2$ is, therefore, $0.04 \times 180 = 7.2$ volts. Note that this is one-third of the sum of the input signal voltages ($3 \times 7.2 = 21.6$). Thus, if the resistors have equal values, the output voltage will always be $\frac{1}{3}(e_1 + e_2)$. With equal-value resistors for the *three*-input circuit shown earlier in B of Fig. 11-4, the output voltage would be equal to $\frac{1}{4}(e_1 + e_2 + e_3)$. If the input resistors are of unequal value, the output voltage can again be found by using Kirchhoff's law though the one-fourth relationship mentioned no longer applies as a simple solution. The analog computer circuitry, however, properly relates the quantities to provide the required solution as subsequently detailed. In such summing networks, the application of negative voltages produces a subtraction process, since a negative voltage will create a current flow in the opposite direction to that caused by positive-voltage signals. The algebraic sum, according to Kirchhoff's law, will then equal the difference between the two values.

### Calculus Functions

In Chapter 1, both *differentiation* and *integration* circuits were discussed and the basic schematics given in Fig. 1-12. It was pointed out that differentiation can be used for obtaining a sharp leading edge for signal pulses and that the circuit has high-pass characteristics. For the integrator, however, low-pass functions are obtained, and some unwanted signal modification could occur if undesired integration is encountered in circuitry having abnormal shunt capacitances. In an analog computer, however, the integration principle is of considerable usefulness in performing calculus operations. Hence, integrator circuits are extensively used in active network systems, as detailed more fully later. For a clearer understanding of integrator functions, the circuit characteristics will be compared with those of the differentiator before discussing complete active systems.

For the differentiating circuit, as pointed out in Chapter 1, the time constant is short compared to the pulse width. The differentiating function comes about because, when voltage is applied to a capacitor, the resultant current flow is proportional to the time derivative of the voltage appearing across the capacitor.

$$i = C \frac{de_c}{dt} \qquad (11\text{-}1)$$

For a short time constant $RC$, certain signal components of the input pulse will find the resistor of the circuit has an ohmic value much lower than the reactance of the capacitor. Hence, the voltage across the resistor is

$$e_R = iR = RC \frac{de}{dt} \qquad (11\text{-}2)$$

For an integrating circuit, the signal voltage applied to the capacitor, $e_C$, and the capacitor signal current $i_C$ have the following relationships:

$$e_C = \frac{1}{C} \int i_C \, dt \qquad (11\text{-}3)$$

where $e_C$ is the signal voltage across the capacitor,

   $C$ is the capacitance, in farads,

   $i_C$ is the capacitor signal current.

Hence, $e_C$ is proportional to the time interval of $i_C$. In the integrating circuit, the time constant $RC$ is long compared to pulse width. For upper signal-frequency components of the pulse, however, the resistance value is higher than the capacitive reactance of the capacitor. Thus, the output signal voltage $e_C$ is proportional to the *integral* of the input signal voltage $e_i$:

$$e_C = \frac{1}{RC} \int e_i \, dt \qquad (11\text{-}4)$$

Since the charge and discharge of a capacitor is linear for only a short period, the integration and differentiating functions are accurate also only within certain limits with a passive network. After a time constant of approximately 0.1, the capacitor charge follows an exponential curve and hence is nonlinear. Similarly, the passive resistive networks attenuate signals and hence also offer some disadvantages in analog computations. To compensate for these *passive*-circuit weaknesses, analog computers use *active* circuits, consisting of special amplifiers having linear characteristics, with controlled feedback. Such amplifiers are called *operational amplifiers* and are of the *direct-coupled* type discussed in Chapter 1.

### Operational Amplifiers

The operational amplifiers are carefully designed to have high-gain (over a million), linear characteristics, a response from d-c to very high signal frequencies, and minimum drift. In addition they have feedback control available from external terminals to permit modification of input impedance or feedback impedance or both for computing purposes. A block diagram representation is shown in A of Fig. 11-5, and the symbolic equivalent is given in B.

In the diagram shown in A, the feedback circuit is designated by the lower-case Greek letter $\beta$, representing the decimal equivalent of the percentage of voltage fed back, as discussed in Chapter 1, Inverse Feedback. The $A'$ symbol in the d-c amplifier is the signal-voltage *amplification with* feedback. The input signal is designated as $e_i$ and the output as $e_o$. For the symbolic representation in B, the triangle is the standard symbol for an amplifier, and on occasion the letter $A$ is shown for additional identification. Resistor $R_f$ represents the feed-

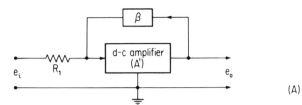

Fig. 11-5. Operational amplifier representations.

(A)

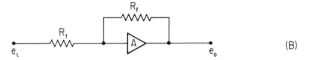

(B)

back loop, and the ground connections are presumed to be present and are not usually shown.

Without feedback, the input signal voltage $e_i$ is increased by the amplification $A$ to produce the output signal $e_o$:

$$e_o = Ae_i \qquad (11\text{-}5)$$

Thus, the amplification without feedback (also referred to as the *open loop* amplification) is the ratio of the instantaneous output-signal voltage and the input voltage:

$$A = \frac{e_o}{e_i} \qquad (11\text{-}6)$$

With feedback, the product of $A\beta$ is the *feedback factor*, and the closed-loop voltage amplification (with inverse feedback) is

$$A' = \frac{A}{1 - A\beta} \qquad (11\text{-}7)$$

As mentioned in Chapter 1, when the feedback factor $A\beta$ is substantially greater than 1, signal-voltage gain is independent of the $A$ factor, and in consequence the output-signal voltage $e_o$ is now influenced only by signal currents in $R_1$ and $R_f$, and the input voltage $e_i$. Thus, in a high-gain operational amplifier with feedback, the output is expressed as

$$e_o = -\frac{R_f}{R_1}e_i \qquad (11\text{-}8)$$

### Multiplication by a Constant

Equation (11-8) illustrates an important function of the operational amplifier; by selection of a specific ratio between resistors $R_1$ and $R_f$, the input voltage will be multiplied by a *constant* factor and the sign changed. By substituting variable resistors for the fixed values, we obtain multiplication by a coefficient which can be varied as required. Fixed and variable (linear) resistors used with analog computers are precision types which are carefully calibrated for maximum accuracy in computations.

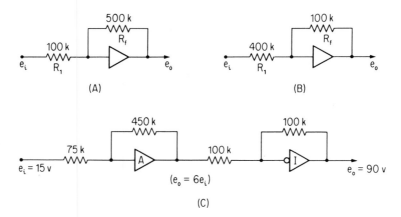

**Fig. 11-6. Multiplication by a constant.**

The operational-amplifier function of multiplication by a constant is shown in Fig. 11-6. In A, resistor $R_1$ has a value of 100 K ohms, and $R_f$ is 500 K ohms. With this ratio the input voltage is multiplied by $-5$ as indicated by Eq. (11-8). In B, $R_1$ has a value four times that of $R_f$, hence multiplication by a fraction is performed ($e_o = -e_i/4$). For multiplication yielding a positive answer, an additional circuit is used to invert the signal and hence change the sign. This inverter has unity gain and thus has characteristics similar to the emitter-follower *not* circuits described in Chapter 3. The symbolic representation for the system is shown in C of Fig. 11-6. Since the $R_f/R_1$ ratio is 6, $e_o = 6e_i = 90$ volts, as shown.

### Summing Amplifier

When the operational amplifier is combined with the summing networks shown earlier in D of Fig. 11-3 and in Fig. 11-4, a *summing* amplifier is formed. With the three-input passive summing network, the output signal is $e_o = \frac{1}{4}(e_1 + e_2 + e_3)$, as mentioned earlier. With the summing amplifier, however, the output signal is

$$e_o = -\left(\frac{R_f}{R_1}e_1 + \frac{R_f}{R_1}e_2 + \frac{R_f}{R_1}e_3\right) \tag{11-9}$$

Thus, the summing amplifier produces an output signal which is equal to the negative algebraic sum of the input voltages. A typical example of the process is shown in A of Fig. 11-7 where input voltages of 8, 6, and 4 are shown. From Eq. (11-9), the output will be equal to the sum of the input voltages, with a change of sign, and hence is $-18$ volts.

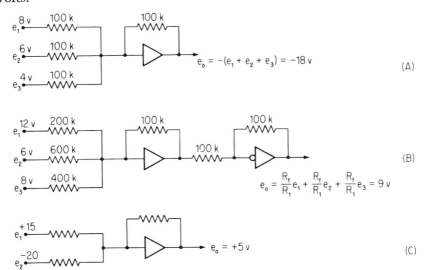

Fig. 11-7. Summing amplifier factors.

The input multiplying factor can be changed by using unequal-value resistors as shown in B. Here, an additional amplifier is used for inversion of the signal to yield a positive answer. Thus, if the input signals are 12, 6, and 8 volts, as shown, the ratio multipliers of Eq. (11-9) yield

$$R_f = \frac{100\,K}{200\,K} = \frac{1}{2} \times \frac{12}{1} = 6$$

$$\frac{100\,K}{600\,K} = \frac{1}{6} \times \frac{6}{1} = 1$$

$$\frac{100\,K}{600\,K} = \frac{1}{4} \times \frac{8}{1} = \underline{2}$$

$$e_o = 9$$

As with the passive networks discussed earlier, negative input signals can be used to represent such numbers as $-6$, $-7$, etc., for subtraction purposes. This is shown in C of Fig. 11-7, where a $+15$-volt signal is applied to one input, and a $-20$-volt signal to the other. The addition gives a sum of $-5$, but, because of the inversion characteristics of the amplifier, a $+5$-volt output signal is obtained.

### Integrating Amplifier

The analog computer's versatility in solving differential equations lies in its ability to perform a series of integrations by adding the passive integrator circuit to the operational amplifier. The basic symbolic representation for the integrating amplifier is shown in A of Fig. 11-8. Here, a capacitor $C_f$ is used as the feedback component in conjunction with the same input resistor $R_1$ used earlier in the other circuits. Without a phase-inverting circuit following the integrator, the output signal $e_o$ will be a negative constant multiplied by the *time integral* of the input signal $e_i$:

$$e_o = -\frac{1}{R_1C_f} \int e_i \, dt \qquad (11\text{-}10)$$

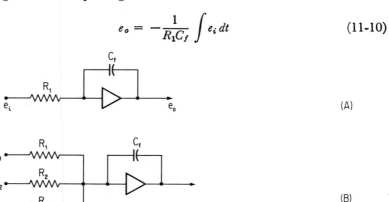

(A)

(B)

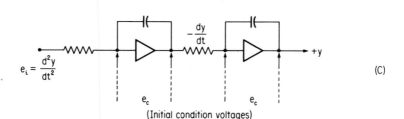

(C)

(Initial condition voltages)

**Fig. 11-8. Integration process.**

The integrating amplifier can also be combined with the summing networks to form a summing integrator as shown in B. The output signal voltage is

$$e_o = -\left(\frac{1}{R_1 C_f} \int e_i \, dt + \frac{1}{R_2 C_f} \int e_i \, dt + \frac{1}{R_3 C_f} \int e_i \, dt\right) \quad (11\text{-}11)$$

Thus, the output signal consists of the sum of the integrated input quantities, divided by the time constants of the respective input circuits for $e_1$, $e_2$, and $e_3$.

Successive integrations can be performed on second- or higher-order derivatives by cascading the integrating amplifiers as shown in C of Fig. 11-8. If, for instance, we wish to obtain the $y$ value for $d^2y/dt^2$, the first circuit integrates and obtains the negative of the integral of the input expression, or $-dy/dt$. This is applied to the second integrating amplifier and the output is $+y$ as a function of time $y(t)$.

For the solution of differential equations, each integrator must have applied to it *initial condition* voltages which are analogs of the arbitrary constants of integration. As shown in C of Fig. 11-8, such voltages are applied across the appropriate integrating capacitors. Voltage sources are available from the power supplies of analog computers for this purpose, and the amplitude is read on the panel meter and adjustments made for obtaining proper values. The analog computer holds the voltages at the prescribed levels until the solution process is initiated at $t = 0$, at which time related switching is made. A real-time plot of the solution may be obtained by plotters, which will display, in graph form, a curve of the solution $y$ as a function of time.

In setting up the analog computer for differential equation processing, certain factors must be kept in mind. First, start with the highest-order derivative, and integrate the required number of times to obtain the desired lowest-order derivative. Each term should be multiplied by the desired constants indicated in the original equation and the terms added as required. Finally, the equation is satisfied by closing the loop, using the necessary terms indicated. As an example, assume the following equation is to be solved:

$$\frac{d^2y}{dt^2} + \frac{dy}{dt} + y = 0$$

Initially, the equation is rewritten, keeping the highest-order derivative at the left:

$$\frac{d^2y}{dt^2} = -\frac{dy}{dt} - y$$

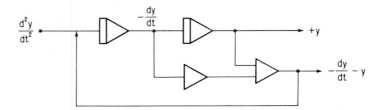

**Fig. 11-9. Differential equation solution.**

The circuitry and connections for the solution of this equation are shown in Fig. 11-9. The first-order derivative is obtained at the output of the first integrator. (This symbol is sometimes used in place of the triangle-capacitor combination.) When the first-order derivative is integrated again, we obtain the $+y$ value. Next, we invert the $-dy/dt$ and add the resultant positive value to the $+y$ in the summing circuit. The output produces the required $-dy/dt - y$ value needed for the equation given above, which must equal the $d^2y/dt^2$ value. Thus, the output is fed back to the input to satisfy the equation. Now, only such voltage changes as satisfy the equation will prevail in the circuit.

An equation of this type could represent certain physical conditions. The variable $y$, for instance, could apply to displacement of a rotating object, and this quantity could be sensed at the output from the second integrator, as shown in Fig. 11-9. The term $dy/dt$ would represent the velocity, with this quantity available from the first integrator. The acceleration of the rotating object is represented by $d^2y/dt$ at the input of the first integrator.

## PROBLEMS

**1.** What are the essential differences between the digital computer and the analog computer?

**2.** What is meant by the *scaling* of variables in an analog computer?

**3.** What is the purpose of a *patch panel* in an analog computer?

**4.** What are the differences between a strip-chart recorder and an *X-Y* plotter?

**5.** How does a passive voltage-divider circuit perform multiplication and division processes?

**6.** Explain how a summing circuit performs addition.

**7.** For an integrator, what are the relationships between the voltage applied to the capacitor and the capacitor current?

**8.** What are the general characteristics of operational amplifiers?

**9.** What characteristics prevail in an operational amplifier when the feedback factor is greater than 1?

**10.** Explain the multiplication process in an operational amplifier.

**11.** What are the $e_i$ and $e_o$ relationships between a three-input passive summing network and a summing amplifier?

**12.** How does an analog computer perform successive integrations on second- or third-order derivatives?

**13.** What factors must be kept in mind when programming differential equation solutions in an analog computer?

**14.** In programming, where are *initial condition* signal voltages applied?

# AUXILIARY
# ANALOG
# DEVICES

**12**

**Introduction.** As do the control consoles of digital computers, the control panel and patch panels of analog computers differ from one manufacturer to another in layout, the number of controls and modules, and the availability of auxiliary equipment. Thus, while the programming of basic calculus problems is fairly simple, the operator must be familiar with the characteristics and methods of module interconnections of a particular analog computer. Hence, it is essential that the manual or instructional booklets accompanying a particular analog computer be studied for an understanding of the patching methodology recommended for obtaining the required solutions of the equations to be programmed.

For the analog computer shown in Chapter 11, Fig. 11-1, for instance, the precision variable resistors are placed in two rows at the top of the console, which are termed the *attenuator row*, as shown in the block diagram for the computer in Fig. 12-1. The area below the attenuators consists of the patch panels for coefficient-setting potentiometers, integrator networks, function switches, and multipliers. The section directly above the control panel is the amplifier row, with patch-panel access to the operational amplifiers.

The control panel has an overload indicator, the null meter, mentioned earlier, on-off switches and voltage-polarity switches,

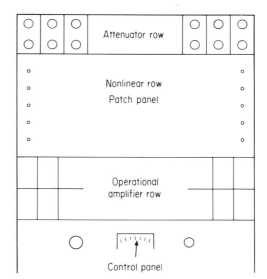

**Fig.  12-1. Analog console layout.**

reset-hold and operating switches, millisecond compute-time dial, additional attenuators, and other controls. Computers by other manufacturers would also have similar controls and patch panels, but with a different layout.

Besides the basic analog-computer modules, auxiliary equipment is available for expediting the programming of complex equations and for performing specific functions, as detailed next. Familiarization with the availability and applications of such equipment is necessary to take full advantage of the wide range of equation programming possible with the analog computer.

## Function Generators

Programming can be simplified considerably for an analog computer if we have available signal voltages representing specific functions. Devices which perform such functions are known as *function generators*. These units can, for instance, accept an input-signal voltage proportional to $\theta$ and furnish an output-signal voltage proportional to $\sin \theta$. The usual circuits are composed of diodes and resistors and are known as *diode function generators* (DFG). In the DFG units, the given function is approximated by discrete straight-line (linear) voltage segments, the composite of which represents the nonlinear function.

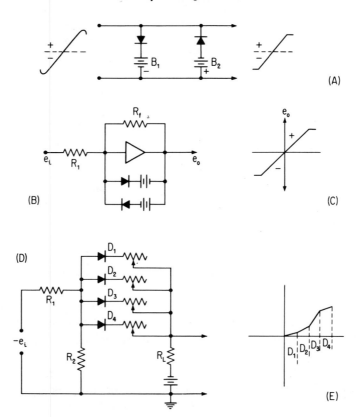

**Fig. 12.2** Function generator principles.

In the variable DFG devices the slope and amplitude of each segment can be adjusted individually to suit requirements. Fixed DFG units are composed of printed-circuit cards, each with specific component values to obtain an individual function. A variety of functions are obtained, among them tan $x$, sin $x$, log $x$, $x^2$, etc.

The basic principles of function generators may be understood by reference to Fig. 12-2. In A is shown a circuit of the limiter-clipper variety discussed in Chapter 1 (see Fig. 1-10). Each diode has a battery in series, with a polarity opposite to that which would cause conduction. If the input signal is negative in polarity and its amplitude gradually increasing, the second diode will conduct when the input signal exceeds that of $B_1$. During conduction, voltage in excess of $B_2$ is shunted because of the low impedance of the conducting diode. Thus, the output is limited to a specific amplitude set by the diode bias.

(This can also be considered as a clipping of the input signal). Similarly, with a positive signal the first diode will conduct when the input voltage exceeds that of $B_1$. Hence, the output waveform is as shown.

When such a circuit is applied to an operational amplifier as shown in B, a basic function generator is produced. If the input signal $e_i$ has a positive or negative amplitude below that of the bias batteries, the circuit functions as a normal operational amplifier. With signal amplitudes above the bias levels, however, the conducting diode circuit effectively shorts out the operational amplifier and the ouput voltage becomes that of the bias-battery potential. The resultant output waveform, shown in C, already exhibits nonlinear characteristics. If a number of diodes are used, each biased at a different level, straight-line voltage segments are produced in sequence to form the function determined by the time and duration of conduction of the individual diodes. A string of diodes can be used to obtain a positive-polarity function, another for a negative-polarity function, or both groups combined for a dual-polarity function.

The manner in which successive diodes conduct to form the function is shown in D of Fig. 12-2. Here the basic principles are shown; the operational amplifier is omitted to simplify the circuitry involved. Each diode has applied to it the correct polarity for conduction, but the variable resistance in series with each diode is set at a different level. When an input signal is applied having a sufficiently high negative polarity to overcome diode conduction, no current flows through the load resistor $R_L$ and hence no output voltage is produced. If the input signal is now reduced (is less negative), a point will be reached when one diode will conduct. If the resistance in series with diode $D_1$, for instance, is such that the positive voltage applied across this diode is greater than the applied input signal $e_i$, this diode conducts and circuit current now flows through the load resistor. The result is an output voltage as shown in E for the $x$ axis area identified by $D_1$. As the input voltage is lowered, the positive potential across $D_2$ is no longer nullified and this diode now conducts. The increased current now flowing through $R_1$ produces another segment of the output waveform, as shown in E. As the input signal is reduced additionally, diode $D_3$ conducts, followed by $D_4$. Thus, a nonlinear function made up of the composite output voltages is obtained as shown.

A specially designed variable resistor can be used as a function generator, as shown in Fig. 12-3. In A the straight resistor is shown to

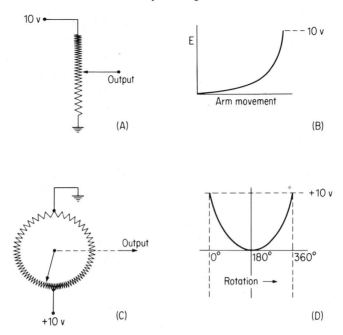

**Fig. 12-3. Resistive function generation.**

indicate the manner of construction. At the top the resistance wires are spaced close together so that very little movement of the variable arm provides a high resistance change. The spacings gradually become farther apart toward the ground end, as shown. With the wider spacings, the sliding arm produces only a small resistance change compared with that with the closer spacings. With a voltage impressed across the resistor, therefore, a continuous movement of the variable arm will produce a nonlinear output voltage, as shown by the graph in B. Such a function in a potentiometer is termed a *taper*, and the slope of the output curve can be predetermined by the characteristics of the taper designed for the resistor.

By forming a resistance strip into a continuous circle, as shown in C, various functions such as $y = x^2$, etc., can also be obtained. For the potentiometer shown, the widest spacing section is grounded and a voltage applied to the area of closest spacing. If the variable arm is now rotated continuously by a motor, for instance, the function shown in D will be obtained and repeated at a rate dependent on the slider-arm rotation. Again, the slope and type of curve can be regulated by the design of the taper.

## Multipliers, DFG and Servo

By using solid-state components as described for the function genera-tors, the product $xy$ can be obtained from inputs of $x$ and $y$. Many such multipliers are of the plug-in type, such as the function genera-tors and other auxiliary equipment. These multipliers make use of the *quarter-square* multiplying principle, as indicated by the algebraic expression

$$
\begin{aligned}
xy &= \tfrac{1}{4}[(x+y)^2 - (x-y)^2] \\
&= \tfrac{1}{4}(x^2 + 2xy + y^2 - x^2 + 2xy - y^2) \\
&= \tfrac{1}{4}(4xy) \\
&= xy
\end{aligned}
\tag{11-12}
$$

Thus, to obtain the product $xy$, the sequence shown in Eq. (11-12) is followed by adding $x$ to $y$, subtracting $y$ from $x$, and squaring the two terms, which proves the validity of the process shown in Eq. (11-12).

As discussed in Chapter 11, and illustrated in B of Fig. 11-3 a poten-tiometer can be used to multiply a variable voltage $x$ by a constant coefficient. To multiply one variable by another, $xy$, two potenti-ometers can be used in a special circuit arrangement such as shown in

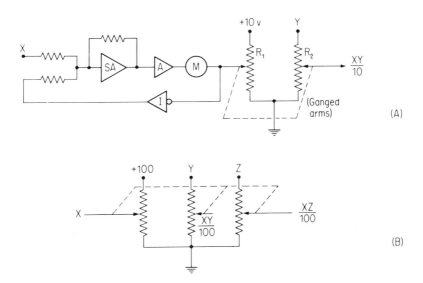

**Fig. 12-4.** Servomultiplier system.

A of Fig. 12-4. Here the potentiometers $R_1$ and $R_2$ have their variable arms ganged together to operate in tantum. The position of the slider arms is controlled by a motor $M$, as shown. Such a system is known as a *servomultiplier*.

A summing amplifier is used to sense the difference in amplitude between two signals and produce an error signal if such a difference exists. The error signal is amplified by a servo amplifier and applied to the motor. The motor now turns in a direction related to the polarity of the signal procured from the servo amplifier. The summing amplifier $SA$ compares the original $x$-quantity input with a sample fed back from the slider arm of $R_1$ and inverted by the $I$ circuit shown. As discussed in Chapter 11 and illustrated in C of Fig. 11-7, if a summing amplifier receives a signal of $+5$ volts at one input and $-7$ at the other, the output will be $+2$ volts. (The positive output is the result of the phase reversal from the input to the output of the summing amplifier.) Thus, if such signals are applied to the summing amplifier shown in A of Fig. 12-4, an error signal is produced and the motor will rotate and move the ganged slider arms of the potentiometers. If, however, the input signals to the summing amplifier are $+5$ and $-5$, for instance, the output would be 0 and the motor would not rotate.

In the system shown in A, a voltage of $+10$ volts is impressed across $R_1$ and the slider arm of $R_1$ taps off a fractional value of this $+10$ volts. If this tapped voltage is not equal to the $x$ value applied to the summing amplifier, an error voltage is produced at the output of the amplifier and the motor turns both potentiometers. When the tap is in the position representing the $x$ value, no error signal is produced and the motor stops.

Note that the $y$ quantity is applied to the top of $R_2$. Since the sliding arm of $R_2$ rotates in unison with that of the arm of $R_1$, both arms follow each change in the $x$ quantity; hence the output from the arm of $R_2$ is proportional to $xy$. Since, however, the voltage applied to $R_1$ is $+10$ in this instance, the actual output from $R_2$ will be $xy/10$. Had the voltage value applied to $R_1$ been $+100$ volts, the output from $R_2$ would have been $xy/100$. For a 1-volt value at $R_1$, the output would be $xy$. Thus, the scale factor is relative to the voltage across $R_1$.

The potentiometers $R_1$ and $R_2$ have a linear taper; hence the resistance changes in straight-line fashion for specific movements of the sliding arms. If, however, special mathematical functions are to be obtained, resistor $R_1$ should be designed with nonlinear characteristics, as shown in A of Fig. 12-3. In such an arrangement the arm would not provide a linear voltage change with equidistant rotations. Hence, the output from $R_2$ would be $f(x)y$. This would indicate the output would now be $y$ multiplied by a function of $x$.

More than two potentiometers can also be used to provide for the multiplication of additional quantities by $x$. A three-potentiometer example is shown in B, of Fig. 12-4 where the third potentiometer has a $z$ value applied to it. Thus, we can obtain outputs of $xy$ as well as $xz$. Since the reference voltage applied to the first potentiometer is $+100$ volts the outputs are actually $xy/100$ and $xz/100$ as shown.

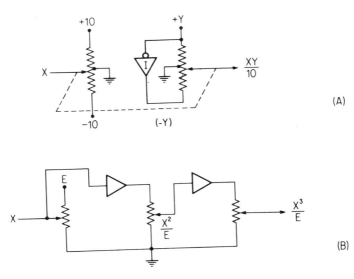

Fig. 12-5. Servomultiplier variations.

In the foregoing examples we have used positive voltage values for the reference voltage applied to $R_1$ and thus restricted our $x$ value to a positive voltage also. If the $x$ value is to be free of polarity restrictions, the circuit shown in A of Fig. 12-5 may be used. Here, the first resistor has a positive polarity at the top and a minus at the bottom, in reference to neutral ground. The $y$ input for the second resistor is inverted, and the resultant negative polarity is applied to the bottom of the resistor as shown. The two variable arm shafts are also ganged and driven by a motor servo as shown in A of Fig. 12-4.

By use of multiple resistors, polynomials can be generated and the versatility of the system extended. As shown in B of Fig. 12-5, the term $x^3$ can be generated by applying the $x$ values to the top portions of the second and third resistors. With 1 volt applied to the first resistor, $x^2$ is obtained from the variable arm of the second resistor, and $x^3$ from the arm of the third resistor.

## Repetitive Operation

Another auxiliary device, available for many analog computers, is a repetitive-operation integrator unit. With such a device the solution time is shortened by changing the $RC$ constants of the integrators and using high-speed relays for rapidly and repeatedly resetting the problem conditions, computing, and resetting again. Thus, the computation is repeated at a rate which permits the output to be viewed on an oscilloscope screen. The curve which appears is retraced sufficiently to remain fixed on the screen and thus display a graph of the solution versus time. This is an important feature for investigating parameter variations in design practices, since the resistance of the potentiometers which represent such parameters can be altered and the resultant changes viewed as they occur.

While an ordinary oscilloscope can be used, special display units are available, which are designed particularly for analog computer outputs. For the Pace TR-20 computer illustrated in Fig. 11-1, for instance, a repetitive-operation display unit is available which can show up to four outputs simultaneously on a rectangular graph screen in a portable (20- by 11- by 8-inch) unit.

## Sine-Cosine Generators

In solving various problems with analog computers, the need often arises for generators which provide for *sine* and *cosine* functions. If we assume the sinewave starts from the 0 point, as shown in A of Fig. 12-6, the cosine wave would be represented as leading the sinewave by 90°. Though the waveforms are similar, it is this 90°-phase difference which is the distinguishing factor between the two a-c signal voltages.

There are several ways in which sine and cosine functions can be generated, and the most basic type is the nonlinear potentiometer with a taper and wiring as shown in B of Fig. 12-6. Since the greatest resistance change occurs when the variable arm is positioned near the grounded sections, if the arm starts to rotate at these points, the voltage

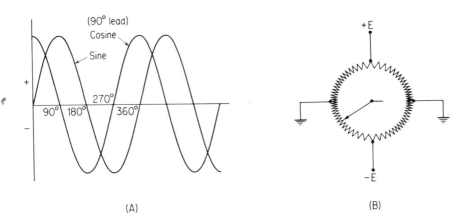

(A)                                          (B)

**Fig. 12-6.** Sine and cosine generation.

appearing at the output of the arm will rise rapidly. If the arm starts at the left ground point and rotates clockwise, a positive-voltage buildup occurs. As the arm nears the vertical position, the resistance change decreases and the waveform rise is less sharp. After the peak positive voltage is reached, the drop is also less sharp initially. As the arm approaches the ground point at the right, the resistance change increases and the decline becomes more pronounced until zero output voltage is obtained. As the arm continues to rotate, the operation is repeated to produce the negative alternation of the sinewave. Thus, for every 360° rotation, one sinewave is produced at the output of the variable arm.

If another arm is added, displaced from the first by 90°, the *second arm* will produce the *cosine* function at the same time the *first arm* provides the *sine* function. (The output ends of the arms are insulated from each other to provide separate output signals.)

Another method for generating both sine and cosine functions by mechanical means is with *resolvers*. These are sometimes called *induction resolvers*, since they have basically a transformer characteristic between their two stator windings and their two rotor windings. Both the rotor and the stator windings are at right angles to each other, as shown in Fig. 12-7. Hence, voltages and currents are 90° out of phase with each other in the stator windings and also 90° out of phase in the rotor windings.

If an a-c signal is applied to the stator winding 1 only, the output $E_1$ from its particular rotor winding will be an a-c signal voltage which

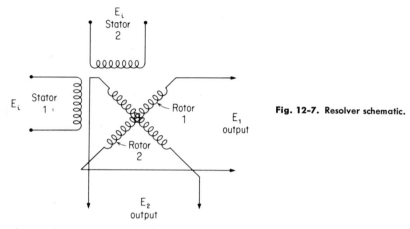

Fig. 12-7. Resolver schematic.

varies as the cosine of the angle it forms with stator winding 1. Though stator winding 2 has no voltage applied to it, the rotor winding 2 cuts the lines of force produced by stator winding 1, and an output voltage $E_2$ is produced which is displaced from $E_1$ by $90°$, producing a sine function.

In similar fashion, if an a-c signal is applied to stator winding 2 only, the output $E_2$ will be a voltage proportional to the cosine of the displacement angle, and the voltage induced in rotor 1 will be proportional to the sine of that angle. Thus, the sine and cosine voltages $E_1$ and $E_2$ are reversed when $E_i$ is applied to stator 2 instead of stator 1.

If a-c signals are applied to both stators, the output voltages $E_1$ and $E_2$ are related to the input $E_i$ voltages by

$$E_1 = E_{i1} \cos \theta + E_{i2} \text{ sine } \theta$$
$$E_2 = E_{i2} \cos \theta - E_{i1} \text{ sine } \theta$$

Nonmechanical sine-cosine function generators are formed with DFG units of the type described earlier. Using up to 20 or more voltage segments, these produce fixed functions of variables for sine and cosine functions when used with operational amplifiers. These are usually available in patch-panel form for plugging into the analog-computer console.

## PROBLEMS

**1.** What are some of the functions obtainable from a function generator?

**2.** Prepare a schematic of a function generator for producing negative voltages to form a function with six segments.

**3.** In what manner can variable resistors be used as function generators?

**4.** What is meant by the *quarter-square* multiplying principle?

**5.** Prepare a schematic of a servomultiplier, showing the input summing amplifier, servo amplifier, and potentiometers, to produce an output $xy$ as well as $xz$.

**6.** What changes must be made in a servomultiplier to produce an output $f(x)y$?

**7.** What changes must be made to the schematics in Fig. 12-4 to make the $x$ value free of polarity restrictions?

**8.** What advantages are obtained with repetitive operations in an analog computer?

**9.** In signal voltages representing waveforms, what is the difference between the sine and cosine function?

**10.** How are sine and cosine functions obtained from a servopotentiometer?

**11.** How are sine and cosine functions obtained from a resolver?

**12.** What outputs are obtained from the rotor windings of a resolver if a-c signals are applied to both stator inputs?

# APPENDIX

## Computer Trainers

For expediting the training of computer personnel, a number of manufacturers have marketed computer trainers, which are, in essence, miniature digital computers containing logic circuits, flip-flop counters, and registers, as well as useful (though limited) storage capabilities. Since such trainers are priced far below commercial computers, they serve as a convenient demonstration and/or laboratory item in schools having computer courses. The design features of such units permit students to be exposed to hardware assembly practices, interconnection of logic components, and the general philosophy of programming techniques. Some of these trainers have available peripheral equipment for read-in and read-out purposes and for facilitating programming procedures. Several such trainers are described briefly here as examples of units and features which are available.

Since analog computers are much lower in cost than large-scale digital types, the analog computers themselves are generally used as trainers as well as completely functional units for solving problems related to research, design, and other areas.

## Philco-Ford Training Materials

The Philco-Ford Techrep Division of the Philco-Ford Corporation has available a number of items for computer lecture-demonstration-laboratory applications. One unit consists of a 19- by 24-inch pegboard and supporting base, supplied with logic modules. Thus, when this unit is used in a school laboratory, the student may interconnect a number of logic-gate circuits as well as flip-flop circuits. Various logic functions can then be observed and characteristics studied. In addition, counters and registers can be assembled for the performance of calculation functions.

Two demonstration racks with storage cabinets are also available. One such unit permits the instructor to demonstrate active circuitry involved in the pegboard laboratory unit. The other demonstration rack consists of a large display board composed of three chalkboard panels (31 by 36 inches) that are bolted together. This assembly is mounted over a storage cabinet, as shown in Fig. A-1.

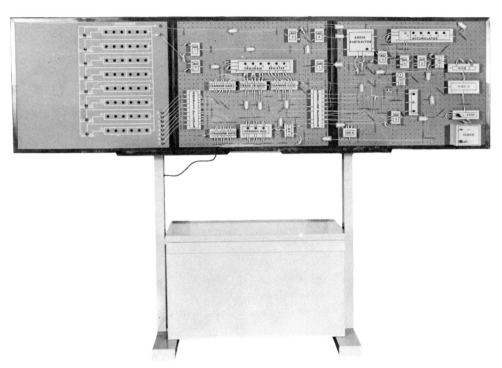

**Fig. A-1.** Philco Corporation computer systems lecture-demonstrations unit.

The demonstration rack is essentially a small computer containing a program register, an address register, an accumulator, an adder-subtractor, a function decoder, an address decoder, a clock, and various transfer and logic gates.

This computer system is assembled on the pegboard structure of the demonstration rack, using prewired modules and preassembled functional units. The program code provides for arithmetic processes, conditional and unconditional branching, and other programming facilities.

### Amperex Digital Trainer

The Amperex DT-100 Digital Trainer is shown in Fig. A-2. This is a small unit with a height of approximately 12 inches, a depth of 17 inches, and a width of 22 inches. This unit consists of 72 of the most common solid-state circuit blocks such as logic gates, flip-flops, pulse shapers, etc. These are installed in such a manner that they can be connected or reconnected as desired. The front panel contains three patchboards with 300 contacts per board for flexibility in connecting digital circuits.

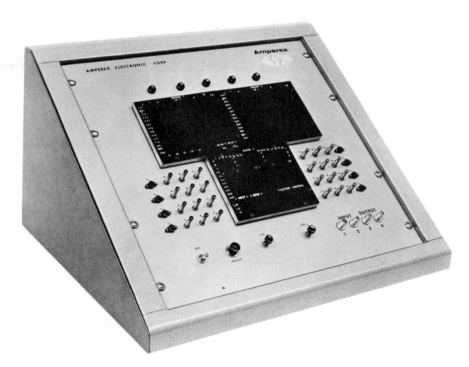

**Fig. A-2.** Amperex DT-100 Digital Trainer.

Visual indication of the outputs of circuits (such as shift registers and counters) can be obtained by connecting any of the five indicator lamps which are located above the patchboards. Twenty-four push-post terminals are also on the front panel for convenience in connecting external components and circuitry. In addition, eight transistor sockets are provided on the front panel. These are connected by internal wiring to the push-post terminals. Switches are also provided for manual input, reset, and voltage-level switching. A maximum of 72 circuit blocks can be used at any one time. Such blocks are mounted on printed-circuit cards which are inserted into the system by plugging them into connectors which are internally wired to the patchboards.

## Fabri-Tek Bi-Tran Six Trainer

The computer trainer manufactured by Fabri-Tek, Incorporated, is shown in Fig. A-3, the Bi-Tran Six Trainer. This solid-state pre-wired unit contains a number of registers, including an accumulator,

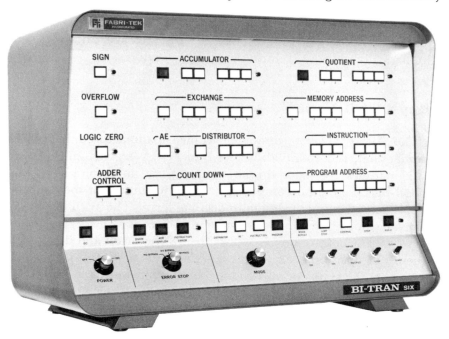

**Fig. A-3.** Fabri-Tek BiTran-Six Trainer.

exchange register, count-down register, quotient register, as well as program-address and memory-address registers. Programming can be done from the front panel by pushing appropriate rectangular switches, which light up to indicate the logic 1. Peripheral equipment can be used for program input as well as read-out, and such auxiliary equipment includes keyboard input, tape punch and reader, and a printer. This is an internally stored program machine.

This trainer contains ferrite-core memory consisting of 128 words of 6 bits each, with random access. The Bi-Tran Six operates as a single-address binary parallel, magnitude and sign, arithmetic system. A versatile instruction repertoire, consisting of 30 operation codes, permits best usage of core storage. Decision and branch type of instructions are included, and the trainer will indicate program errors, overflow, and the status of the operational registers at all times. Thus, it can be considered as a large-scale computing system in miniature.

This trainer contains seven logic-circuit boards and a logic-memory board, each approximately 22 inches wide and 17 inches high. These are accessible from the top of the unit and can be raised to an upright position for circuit inspection, demonstration, and circuit testing. Various program modes may be used to facilitate logic-circuit and program progression analysis. Storage addresses are automatically sequenced during loading procedures.

## Arkay CT-650 Trainer

The Arkay CT-650 computer trainer manufactured by Arkay International, Incorporated, is shown in Fig. A-4. This unit consists of six modules corresponding to the six basic units found in most general-purpose digital computers. The input unit is at the extreme left and accepts numerical data in decimal form. The arithmetic unit performs calculation functions under the direction of the computer program. The control unit is located below the drum and directs the sequence of operations for all the computer units. Various indicator lights show the status of operations. The output unit is at the lower right and displays the output in decimal form. Selector knobs for the scale factor are present.

The memory shown at the upper left is a simulated core type of scratch-pad storage. It has a capacity for storing five four-bit words. The drum storage shown at the upper right is capable of holding 100

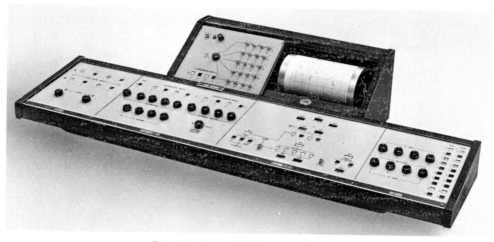

**Fig. A-4.** Arkay CT-650 Computer Trainer.

programmed instructions. Programs are laid out on perforated mylar sheets precut to the drum width. After the sheets are programmed, they are placed around the drum surface and locked in place. Holes in this memory sheet represent logic-1 digits. Complex mathematical functions can be programmed with an instruction repertoire typical of those used in standard computers.

# INDEX